*Emilio Rabasa and the Survival of
Porfirian Liberalism*

Emilio Rabasa and the
Survival of Porfirian Liberalism

The Man, His Career, and His Ideas, 1856–1930

Charles A. Hale

STANFORD UNIVERSITY PRESS

STANFORD, CALIFORNIA 2008

Stanford University Press
Stanford, California

Printed in the United States of America on acid-free, archival-quality paper

Library of Congress Cataloging-in-Publication Data

Hale, Charles A. (Charles Adams)
Emilio Rabasa and the survival of Porfirian liberalism : the man, his career, and his ideas, 1856–1930 / Charles A. Hale.
p. cm.
Includes bibliographical references and index.
ISBN 978-0-8047-5876-5 (cloth : alk. paper)
1. Rabasa, Emilio, 1856–1930. 2. Mexico—Politics and government—1867–1910. 3. Mexico—Politics and government—1910–1946. I. Title.

F1233.5.R33H35 2008
972.08'1092—dc22
[B]

2007038752

Typeset by Thompson Type in 10/12 Sabon
Frontispiece: Portrait of Emilio Rabasa Estebanell. Courtesy of ELD.

In Memory of Hugh M. Hamill, Jr. (1928–2005).
Fine Scholar and True Friend for More than Fifty Years

Contents

List of Photographs

Acknowledgments

This book has depended over many years on the collaboration and support of numerous friends and colleagues. Jaime del Arenal has been my principal consultant on the juridical world of Emilio Rabasa and on the institution of which he was a cofounder. Alicia Salmerón has been exceptionally generous by sharing many relevant materials drawn from her own work, which I would never have found myself. A number of others have also aided by sending me books, documents, photos, or giving me valuable suggestions for research and interpretation. I note particularly Jon Benfer, Thomas Benjamin, Carlos Bravo Regidor, Roderic Ai Camp, Rafael Estrada, Paul Garner, Linda B. Hall, T. M. James, Friedrich Katz, Bert Kreitlow, Asunción Lavrín, Alonso Lujambio, María Luna Argudín, Josefina Mac Gregor, Pablo Piccato, Jan Rus, Elisa Speckman, Mauricio Tenorio, and Jan de Vos. In years past I had excellent research assistance from David Gilbert and Patrick J. McNamara; more recently Matthew Barton and Keith Hernández have also helped. Pablo Mijangos compiled the index. Cynthia Steele willingly aided in the translation of a number of passages and texts, both literary and otherwise. Juan Manuel Casal has acted for many years as my skilled translator into Spanish. My niece Leslie Hale provided professional help with the illustrations.

Ricardo de Villafranca Rabasa was a mine of Rabasa family information and anecdotes and spent many hours enlightening me. I also received help from other family members, Emilio O. Rabasa, Emilio Rabasa Gamboa, and Manuel Rabasa. Marcia Almquist provided additional information on the Villafranca family.

Andrés Lira González read the manuscript and made many valuable comments, particularly pertaining to juridical matters. Consistent encouragement for this project came from Jeremy Adelman, John H. Coatsworth, Javier Garciadiego, Emilio Kourí, Enrique Krauze, Cecilia Noriega, Steven Palmer, Erika Pani, Eric Van Young, and Josefina Vázquez.

The book has benefited by grants from the National Endowment for the Humanities, the Bellagio Study and Conference Center of the Rockefeller Foundation, and the David Rockefeller Center for Latin American Studies, Harvard University. The staff of many libraries and archives have welcomed and aided me. I note especially those of the Latin American library of the University of Texas, Austin, the Centro de Estudios Históricos, Condumex, and the Escuela Libre de Derecho. El Colegio de México and the University of Washington favored me by appointments as Visiting Scholar.

Among the many fine colleagues and good friends at the University of Iowa over a generation, Claire Fox, Lawrence Gelfand, Michel Gobat, Laura Gotkowitz, Linda Kerber, John Reitz, Alan Spitzer, and Shelton Stromquist have taken a special interest in this book and have sustained me in its completion. I will never forget that Iowa's Department of History has been my firm academic anchor through most of my career.

My children and grandchildren have been an immeasurable source of strength and understanding of my scholarly obsessions; in addition, my son Charles not only gave the manuscript a careful critical reading, but has for many years engaged me in valuable dialogue arising from our differing interests and scholarly disciplines. Finally, words cannot adequately express the fount of constructive criticism, good judgment, and unbounded love that has poured forth from my life companion Lenore.

Preface

This study was originally designed as a sequel to my earlier work on nineteenth-century Mexican liberalism, which would trace the experience of liberalism in the era of political and social upheaval after 1910. I had thought to focus, as I did earlier, on the ideas of key individuals, in this case intellectuals of the revolutionary era whose ideas when placed in broader context epitomized the changes brought about by the Revolution. As I proceeded, I realized that my interests moved more naturally toward continuity rather than change (or continuity within change), and I hit upon Emilio Rabasa, a man of the old regime caught up in the maelstrom of revolution. And yet Rabasa was not simply a figure that the changes of history passed by. He and to some extent his ideas survived; he was a man who by choosing exile continued to write and think critically about Mexico, its problems, its past and future. Ultimately returning to his country, Rabasa accepted the new order and adapted himself to its exigencies with only a modest change in his ideas. My earlier studies of liberalism focused on José María Luis Mora in the early nineteenth century and on Justo Sierra in the later period. However, in both cases my central concern was to probe a set of ideas rather than the thought (or the lives) of the individuals themselves. However, as the present study progressed, it became increasingly biographical, in part because the man I had chosen, besides representing intellectual continuity, was in himself of great interest, a man whose career, ideas, and personality were filled with enigma and even contradiction. Of course, I was also drawn to biography by the discovery of new evidence that uncovered a figure of great public importance whom we knew only superficially. The result is that except for Chapter 7, devoted to Emilio Rabasa's later juridical thought and action, the chapters of this book basically follow the stages of his life and multiple careers, intertwined with analysis of his ideas.

ABBREVIATIONS

The following abbreviations are used in the text, the Notes, and the Bibliography.

AIC	American International Corporation
BNM	Banco Nacional de Mexico
BR	Archivo Bernardo Reyes
CONACULTA	Consejo Nacional para la Cultura y las Artes
DDCC	*Diario de debates del Congreso Consituyente (1916–17)*
DDCD	*Diario de debates de la Cámara de Diputados*
DDCS	*Diario de debates de la Cámara de Senadores*
ELD	Escuela Libre de Derecho
ENJ	Escuela Nacional de Jurisprudencia
ER	Emilio Rabasa Archive
FCE	Fondo de Cultura Económica
IBC	International Bankers Association
INEHRM	Instituto Nacional de Estudios Históricos de la Revolución Mexicana
JYL	Archivo José Yves Limantour
PD	Archivo Porfirio Díaz
RVR	Archivo Privado de Arq. Ricardo de Villafranca Rabasa
SJF	*Seminario Judicial de la Federación*
SMU	Buckley-Garrison Collection, Southern Methodist University
UNAM	Universidad Nacional Autónoma Mexicana
UNICACH	Universidad de Ciencias y Artes del Estado de Chiapas
WFB	William F. Buckley Archive

Emilio Rabasa and the Survival of Porfirian Liberalism

CHAPTER ONE

Introduction

The Nineteenth-Century Heritage

For the historian of Mexican thought and politics and for the biographer, Emilio Rabasa is not only a figure of central importance but an enigmatic and contradictory one as well. It is widely acknowledged that Rabasa exerted a strong influence on the formation of the Constitution of 1917, the Magna Charta of the Mexican Revolution. And yet this influence came from a man who was politically antirevolutionary and socially conservative. As a senator in 1912 he opposed Francisco I. Madero, the "apostle" of the Revolution. As a diplomat he served Victoriano Huerta, the "usurper." As a close associate of the *Científicos*,[1] Rabasa in his historical writings of 1912 and 1920 took a benign view of the regime of Porfirio Díaz (the Porfiriato) and has been often labeled its apologist. As governor of his native state of Chiapas in the 1890s, Rabasa introduced measures to divide indigenous communal property; and these policies continued to guide his social ideas during the revolutionary and postrevolutionary eras. Yet as a jurist, Rabasa became not only the phantom member of the Constitutional Congress of Querétaro but also the revered modern master of Mexican constitutional law, idolized by the juridical community. In addition, Rabasa is celebrated for his literary works of 1887 to 1891 and recognized as the pioneer of the Mexican realist novel. Although some aspects of his career have been the subject of study by historians, legal scholars, and literary critics, other aspects have been slighted or overlooked entirely. Aided by both known and heretofore unknown evidence, I present (as far as possible) a full biographical portrait of this major figure in Mexican history, whose life spanned three critical but distinct periods: the era of Porfirio Díaz (1877–1911), the Revolution (1910–20), and the reconstructive years of the 1920s. Rabasa is of particular interest to me because his ideas and

career constitute intellectual continuity and survival from the old regime to the new regime.

Within the constraints and peculiar obsessions of the biographical mode, I have tried to follow the methods of my earlier work. My
central objective has been to examine Mexican political ideas within a
broader Western context, both in terms of influence and comparison.
The world of the nineteenth-century intellectual and governing elite was
Europe, mainly France and Spain, but also England (usually filtered
through a continental lens), and as the twentieth century wore on, the
United States. One of my central questions has been: why were certain
ideas, policies, and political configurations influential in Mexico and
not others? I have found the answer to be that intellectual influence is
based on the relevance of those European and North American ideas to
Mexico and thus adapted to Mexico's social and political peculiarities.
I have always rejected the notion that the ideas of the Mexican (and
by extension Latin American) intellectual elite are a mere "reflection"
of foreign thought; moreover, I have refused to enter the sterile debate
over "imitation" versus "authenticity" in the intellectual life of the con-
tinent. Thus, my concern has been consistently comparative. In the case
of Emilio Rabasa I have tried to identify ideas and authors that guided
his thought, seek out sources (even though his references are often vague
and his documentation casual), and to find the reasons why he found
them relevant. Therefore, my method has been comparative throughout this book, a method that is particularly appropriate in the case of
Rabasa, who himself was a master comparativist.

In terms of reputation and continuing influence, it might be useful to
compare Rabasa to other important Porfirian intellectuals. In his notable defense of the Constitution of 1857, Daniel Cosío Villegas identified
Rabasa and Justo Sierra as the major critics of the document and as the
principal defenders of the Porfiriato. He correctly identified Rabasa's *La
Constitución y la dictadura* of 1912 as an elaboration of ideas enunciated by Sierra in the newspaper *La Libertad* from 1878 to 1880.[2] The
reputation of both Sierra and Rabasa has seen a strong revival since the
1940s, yet we should resist too close a comparison. Though both men
were born in remote provinces, Sierra in 1848 in Campeche and Rabasa
in 1856 in Chiapas, Sierra was taken to Mexico City at an early age
and experienced the heroic civil and ideological wars of the 1860s as a
student in the capital. Rabasa was sent to school in Oaxaca during the
years following the restoration of the Republic in 1867. He did not go
to Mexico City until 1886 when the regime of Don Porfirio was fully
consolidated. Thus Sierra, more than Rabasa, retained a lingering attachment to classic political liberalism and to the "old" liberals of the

Constitutional Convention of 1856–57. One of these liberals was Ignacio Altamirano, the literary mentor of Sierra's youth. The young Rabasa, by contrast, is credited with being the first post-Reforma novelist not to be sponsored by Altamirano.

Though Rabasa and Sierra shared many ideas, Rabasa's age and the experience of his formative years made him a Porfirian liberal without the degree of ambivalence Sierra revealed toward the regime. In fact, in the early 1890s Rabasa was essentially appointed by Porfirio Díaz to be governor of Chiapas. Also critical in comparing the subsequent reputations of Sierra and Rabasa is the fact that Sierra died in 1912, while ambassador from the Madero regime to Spain, and thus was not forced, as was Rabasa, to take a political stand during the turbulent years 1913–20. How would later generations of Mexicans have regarded Sierra if he like Rabasa had first accepted Huerta and then spent the rest of the decade in exile?

Rabasa's political ideas and his defense of the Porfirian regime might also be compared to those of Francisco Bulnes. Yet Bulnes, who lived until 1924, was so much the polemicist that his attacks on Benito Juárez and his subsequent defense of Porfirio Díaz identified him thoroughly with the old regime in the eyes of later generations. As for Rabasa's influence on the Constitution of 1917, only Andrés Molina Enríquez surpasses him. However, Molina was a decade younger, and his major work of 1909 was a critical treatment of the land problem, a problem Rabasa viewed in classic liberal terms and even questioned its existence. Molina's *Los Grandes Problemas nacionales* made him the reputed precursor of revolutionary agrarianism, an official consultant on agrarian issues, and presumed author of Article 27 of the Constitution.[3] Though Rabasa's reputation has not achieved the exalted status of Justo Sierra and Andrés Molina Enríquez, it certainly has surpassed that of his *Científico* contemporaries. For example, there were the brothers Macedo, whose ideas were either too confined within the narrow official boundaries of the late Díaz regime (in the case of Pablo) or sufficiently technical to arouse little continuing interest (in the case of Miguel). In short, Emilio Rabasa emerges as an unusual figure among those Porfirian intellectuals whose ideas were subjected to the ideological onslaught of the post-1910 years.

Clearly a major source of Rabasa's reputation and continuing influence is the respect he has come to command among members of the legal profession. This status stems in large part from the experience of Mexico City's lawyers and legal educators during the revolutionary decade. The juridical establishment of the capital was closely identified with the regime of Porfirio Díaz and showed little enthusiasm for the triumphant arrival of Francisco Madero in mid-1911. One prominent figure was Francisco León de la Barra (1863–1939), eminent lawyer, ambassador to the United States, minister of Foreign Relations, and interim president of the Republic from 25 May to 6 November 1911. Another was Demétrio Sodi (1866–1934), distinguished jurist and Supreme Court justice from 1908 to 1911, who served as Diaz's final minister of justice. Sodi declined a cabinet post offered by Madero. Another leader of the legal community was the aforementioned Miguel S. Macedo (1856–1929), prominent Científico, expert on criminal law, and sub-secretary of the Interior from 1906 to 1911. All three had close ties to the Escuela Nacional de Jurisprudencia, directed from 1904 to 1911 by Miguel Macedo's brother Pablo (1851–1918), chief publicist on development issues during the final decade of the Porfiriato.

The critical event that solidified Rabasa's central place in the metropolitan juridical community was the founding of the Escuela Libre de Derecho (ELD) in July 1912, a subject I discuss in detail in Chapter 4. Although a student strike against Luis Cabrera, the new director of the Escuela Nacional de Jurisprudencia, provided the spark, the idea of a "free school" (that is, free from direction by the revolutionary government) soon found considerable professorial support and became a reality within two months. Emilio Rabasa was perhaps the most significant figure in the ELD of 1912. Among the other professorial founders were men I have just mentioned, Francisco León de la Barra, Demétrio Sodi, and Miguel S. Macedo, as well as Jorge Vera Estañol, a popular professor. The school rapidly gained prestige, in part because its founders were the country's leading lawyers and jurists. Though its degrees were not given official recognition until 1930, the political antagonism between it and the official school soon faded, especially after the fall of the regime of Victoriano Huerta in July 1914. Emilio Rabasa's professorship in the early ELD was brief, yet by the time he left Mexico in May 1914 as chairman of Mexico's delegation to the conference in Niagara Falls, Canada, mediated by Argentina, Brazil, and Chile (ABC), his reputation was established as the country's premier expert on constitutional law. His two works, *El Artículo 14* (1906) on the defense of individual rights and his more general *La Constitución y la dictadura* (1912), were standard texts for the new generation of law students.

Rabasa's influence on the legal community was based on more than technical expertise. His juridical studies and his teaching of constitutional law were informed by a keen historical sense, which broadened his vision and strengthened his argument. As Cosío Villegas acknowledged, despite disagreeing fundamentally with his substantive interpretation of the Constitution of 1857, "Rabasa knew history and knew law," something that "is rare in México."[4] Rabasa was the major exponent in the post-1910 period of the dominant political doctrine of the Porfiriato, a transformed liberalism that rested on the contemporary concept of "scientific politics" and on a historical or traditional constitutionalism already rooted in nineteenth-century Mexico.

To demonstrate Rabasa's adherence to these elements of Porfirian liberalism, we must consider the well-known aspects of his career and writings but also look beyond to aspects that are less studied or heretofore ignored. These include his policies as the modernizing governor of Chiapas from 1891 to 1894, his role in the Senate of the Republic from 1894 to 1913, his anonymous contributions from 1916 to 1918 to the émigré journal, *Revista mexicana,* and his career and writings following his return to Mexico in 1920. Also of major importance was his close business and legal association with William F. Buckley, Sr., an American lawyer and oil entrepreneur, working in Mexico from 1908 to 1921. Additional major insights into Rabasa's career, his concerns, and his ideas come from an extensive and intimate correspondence from 1910 to 1920 with José Yves Limantour, the exiled finance minister of the late Díaz regime. In particular, this correspondence opens up for us Emilio Rabasa's previously unknown exile experience. In short, Rabasa's ideas, based on the transformed liberalism of the late nineteenth century are further revealed in a multifaceted career that in the absence of a Rabasa personal archive has remained largely obscure to historians. The correspondence with Buckley and Limantour also uncovers the personal side of a man who made a concerted effort to avoid public scrutiny.

The concept of scientific politics was put forth by Justo Sierra and the other editors of the newspaper *La Libertad* in 1878. Drawn from the positivism of Henri de Saint Simon and Auguste Comte, scientific politics entailed a critique of classic liberal and particularly egalitarian ideas. Politics must not be based on abstractions, but upon science, that is, upon empirical study, history and social reality, and practical economic objectives. Furthermore, argued *La Libertad,* politics is the science of the possible; dogmas, theories, and legal formulas must give way to observation, patient investigation, and experience as the guides to statesmanship. The self-styled "new generation" of intellectuals of *La Libertad* contrasted scientific politics with the "metaphysical politics" of the "old" midcentury liberals, whose ideas in their view had led only to revolution and anarchy. Sierra and his colleagues called themselves "new" or "conservative" liberals, following the founders of the Third Republic in France and the First Republic in Spain, particularly Adolphe Thiers, Jules Simon, and Emilio Castelar. Articles by and about these "conservative-liberal" leaders filled the pages of *La Libertad* in the years 1878 to 1880. The term *conservative-liberalism* became the correlate of "scientific politics," in Mexico as in Europe.

The idea that administration must take precedence over political contention, central to scientific politics at its origin in the thought of Henri de
Saint Simon, had great appeal for the writers of *La Libertad*. The ultimate
success of the Díaz regime, they argued, will depend on the formation of
a "scientific plan of administration and politics, based on knowledge of
the biological, social, and economic conditions of the country."[5] Another
major feature of scientific politics in Mexico was the now commonplace
idea that society was an evolving organism to be understood historically.
From Herbert Spencer came the idea of the social organism, its evolution
and inevitable progress. From Auguste Comte came the emphasis on history as the proper way to study the science of society. Strong government
through practical administration, a biological and historical sense of society, a faith in progress: these were all key elements of scientific politics.

In addition, Sierra and his colleagues also sought constitutional reform and regarded themselves very much as constitutionalists. These
advocates of scientific politics called for a constitution that was in accord with the country's political and social realities. In short, their constitutionalism was historical or traditional as opposed to the doctrinaire
constitutionalism of 1856–57. The doctrinaire tendency reflected a belief
that rigid adherence to or imposition of the precepts of the written document could guarantee the realization of constitutional order. Doctrinaire
constitutionalists often took a radical or democratic political stand, believing it was necessary to change society to conform to the constitution.
Historical or traditional constitutionalists, on the other hand, sought to
change constitutional precepts they found abstract or unrealizable in
Mexico. They tended to be politically moderate and socially elitist, calling for strong government within the constitution, at the same time resisting personal presidential power. The assumptions of historical constitutionalism came to guide Emilio Rabasa's political thought, and he
carried them into the revolutionary decade. Thus Emilio Rabasa, like
Justo Sierra, can be rightly called a constitutionalist and a liberal, as
well as a positivist. The terms are not mutually exclusive and reflect the
ideological consensus that prevailed among the intellectual and governing elite of Porfirian Mexico.[6]

The constitutionalism that guided Rabasa was well established in
Mexico. Throughout the nineteenth century there were continual unsuccessful attempts by liberals to establish a system of "constitutional
balance" that would prevent the extremes of "anarchy" and "despotism." The elements of this system were an effective separation of powers, an ambivalence if not hostility toward popular sovereignty, and a
tie between individual rights and propertied interests as the guaran-

tee of stability. The system was elitist, antidemocratic, and theoretically antistatist, though it came to include a strong state if properly limited by constitutional means. It drew inspiration from a current of French political thought that had its origins in Montesquieu and was put forth in the nineteenth century by Benjamin Constant, Alexis de Tocqueville, Edouard de Laboulaye, and even in a sense by Hippolyte Taine. French constitutionalists idealized English (and in one instance, North American) institutions and made their point of departure a critique of the French Revolution and the egalitarian or "jacobin" revolutionary tradition. The Mexican version of historical constitutionalism is revealed in three episodes from the 1820s to the 1890s.[7]

The first episode came in the aftermath of the Revolution for Independence and can be traced in the ideas of José María Luis Mora, Mexico's leading liberal theorist of the postindependence generation. Besides his writing, Mora was a leader in drawing up the first constitution for the state of México, by far the new nation's most populous entity within the federal system established by the Constitution of 1824. Though liberal Spain provided much of the specific guidance for Mexican constitution makers of the 1820s, including Mora, postrevolutionary France through the ideas of Benjamin Constant provided the theoretical impulse. Constant was the classic continental constitutionalist, who from 1796 to 1830 upheld the defense of individual liberty against the invasions of arbitrary authority in widely differing regimes. Following in the spirit of Montesquieu, Constant's model was England, leading him to emphasize the need for "numerous and independent representation" and for "intermediate bodies" to act as positive safeguards between the individual and the state.[8]

'It was Constant's ambivalence toward the French Revolution that made his thought directly relevant to Mora's Mexico. Constant shared Tocqueville's later dictum that "in the French Revolution there were two impulses in different directions, which must never be confounded, the one favorable to liberty, the other to despotism."[9] Mora did not categorically deny popular sovereignty. Like Constant, he could not have done so and remained a liberal. Yet both began with a critique of Rousseau and the misuse of his ideas by French revolutionary governments after 1792. "As the celebrated Constant observes," wrote Mora, "the horrible outrages against individual liberty and civil rights committed in the French Revolution arose in large part from the vogue of Rousseau's doctrine, which is not only illiberal, but the fundamental principle of despotism"[10]

At the heart of Mora's constitutional liberalism was the idea that individual liberty could be best guaranteed if the political process were entrusted to property holders, an idea he expressed forcefully in the debates over the electoral law for the state of Mexico. Mora's attachment to property revealed aristocratic leanings, and he even used the term *aristocratic* favorably in 1830, revealing a Creole elitism that became a central feature of Mexican constitutionalism.

The weakness of constitutional liberalism as a political program became apparent to Mora after 1830. As a liberal he could no longer overlook, as he had in the 1820s, the reality of entrenched corporate privilege, epitomized by the juridical privileges of the church and the army and by the vast ecclesiastical property holdings. Mora realized that the state, instead of being further restricted, must be strengthened if individualism and equality under the law were to have meaning. Thus he turned away from constitutionalism and from Benjamin Constant, finding guidance instead in the Spanish Bourbon reform tradition. As theorist for the first Mexican reform government of 1833, Mora sensed that the "constitution" had to give way to a fiscally strong administrative state which could secularize society, institute legal equality, and yet avoid the democratic extremes of the French Jacobins or of the Spanish radicals of Cádiz.

The second constitutionalist episode came in the aftermath of the Reforma, Mexico's midcentury ideological and civil conflict. With the restoration of the Republic in 1867, the government of Benito Juárez issued the *convocatoria,* a call for elections, which marked the official return to constitutional government following the de facto wartime dictatorship. However, the convocatoria aroused great hostility because it included a proposal to modify the Constitution of 1857 that had been the banner of the liberal cause. In defending the changes, Minister Sebastián Lerdo de Tejada argued that to complete the Reforma Mexico must abandon "convention government" in favor of "good administration" and "constitutional balance." The Constitution had proclaimed popular sovereignty and had provided for a parliamentary regime on the French model of 1848. Under the Constitution, said Lerdo, the unicameral legislature was everything, the executive nothing. As a vehicle of "social reform" in the trying circumstances from 1857 to 1863, convention government might have been justified, but "in normal times the despotism of a convention can be as bad as the despotism of a dictator, or worse."[11]

The only reform proposal eventually to succeed called for the recreation of a senate, provided for in 1824 but abandoned in 1857. Lerdo argued that the Senate was a way to "consolidate our institutions" in the post-Reforma era. It would allow the states more authority to legislate and to curb the rash of local rebellions. The Senate would also have the power to call for federal intervention in a state whose constitutional powers had "disappeared." Thus "consolidation" in effect meant the strengthening of central authority as well as the controlling of excessive democracy. After several years of congressional debate, the Senate was finally adopted in 1874.

In promoting the Senate, the Juárez government published in 1870 a Spanish-language edition of Edouard de Laboulaye's *Histoire des États-Unis,* translated by Manuel Dublán, a stalwart of the regime. Moreover, approximately half of the congressional committee's recommendation of December 1869 consisted of sections from Laboulaye's discussion of the Senate in the United States Constitution.[12] Writing in the wake of the democratic Revolution of 1848, Laboulaye said that the experience of the United States might demonstrate "what the lasting conditions of liberty were and how a country [like France] that suffers from anarchy can reform its institutions."[13] Laboulaye saw the French Constitution of 1848 as abstract and unworkable, one that had inevitably led to Caesarism because a single chamber could provide no resistance to tyranny. The Mexican constitutional reform committee maintained that the nation's history fully confirmed the theories of Laboulaye. If a Senate is adopted, said the authors, "dictatorship will be less frequent among us."[14]

Laboulaye was a constitutionalist in the tradition of Montesquieu, Constant, and Tocqueville. Besides producing two editions of Constant's works in 1861 and 1872, Laboulaye published an important essay on Tocqueville and a seven-volume edition of Montesquieu in 1875. He argued the relevance of Montesquieu, who had survived all France's revolutions and "reappears whenever France takes up liberty anew."[15] Laboulaye's attachment to Constant was even stronger than it was to Montesquieu. Yet Laboulaye was less legalistic than Constant, for he also adhered to the German historical and comparative school of law derived from Friedrich Carl Von Savigny. Therefore Laboulaye was not in principle hostile to the state, which, representing nationality and justice, "encompasses what is great and most sacred within human institutions."[16] He spoke of the reconciliation of power and liberty, distinguishing like the Mexicans who cited him between dictatorship and strong government. The Senate was an important part of his vision, because through it men of merit, moderation, and substance could complement as well as limit administrative authority. France, he wrote in 1872, "wants to found a government that will assure public peace, while providing a solid guarantee for every interest and every right."[17] Such phraseology, joining interests, guarantees, and the authority of the state, struck a responsive chord in the liberal establishment of post-Reforma Mexico.

The third constitutionalist episode, which took place in the early 1890s and was closely related to the second episode, reflected the flowing together in Mexican political thought of historical constitutionalism and the new doctrine of scientific politics. In emphasizing administration and strong government, advocates of scientific politics regarded the convocatoria proposals of 1867 as a precedent; they upheld the newly reestablished Senate; and they quoted Laboulaye with approval. They found relevant the confluence in France of formerly antagonistic elements of political liberalism: the system of constitutional guarantees and the centralized state. Theirs was the language of an intellectual and social elite, which infused "science" into liberal discourse, producing an amalgam of formerly conflicting concepts.

The third episode entailed the founding of the National Liberal Union in 1892 and the subsequent campaign from within the official circle to reform the Constitution. The leader of this campaign, as in 1878, was Justo Sierra who, joined by some old and some new colleagues, used the scientific arguments of *La Libertad* to propose reforms that would limit, not enhance, the power of Porfirio Díaz. The advocates of scientific politics were still calling for strong government within the Constitution, but their sense of it had changed with the political situation. The weak executive of 1878 had now become too strong. The key reform proposal was to make judges irremovable, that is, appointed for life rather than being popularly elected (and thus subject to political manipulation), as provided for in the Constitution of 1857. The proposal sparked a major debate in Congress and in the press, in the course of which the reformers were labeled "científicos" (for their use of "scientific" language), and the opponents of reform, defenders of the pure constitution, "jacobinos." Thus 1893 marked the entry of these two epithets into the vocabulary of Mexican politics, to be used constantly thereafter.

The Científicos presented the elements of historical constitutionalism in the language of the new sociology. Justo Sierra argued that the effective separation of powers was no more than the creation of a healthy autonomy among the interdependent vital organs of a vigorous social body. *El Universal*, the principal journalistic advocate of irremovable magistrates, called the doctrinaire defenders of the Constitution "new reactionaries," attempting to stop evolution as if they were zoological organisms trying to retain their rudimentary members. Liberty, it continued, is not the product of "metaphysics," but rather of "positive facts."[18] The reformers also used the terms of historical constitutionalism. Justo Sierra recounted the epic struggle for a free judiciary through history, emphasizing that in France it had taken a century to surmount the ravages of Jacobin and Napoleonic tyranny that had laid waste to an independent judiciary.

Sierra's reference to the French Jacobins reminds us that the case for irremovability included an assault on popular sovereignty and a suspicion of democracy, as well as a resistance to dictatorship. Constant had emphasized the need for irremovable judges instead of the popularly elected judges of the Revolution, a guarantee of liberty repeated by Laboulaye in his critique of the Constitution of 1848.[19] In his eloquent remarks to the Mexican congress, the Científico Francisco Bulnes warned against committing the error of the opponents, "the same one committed by the Jacobins of 1893, that is, believing that liberty and democracy are the same thing or that liberty necessarily emanates from democracy."[20] As the advocates of scientific politics had done in 1878, Bulnes was linking his opponents' adherence to popular sovereignty to their defense of the Constitution of 1857. Now, however, the former label "metaphysical" was giving way to the new label "jacobin," reflecting yet another influence on Mexican political discourse, the ideas of Hippolyte Taine. Already evident in 1893, Taine's influence, as we shall see, was an important ingredient of the thought of Emilio Rabasa.

Thus concluded the third of the nineteenth-century episodes of historical constitutionalism, the campaign of 1893 to reform the Constitution. It failed but did not die, kept alive after 1900 in large part by the efforts of Emilio Rabasa. As we have noted, Rabasa probably would have been a party to the debate of 1893 had he not been serving as Porfirio Díaz's handpicked governor of Chiapas. As such, he was attempting to apply the other principal element of Porfirian liberalism, scientific politics, in this remote state. We will examine Rabasa's work as a Porfirian liberal governor; but before we do, let us turn in Chapter 2 to his earlier life and career (including a brief but impressive foray into literature), during which he assembled intellectually the principles of scientific politics.

CHAPTER TWO

Forming a Porfirian Career: Oaxaca, Mexico City, and Chiapas (1856–1894)

Emilio Rabasa was descended from two extensive and tight-knit merchant families of Catalan origin, who migrated from Spain to New Orleans, probably in the early 1820s, and later to Chiapas. These families were joined when Emilio's father, José Antonio, married his sister-in-law, Manuela Estebanell, in 1848, both having been widowed a few years earlier. Manuela's first husband, Silvestre Acebo, and Jose Antonio had worked in a New Orleans firm, Courval and Estebanell, cofounded by Manuela's father, José. On his death, José Estebanell bequeathed the business, which dealt in *ultramarinos* (imported foodstuffs), to his two employees, both of whom ultimately left New Orleans for Chiapas in 1836. Oriented toward the sea, José Antonio and his brother Isidro saw the opportunity to develop a port for remote Chiapas at Paredón, adjacent to Tonalá. After promoting the idea for three decades, they finally won over the governor, Angel Albino Corzo, and ultimately President Benito Juárez, who from Veracruz designated Tonalá officially as "Puerto de Cabotaje y Altura" in 1863. Isidro had died in 1860, but José Antonio Rabasa lived on, extending his activities into agriculture and commerce in the region of Tonalá and Tuxtla Gutiérrez, including the acquisition of a large property near Ocozocoautla. As early as the 1850s, we are told, José Antonio had accumulated "a well-preserved fortune."[1]

Emilio Rabasa Estebanell, the youngest of four children of José Antonio Rabasa and Manuela Estebanell, was born on 22 May 1856 in Ocozocoautla. Besides his three siblings, Emilio also acquired four half-brothers and sisters, Acebos and Estebanells, from his parents' first marriages. From this prosperous commercial and landed ancestry came the less known dimension of Emilio Rabasa, the man of practical legal and entrepreneurial affairs, as well as the more famous Rabasa, the jurist, politician, diplomat, and intellectual. He was the most eminent member of a clan that wielded great influence in the State of Chiapas for at least a generation.

After primary schooling at home and in Ocozocoaulta, Emilio was sent to Oaxaca at age twelve and enrolled in the Instituto de Ciencias y Artes del Estado. We don't know why he was sent to Oaxaca instead of to Spain and Germany like his older brother, Ramón, but the decision was significant for Emilio's future. Beginning his studies in 1868, he was exposed to the resurgent liberal republican civic culture of the Oaxaca that had sent Benito Juárez and Porfirio Díaz to triumph over the French army, Maximilian, and the Conservatives. The teenage Rabasa also immersed himself in the Spanish literary classics and in the fashion of the day took to writing romantic poetry. One creation of these early years was an unpublished series of thirty short poems of unrequited love, "To Ynes":

> Disdain! What does it matter to suffer your disdain!
> How sweet it is that my heart aches for you!
> Seeing disdain in your eyes,
> My soul wounded by cruel stings,
> I bless my love.[2]

Also, at age sixteen, he published an ode to Emilio Castelar, the great Spanish orator and republican statesman whose influence in Mexico was immense.

> Look upon Castelar! Regard the giant
> Who freed the Iberian people
> And raised his head in pride
> Before the arrogant monarch
> Who sought to subject them.[3]

Rabasa then turned to law, receiving his *licenciatura* in 1878. That same year he was discussing with his companions (and future Científicos) Rosendo Pineda and Emilio Pimentel articles from *La Libertad,* which was launching the doctrine of scientific politics in Mexico City. This may have been Rabasa's introduction to positivism, for Auguste Comte's hierarchy of the sciences, adapted by Gabino Barreda as the curriculum of the Escuela Nacional Preparatoria in Mexico City, was not introduced in the Oaxaca Institute until 1885.[4]

The precocious twenty-two-year-old was soon making his way in the legal, political, and social world of both Chiapas and Oaxaca. He seemed to have already gained prominence (and even notoriety) by 1880 when he successfully sought an *amparo* (a suit for protection of individual constitutional rights) against an 1861 Chiapas law requiring him on request and without pay to defend an accused criminal in a lower court. The State Tribunal decided against him, fined him, and threatened to remove his title. Following amparo procedure, Rabasa appealed to the Federal Supreme Court, which ruled unanimously in his favor. Chief Justice Ignacio Vallarta wrote a well-documented thirteen-page opinion (*voto*). The case was notable in that Rabasa had the Supreme Court judgment reprinted in Oaxaca, with a preface of explanation (and vindication) because "the matter raised commotion," and because he found it necessary to dispel the rumor that his title had been actually removed by the Chiapas tribunal.[5] Moreover, one can assume that the eminent jurist Ignacio Vallarta took note of this young lawyer. In 1881 Rabasa was named to the Ayuntamiento of Tuxtla and for two years was its deputy to the Chiapas state legislature, as well as serving as director of the Instituto del Estado, where he was credited with introducing a "modern" curriculum.[6]

Keeping close personal ties with the neighboring state, on 11 September 1882 Emilio Rabasa married Mercedes Llanes de Santaella, from a prominent Oaxaca family. However, it was a wedding beset with tragedy, for both Rabasa's parents died of cholera in Chiapas during the short interval between the civil and religious ceremonies. His son Oscar later wrote that Emilio learned of the first death, his father's, "moments before entering the church."[7] In a long romantic poem, "Memorias. A Mercedes" (1884), Rabasa recalled the loneliness of his early student years, the excitement of returning to the family hacienda for vacations (an arduous fifteen-day ride on horseback from Oaxaca), his joy at meeting his future wife, and the family tragedy. He concluded:

> My loving heart is with you;
> It is your sweet shelter
> And, loving you, it forgets the past
> Come with me and leaving behind your pain
> Let us fearlessly cross
> Through this painful vale of tears![8]

From 1882 to 1886, Rabasa practiced and taught law in Oaxaca, was a civil judge, and also a deputy to the state legislature. In 1885 he was chosen by that legislature to deliver an oration to mark the return of the remains of the Oaxacan hero, Colonel José María Ordaz, who died in the wars of the Reforma. Rabasa did so in florid Castelarian prose, vastly different from his later precise and carefully crafted literary and juridical style.[9] Rabasa also served briefly as private secretary to Governor Luis Mier y Terán, previously a notorious figure from the late 1870s in Veracruz. Rabasa soon resigned the post, "because he could not mould himself," we are told, "to the excessively restless character of the governor"; but the experience provided him material for his later novel, *La Gran Ciencia*. This whirl of activity in Oaxaca apparently caught the eye of Porfirio Díaz, for by the end of 1886, the young provincial lawyer and politician had arrived in the capital, his career now in full ascent.

Rabasa's initial period in Mexico City from 1886 to 1891 was basically devoted to expanding the activities of his earlier provincial years—in law and literature, with an added incursion into journalism and to a lesser extent into teaching and national politics. He was appointed to several judicial positions pertaining to criminal and private law, and he served as a substitute deputy to the national legislature. He also taught political economy at the Escuela Nacional de Comercio in 1889. Along with Victor Manuel Castillo, a relative from Chiapas, Rabasa founded the *Revista de legislación y jurisprudencia*.[10] These years were also for him an intense period of literary production, which included five short novels and some literary criticism, most of which appeared in *El Universal,* a daily newspaper of which he was presumably a cofounder in 1888. Of these multiple activities, let us turn first to the law. The short-lived *Revista* included technical articles by prominent jurists, including several by Rabasa. The publication, wrote the editors, responds to the need to advance the new "science of law." Positivist philosophy was beginning to permeate Mexican legal thought, just as it was political and social thought. Law, according to positivist philosophy, should adhere to a strictly scientific method, based on empirical examination of facts, social reality, the use of clear and precise language, and not upon "metaphysical" abstractions, such as universal natural rights.

In what Rabasa called "a philosophical examination" of "La Prisión preventiva" (protective custody without bail pending a trial), he argued in an article of that title that the concept did not have a legal character. However, it was a prudent judicial practice, if not applied arbitrarily, but based on sufficient proof of a criminal act.[11] The article appeared to have been drawn from a case recently brought to his criminal court, the Juzgado Primero de Instrucción. Lic. Luis Huller, an employee of the Mexican Land and Colonization Company was accused of defrauding the company. Rabasa ruled that Huller was innocent of the charges against him and that he had also been imprisoned improperly pending trial. Rabasa brought the case to public attention, as he had done with his amparo in Chiapas in 1880. He requested that Joaquín Baranda, minister of Justice and Public Instruction, publish it because "the newspapers continue to deal with this matter, without the indispensable facts to duly evaluate it." This was clearly a high-profile case, in part because Luis Velasco, a former minister and deputy, was the prosecutor and Huller's defender was Emilio Pardo, also a deputy and a future Científico. This episode is further evidence of Rabasa's entry by 1889 into the Porfirian establishment.[12]

Other articles in the *Revista de legislación* were probably also drawn from his judicial practice. In "Arbitrio judicial," Rabasa carried on a lengthy debate with Lic. Prisciliano Díaz González over individual rights versus the rights of society. If the individual is placed above society, argued Rabasa, the latter will dissolve. Moreover, prompt judicial punishment for a crime is what contributes to upholding constitutional guarantees. In yet another article, "El Caso Estrella," Rabasa called for more flexibility in criminal law as the only road to justice, in order to avoid two judgments for the same crime. Moreover, he said, a sentence should be annulled if subsequent proof of innocence appears. In each of these articles Rabasa revealed erudition (for example, he referred in "El Caso Estrella" to four different French commentators on criminal law), precision, and a proclivity for legal comparison, even though there was as yet little indication of his future eminence in public and constitutional law.[13] However, the *Revista* caught the attention of Bernardo Reyes, the prominent governor of Nuevo Leon, who sent information to the editors on laws of that state, as well as recommending the publication to state judicial officials.[14]

In the world of journalism, we are often told that Rabasa was a co-founder of the revived daily *El Universal*; however, his name did not appear on the paper's masthead, perhaps because of his perennial desire to keep a low public profile. It is clear, however, that he collaborated closely with Rafael Reyes Spíndola, the director of *El Universal*, a Oaxacan who had been a fellow student at the state Institute's Escuela de Derecho. The paper, later sold to Ramón Prida y Arteaga, became the chief journalistic advocate for the judicial and constitutional position upheld by the Científicos in the major debate of 1893. *El Universal* announced that on 1 August 1888 it would begin publishing works of major novelists, including Benito Pérez Galdos, José María Pereda, Juan Valera, Alphonse Daudet, and Guy de Maupassant. The first was to be *Miau* by Pérez Galdos, which had appeared in Madrid a few months earlier. It may well be that this literary initiative was the work of Emilo Rabasa and that he became the de facto literary editor of the paper. His personal contributions, which included criticism, at least one poem, a few stories, and the last of his short novels, were all signed by "Pio Gil"; thus Rabasa began a practice of supposed anonymity that he followed in all his literary writing. He of course made little effort to keep a low profile in his judicial work, in fact, as we have seen, quite the opposite. Moreover, he was named by the Junta Liberal de Periodistas Liberales to deliver an oration on the anniversary of the death of Juárez, published prominently in *El Universal* the following day (19 July 1888). He also signed a contribution to *La Escuela moderna* the following year, emphasizing the need for better teaching of national history.[15] Why Rabasa insisted on attaching pseudonyms to his literary creations remains something of a mystery.

Rabasa arrived in Mexico City well prepared for his brief and spectacular foray into the world of literature. Not only had he written poetry as a youth in Chiapas and Oaxaca, but also on the eve of his departure for the capital he edited *La Musa oaxaqueña,* an anthology of Oaxacan poets from the colonial era to Rabasa's time. He berated the tendency toward imitation, by national writers of Europeans and by provincial writers of those in the capital. Although Mexican letters form part of Spanish literature, he argued, we can achieve our own personality. If we seek our own traditions and seek inspiration in nature, our poetry will spring forth, "even if as a chaotic torrent, pure, magnificent, rich in colors, and perfectly individualized by the character of the people." This, he added, is the only true origin of a national literature.[16] Rabasa said the purpose of his work was to make Oaxacan poets known beyond the borders of the state. Among living poets, he included works by two women and two Santaellas, possibly relatives of his wife. Unfortunately, Rabasa's good intentions went unnoticed in Mexico City, and the book, published in Oaxaca, soon became virtually unobtainable.

However, in *El Universal,* "Pio Gil's" literary articles were very much noticed, for Rabasa did not shirk from criticizing the work of major figures. He rebelled against what he called the tendency in the newspapers to simply praise writers and to indulge in "mutual praise"; and he proceeded to attack the poetry of Ramón Valle. "Señor Valle is not a poet," concluded Rabasa. According to Rabasa, Valle abuses grammar and misuses verbs. He lacks interior fire, a vigorous imagination, and the ability to "portray what he feels." Moreover, "his verses suffer from a worse defect: they have no beauty."[17] Rabasa was kinder to Justo Sierra, whom he basically admired, though he again mentioned the poet's grammar, his use of verbs, and his tendency "to put on airs (*encumbrarse*)."[18] Rabasa then entered into a heated exchange with Francisco Sosa over *Miau* by Pérez Galdos, a work he greatly admired. I envy Spanish literature, he said, and I wish we could equal it. Although Pérez Galdos had presumably written his four famous novels before *Miau* was published, it is clear that the realistic social criticism and satire of his previous volumes in the series *Episodios contemporaneos* strongly influenced Rabasa.[19] In fact, his short story, "Juan B. Perez," in *El Universal* may have been modeled on *Miau,* for Rabasa's servile office seeker facing an indifferent minister was not unlike Ramón Villamiel, the *cesante* in *Miau,* who lost his government job and could not get reinstated.[20] Perhaps the most opinionated and moralistic of Rabasa's contributions to *El Universal* was

"La Cosa juzgada," in which he was at odds once again with Francisco Sosa. This time, it was over what Rabasa saw as the clear suggestions of incestuous relationships between Paul and Virginie in the novel of the same name by Bernardin de Saint Pierre and between María and Efraín in Jorge Isaac's famous Colombian novel *María*. Rabasa cited Proudhon ("a socialist!"), Bentham, and the Spanish writer Juan Valera in support of his strong attack on works that seemed to affirm incest, perhaps even encouraging such behavior by their readers.[21]

The culmination of Emilio Rabasa's literary career came in his thirties, with the publication in 1887 and 1888 of the four short volumes he called *novelas mexicanas,* followed by a novelette, "La Guerra de tres años," which appeared in *El Universal* in July 1891. When asked, just before his death in 1930, why he turned away from literature after 1891, he replied that his "work as a novelist had been a youthful whim."[22] Rabasa apparently conceived of the first four novels when he was still in San Cristóbal, Chiapas, and, despite his professed fear of the literary public, received continual encouragement from Rafael Reyes Spíndola during his Oaxaca years. Rabasa obviously had overcome his inhibitions by the time he arrived in Mexico City in 1886, and at his friend's urging that he write the first one in a month, he set to work. Rabasa's varied and prodigious activity in these years seems a wonder to our generation: as a father of two young children, he was writing his novels while carrying on three judicial positions, teaching, editing the *Revista de legislación* and *El Universal,* and writing articles regularly for both. Rabasa's Chiapas compatriot Angel Pola described his work surroundings: his study is "a small bare room . . . where he passes the time reading and writing, hour after hour, day and night." On his writing table are only "his weapons: inkwell, pen, the first volume of the works of Fr. Luis de Granada and the *Diccionario de la Academia.*"[23] This Spartan environment seemed to permeate not only his work habits but his character and personality as well.

Rabasa's major literary effort was of course the famous serial novels signed by "Sancho Polo," *La Bola, La Gran Ciencia, El Cuarto Poder,* and *Moneda falsa,* in effect one novel in four parts. In them are revealed Rabasa's penchant for political and social observation and satire, his spare style, and his positivist conviction that all knowledge comes from experience. There are clear autobiographical elements in the tale he tells. The novels trace the career of an honest and intelligent villager, Juan Quiñones, who is swept along by events from his town of San Martín de la Piedra to the state capital and ultimately to Mexico City.[24] Initially an unwitting participant in a local rebellion (*La Bola*), Juan then becomes a clerk in the office of the governor and experiences provincial politics (*La*

Gran Ciencia); he later finds success in the metropolis as a journalist (*El Cuarto Poder*). In his innocence, Juan is continually shocked by the duplicity, intrigue, and corruption of politics and journalism. But he gradually yields to ambition, abetted by his passionate hatred for the crude *cacique* Don Mateo Cabezudo (Pighead), leader of the successful local rebellion and later a rising urban politician. Juan's hatred for Cabezudo clashes with his love for Cabezudo's niece and jealously protected ward, Remedios, whom Don Mateo brings with him to the capital. With the ultimate reversal of the fortunes of the blood enemies Juan and Don Mateo, both return disillusioned to San Martín and become reconciled. Juan and Remedios are married with Don Mateo's blessing. Although Remedios dies young, she leaves Juan a daughter, also Remedios; and Juan finally realizes that she and the village are "pure gold," the world he has left *Moneda falsa* (false coinage).

La Guerra de tres años (The Three-Years War) tells a somewhat different story, written "with the wit and elegance that were characteristic of Rabasa."[25] Except for the concluding paragraphs, it takes place exclusively in the village of El Salado, where the church-state conflict of the post-Reforma years is played out at the local level. The subject of contention is a religious procession for San Martín, planned by Doña Nazaria, the zealous church mouse (*beata*). Don Santos Camacho, the imperious district boss (*jefe político*), a good anticlerical liberal, is determined to stop the procession. The town folk are divided, many caught between their liberal politics and their religious sentiments. The conflict is fueled by the fact that Don Santos, who had courted the widow Nazaria, suddenly drops her for the younger Luisa. In the absence of Don Santos, who happens to be away at a cockfight, the procession begins. He returns quickly, stops the procession, levies a fine on the organizers, and imprisons the priest. Doña Nazaria then appeals to the pious wife of the governor to lift the fine and to remove Don Santos. The governor, who had recently received a directive from Manuel Romero Rubio, minister of the Interior, to enforce the Reform Laws, finds an intermediate solution. He praises Don Santos, upholds the fine, makes a contribution "charged to extraordinary war expenses," and then promotes the jefe político to an ambiguous state position. "This is all that happened in El Salado. This story may be insipid (*sosa*), but I can't be blamed if great things don't take place in El Salado."[26] Thus Rabasa ends the tale.

It has been argued that Rabasa's novels are an overt apology for the Porfirian political system, an argument that has some truth.[27] The rise and fall of both Juan Quiñones and Don Mateo Cabezudo and their return to quiet village life, disillusioned by the moneda falsa of the broader world of journalism and politics, can be taken to suggest that the affairs of the country are best left to a paternalistic dictator. If peace is not enforced from the top, goes the argument, politics could become a perpetual *bola*. Moreover, as demonstrated in El Salado, the Constitution and the Reform Laws embedded in it are not to be seriously enforced, if they undermine the peace. Rabasa clearly was an aspiring figure in the Mexico of Don Porfirio, and the doctrine of scientific politics to which he adhered was an elitist call for strong government and adaptation of the Constitution to social realities.

However, Rabasa's novels and the ideas revealed in them are more than a Porfirian tract. They are a fine depiction of political and social realities on three levels, the village, the province, and the metropolis.[28] Rabasa clearly drew from his own experience, growing up in Chiapas and Oaxaca, as secretary to the problematic Governor Mier y Terán, and presumably from his first experiences in Mexico City (which of course did not include politics at the highest level). We have no record of his direct contact with the problems of enforcing the Reform Laws on the local level, but cases like those he depicts in El Salado are well known. On one level, Rabasa seemed to stand apart from the life he portrayed, a somewhat bemused observer and master satirist, trying to pinpoint (often quite humorously) reality as he saw it. On another level, he is, as Emmanuel Carballo puts it, "a novelist with a message," advocating through his characters a political and social order "at once more rational and effective."[29] Though clearly a supporter of the Reforma (unless his 1888 eulogy on Juárez was sheer hypocrisy), Rabasa realized the legitimate conflict their imposition caused in society. He was not militantly anticlerical; for example, he portrayed Padre Benajmín Marojo in *La Bola* sympathetically as the spiritual and moral buttress of San Martín de la Piedra.

A provincial lawyer said early on to Juan Quiñones, "in politics there are no scruples that are worth anything, and the *gran ciencia* consists of not losing, not falling."[30] From Rabasa's novels emerge his conviction that what the country needed was strong executive authority, supported by an enlightened elite. This would be in effect a true implementation of scientific politics to counter "*la gran ciencia*" of the novels—that is, the provincial *bolas* and the pointless strivings of petty urban politicians and corruptible journalists. Scientific politics for Rabasa was quite different from mindless support for a personalistic dictatorial regime, just as it came to be for the Científicos of 1893. As noted above, with the publication of "La Guerra de tres años," Rabasa left his literary career behind, though we will see that traces of it reappeared unexpectedly twenty-five years later.

During his five years in Mexico City, Emilio Rabasa maintained ties with his home state through the periodic meetings of the Chiapas colony of the capital. The remoteness of Chiapas from Mexico City, the monumental problem of travel, and the close-knit elite (*familia chiapaneca*), probably brought the group together more so than those from other regions. *El Universal* reported on 18 July 1888 that resident *chiapanecos* were meeting to take part in an enthusiastic recognition of Benito Juárez. Rabasa was elected president of the Executive Committee, and also as we have noted delivered a eulogy on the hero of the Reforma. Two of Rabasa's relatives, Victor Manuel Castillo and Juan M. Esponda were also on the committee. Among others at the July meeting was Angel Pola, regarded as the patriarch of the Chiapan colony.[31] Rabasa's leadership among his countrymen, his notable juridical talent, his literary fame (particularly his exposure of *caciquismo*), and his ties to the emerging Científicos of Mexico City were clearly all reasons that prompted Porfirio Díaz to select him (among five candidates) to run for election as Governor of Chiapas.[32] He was to replace Manuel Carrascosa, whose term had been tarnished by financial and personal scandal. At age thirty-four, Rabasa became the youngest of Mexico's governors, well prepared to implement with vigor the principles of scientific politics in the country's most underdeveloped state. In the words of Thomas Benjamin, the only historian to probe the Rabasa governorship in detail, "the history of modern Chiapas, in a political and economic sense, begins with his reforms."[33]

The young governor returned in late 1891 to a state that had experienced throughout the nineteenth century intense conflict between its two major economic and social regions, the traditional highlands and the lowlands in the valley of the Grijalva River. The highlands were the center of the majority indigenous population and included the state capital San Cristóbal de las Casas. The less populated but more fertile and economically progressive lowlands had as their center the city of Tuxtla Gutiérrez. Emilio Rabasa, his ancestors, and his extended family, were of course rooted in the latter region. Although elite contention was basically over regional issues, especially the access to Indian lands and labor, the church was also a point of conflict. It held extensive rural properties (at least 30 percent of the total before 1856) and a traditional sway over Indian communities. The two *ladino* (non-Indian) factions were drawn into the national midcentury political and ideological conflict, lowlanders becoming anticlerical Liberals and those of the highlands prochurch Conservatives. From 1855 to 1861 Angel Albino Corzo, son of a lowland sugar planter, became governor. Under his regime, many

Governor Emilio Rabasa ca. 1892. Courtesy of RVR.

properties were transferred to Liberal hands, including rich estates of the Dominican order and *baldios* (traditional indigenous property outside the confines of the community proper). The local attack on church lands was bolstered by the 1859 nationalization decree of the Liberal government under Benito Juárez at Veracruz. Continual Conservative rebellions against Governor Corzo and his successors also marked the period of national civil war until the ultimate triumph of the Liberal Republic in 1867. Symbolic of the political conflict in Chiapas before 1867, the Liberals were forced to move the state capital several times from San Cristóbal to Tuxtla Gutiérrez and from 1867 to 1872 even to the town of Chiapa.

The 1870s and 1880s saw a marked economic expansion in the state, particularly in the central lowlands, as new external markets emerged for coffee, cacao, sugar, and mahogany, along with traditional ranching. Emilio Rabasa's father and uncles took part in this expansion, as we have seen. Economic opportunity also brought immigrants, especially Germans who became coffee planters in Soconusco and neighboring Guatemala. The overall population of the state grew by 50 percent from 1870 to 1890. Amid this expansion, labor became increasingly scarce, which led to an increase of indebted servitude (peonage), because, in contrast with the north, there were few alternative opportunities for laborers. The post-Reforma era also saw the increase of *caciques,* local bosses whose power greatly weakened the state government. An anonymous report to the Minister of Finance Matías Romero, in 1878, indentified a system of "indescribable chaos," one "in the hands of arbitrary *jefes políticos,* ignorant school teachers, and corrupt priests."[34] In short, an "intractable malady," the report concluded. Jesús Rabasa, a rancher and relative of Emilio's, wrote a year later that only the central government could correct the reigning disorder. By 1891 Porfirio Díaz apparently came to the same conclusion and thus turned to the rising young intellectual and jurist.

Rabasa's agenda was ambitious from the start: nothing less than to integrate Chiapas with the nation. It was a state without modern transportation, communications, or schools, and one as we have seen in which local caciques were powerful, the state government weak. Ties with Guatemala, particularly in the highlands, were stronger than with Mexico.[35] Governor Rabasa set out to change these conditions. In doing so, he accepted Porfirio Díaz without question as "the essential man" carrying the nation beyond mere political struggle characteristic of "the state of anarchy" to the economic principles upheld by "civilized peoples."[36] Though he did not articulate these thoughts until 1912, it is evident from his constant correspondence with Díaz while governor that they were assumptions that guided his administration. Although Rabasa definitely had the confidence of Porfirio Díaz, he found it necessary to seek "instructions" frequently and to report in detail to the president on even minor actions he took. He did this perhaps in part because he could not return frequently to Mexico City to confer personally with the president, as did other governors. The arduous voyage from Chiapas made that impossible. Two modern authors refer to Rabasa as Díaz's "proconsul" in Chiapas; a third calls him "a local Díaz."[37]

One of Rabasa's early initiatives was to transfer the capital of Chiapas from San Cristóbal de las Casas to Tuxtla Gutiérrez. As we have noted, moving the capital was not a new idea. From 1858 to 1861, during the national Three-Years War, and again in 1863 during the French Intervention, resurgent Conservatives forced Liberal Governor Corzo to retreat to Tuxtla. With the national amnesty of 1867, all state capitals were to return to their original sites. Nonetheless, Governor José Pantaleón Domínguez defied the agreement and chose to make the intermediate town of Chiapa his capital, fearing renewed control of government by the *cristobalenses*. He finally returned to San Cristóbal in 1872. During the subsequent two decades, the economically prosperous central valley elite increasingly saw the advantage of having Tuxtla Gutiérrez as the state capital. Whereas San Cristóbal was the traditional trade route to Guatemala, Tuxtla was the potential gateway to Oaxaca and to Mexico City. Thus Governor Rabasa's action, while decisive and an integral part of his program of modernization, was built upon ample precedent.[38]

Although Porfirio Díaz probably saw the move as beneficial, Rabasa nonetheless felt obliged to make a strong case over several months. He emphasized the great scarcity of food in San Cristóbal, most of which had to come over nonexistent roads from *tierra caliente*. Hard-pressed government employees were threatening to leave, he said, and even Rabasa asked to be relieved of his post and given a seat in Congress. Rabasa in addition used the "Indian problem" to reinforce his argument for transfer of the capital and his ongoing diatribe against San Cristóbal. The Chamulas, "the most wretched and submissive Indians of the Republic," he wrote, are the eternal victims of maltreatment by the *cristobalenses,* maltreatment, for example, that the "highlanders (*serranos*) of Oaxaca" would not tolerate. He added that in 1869 there was no "Caste War" (a view he was to repeat publicly a year later); the term "is a pretext. What happened is that the Indians wanted to destroy San Cristóbal." The Chamulas even bring their produce and artifacts willingly to Tuxtla, Chiapa, and Comitán, because they are abused and cheated in San Cristóbal.[39] Rabasa's campaign was obviously successful, despite many protests to Díaz from disgruntled cristobalenses, for Tuxtla Gutiérrez became the official capital of Chiapas on 11 August 1892. Rabasa's initiative naturally produced intense cristobalense hatred toward Rabasa and *rabacismo* for many years. There were several efforts after 1894, including an armed rebellion in 1911, to bring the capital back to its previous site, but the Rabasa action prevailed, in part because of his continuing influence and that of his brother Ramón over affairs in their native state.[40]

The moving of the capital allowed Governor Rabasa to replace the bureaucracy of the Carrascosa regime. Many of Rabasa's appointments were Oaxaqueños he knew, men without local ties. This new bureaucracy made it possible to enhance the efficiency of public finance, to improve accounting practices, and to increase tax revenue. Rabasa also established a rural police force (*seguridad pública*) dependent on the governor and a post of *visitador* (inspector) *de jefaturas* to control local authorities.[41] His most successful attack on *caciquismo* was to appoint Manuel Figuerro of Oaxaca as jefe político of Soconusco in 1892 in order to limit the power of long-time cacique Sebastián Escobar. Rabasa's plan was facilitated by the chance assassination of Escobar in late 1893. Rabasa could report to Porfirio Díaz that because of the assassination, the new jefe político "will take this opportunity to make sure that Soconusco will have no more *caciques*."[42] His success was less dramatic elsewhere in the state, for example in Chiapa, where Julián Grajales continued strong, despite the creation of a new adjacent department, Mescalapa, in order to limit his power. Although Rabasa wrote to Díaz in January 1894 that Pichucalco (also adjacent to Mescalapa) and Soconusco were "now entirely submissive," there is no specific evidence of intervention by Rabasa in Pichucalco.[43] Nonetheless, a later respected revolutionary leader concluded that Rabasa "developed and put into practice a completely new program of government, which until then was unknown in Chiapas."[44]

It would seem natural that Governor Rabasa, an already established judicial authority on the national level, would turn to a reform of the state's Constitution of 1858. What emerged under his guidance on 15 November 1893 was in essence a new, much simplified document. The 1893 Constitution was two-thirds the length of that of 1858 and in a sense codified the scientific administrative orientation of the Rabasa regime. Moreover, the 1858 Constitution, promulgated during Governor Angel Albino Corzo's chaotic term, was issued from the temporary capital of Chiapa during the national Three-Years War. It had also been subject to many amendments and changes by decree in subsequent decades, constituting more pages than the original document.[45] The principal substantive change in the 1893 document was the enhancement of the executive power. Jefes políticos were to be appointed by the governor, rather than elected by the city governments (*ayuntamientos*), thus codifying the practice already initiated by Rabasa. The new constitution also omitted much detail on matters of governmental function, elections, and restrictions on officials. The 1858 document seemed to reveal a persistence of the spirit of the colonial laws of the Indies, that is, "confusion between the fundamental laws and the details, which in the modern age have been entrusted to the regulatory power."[46] In any case, the 1893 Constitution of the State of Chiapas was a spare document, reflecting the juridical precision that Emilio Rabasa was to bring to his subsequent constitutional writing.

If one pillar of Rabasa's governorship was strong and efficient government, put on a modern and "scientific" basis, another was the establishment of infrastructure to unleash the spirit of enterprise (particularly in coffee and cattle) of the *tuxtaleño* elite in the agriculturally rich central valley. Rabasa began construction of the first modern road in Chiapas, from the border of Oaxaca at Arriaga through Tuxtla and San Cristóbal to Comitán and Guatemala. The first section, from Arriaga to San Cristóbal was completed during Rabasa's term, the rest carried on by his successors.[47] Díaz authorized the use of the army for construction; previous efforts to establish private contracts for road building had come to nothing, in part because the cristobalense elite preferred Indian carriers as a cheaper alternative. Rabasa was painfully aware from personal experience of the need for roads, for he had traveled numerous times by mule to and from Oaxaca during his years of schooling, marriage, and early career, a journey of two weeks. Shortly before his death, Rabasa described in detail his trip in November 1891 from Mexico City to take up the governorship. It involved traveling overland to Veracruz, then by boat to the port of Frontera in Tabasco, inland to the capital at San Juan Bautista (later Villahermosa), down the Grijalva river to Pichucalco, and finally on to San Cristóbal. He made this trip with his family and several friends, spending one eventful night at the Indian village of San Bartolo Solistahuacán.[48] In fact, this route from San Cristóbal to San Juan Bautista was the preferred plan for road building before Rabasa's arrival. As governor, Rabasa also expanded the telegraph network begun in 1886 and installed the first telephone line; he further developed the port facilities promoted by his father in the 1850s at Paredón (Tonalá) as well as at San Benito (Tapachula.)

The modernizing accomplishments of Emilio Rabasa's governorship were in effect set forth by his older brother Ramón (1849–1932) in an official detailed geographical and statistical almanac of the State of Chiapas, undoubtedly commissioned by Porfirio Díaz, and published in Mexico City. The two-hundred page volume included the principal geographical features of the state, a full description of the political divisions of the country, its agricultural products, its communications, distances between communities, and a breakdown of the population of each department between its principal towns and rural properties, all based on a census of 1892. The volume also listed an impressive number of tax laws and decrees issued by Emilio Rabasa's regime. Though the tone of the volume was factual rather than promotional, it was clearly designed to point up the progress of the state.[49] Ramón Rabasa served as state treasurer from 1899 to 1905, as well as manager of the newly created Bank of Chiapas. He was governor of the state from 1906 to 1911.

Education was also an important part of the infrastructure Rabasa sought for a modern Chiapas. He wrote to Governor Bernardo Reyes of Nuevo Leon that he was much impressed with the advances of public education in that state, and he sought general information, plus specifics on buildings, maintenance, and methods of instruction. Reyes responded with a three-page report, which described these matters, as well as the new Normal School and the General Executive Committee for Public Instruction.[50] The educational budget of Chiapas under Rabasa's guidance was increased from 7,000 to 40,000 pesos. Despite great obstacles—the lack of teaching materials and miserable pay for teachers—he could announce in 1893 the establishment of 167 primary schools, where virtually none existed previously, as well as two new preparatory schools in Tuxtla and Comitán. Nonetheless, Rabasa did not regard education as a cure-all for social development (unlike, for example, Justo Sierra). This point was made by *El Universal* (19 October 1893) in Mexico City, the newspaper that supported the Científicos and was directed by Rafael Reyes Spíndola, Rabasa's school friend from Oaxaca and publisher of his novels.[51] When Rabasa reported to the Chiapas legislature in 1892 that the state could count on "powerful forces that can be utilized for development of the state," his particular emphasis was on "those [forces] of private initiative developing uniquely in some departments."[52]

Emilio Rabasa adhered to the nineteenth-century liberal bias against rural communal property, which he regarded as an obstacle to progress. He was determined to "offer lands to enterprising men" by dividing communal properties, granting individual portions to the poorest rural inhabitants, and selling the remainder. As in the case of other Rabasa initiatives, he built upon precedent, providing the decisive culmination of policies pursued by previous governments. One precedent was the midcentury national alienation of corporate ecclesiastical property, a process that was essentially completed before Rabasa took office. Another precedent was the alienation over many years of indigenous *baldíos*, lands, we have noted, outside the communities proper. These measures, as Jan Rus has argued, were a major cause of the so-called "Caste War" of 1869–70, when Indians rose up against ladinos and were only defeated when the two contending elite groups, those of the highlands and those of the Central Valley, put aside their differences to meet a common threat. The threat of renewed uprising by "barbarous" Indians against "civilization," what Rus calls "the myth of the Caste War," was a major preoccupation after 1870, fed by journalists and at least two prominent historical accounts.[53] Rabasa was clearly aware of this history when he began his speech to the state congress in 1893. He dismissed concern over vague reports of uprisings in Palenque and Chilón, "which are often called 'caste wars,' but are now little more than a myth." He emphasized the "peaceful condition" of the Indians of the center and northeast, if only they are treated with "an attitude of simple humanity."[54] This apparent sympathy for the indigenous majority did not affect Rabasa's land policy or (as we will see) his labor policy.

Rabasa's "agrarian reform" was not only built on specific local precedents, but it also formed part of a general national policy of identifying titles to occupied lands, and of surveying unoccupied public lands (*terrenos baldíos*). These baldíos were generally distinct from the indigenous baldíos in Chiapas mentioned above. The national policy toward public lands was governed till 1894 by the Juárez law of 1863, by which individuals could survey and make claim to (*denunciar*) up to 2500 hectares of unoccupied lands at a price set by the government. In 1883, in order to speed up this process in the interests of development, the survey of public lands was contracted out to private (including foreign) companies, which received grants of one-third of the lands surveyed. Stimulated by a general fever for development, this policy produced a surge of public land transfers, reaching a peak in the early 1890s; and it often ran roughshod over indigenous communities.[55] Thus Rabasa's agrarian policy, as laid out in a series of decrees issued in 1892 and 1893, followed a national trend, and was designed, he said, to "take extensive portions of land from their present abandon and turn them over to be worked."[56] Moreover, Rabasa's decrees coincided with (and actually preceded) a new national legislative initiative in 1893, which would further facilitate the alienation of terrenos baldíos, by removing the 2500-hectare limit for individual claims. This initiative was promoted by several of Rabasa's Científico friends, including Justo Sierra, Rosendo Pineda, and Emilio Pimentel, and was passed into law in 1894.[57]

Rabasa's plan in Chiapas was to use the receipts from the sale of communal lands to finance schools and public building in rural communities, but its success was modest. Although Chiapas before the 1890s was not basically a region of latifundia, there was considerable land grabbing by larger property owners. The effect of the distribution (*reparto*) on villages was devastating. Class divisions in the countryside increased. Many communal properties disappeared because poor *campesinos* could not afford minimum payments. Better-off farmers were able through purchase to increase their holdings, and the number of ranchos more than doubled from 1890 to 1910. Rabasa said he had hoped that distribution would be the best way of preventing larger landholders from appropriating all communal land at the expense of traditional villagers who could not prove ownership. But he admitted years later that he erred in not making the smallest plots inalienable.[58] In effect, Emilio Rabasa's agrarian reform program was, according to Benjamin, "an economic success and a social disaster," again not unlike results on the national level.[59] A recent study by Sarah Washbrook goes further and argues that Emilio Rabasa's policies initiated a practice of facilitating the acquisition of land, especially in Soconusco, Pichucalco, and Palenque, by the elite of the central valley, with which Rabasa had close relations, and by foreign investors. Critics, especially those from the church and the displaced leadership in San Cristóbal, came to brand as rabacismo these explicit government efforts by Rabasa and his successors (which included his brother Ramón).[60]

Governor Rabasa, ever mindful of the need to promote economic development in the state, also pursued a campaign to "free" labor from the traditional bonds of indebtedness. Until 1890 peonage was regarded as basic to the state's economy. However, the shift of the political and economic center of gravity from the highlands to the central valley brought a call for labor reform. The major impetus for the change, according to Jan Rus, was the rapid expansion of coffee plantings in the late 1880s and early 1890s in Soconusco and the resulting need in this underpopulated region for workers to harvest the beans.[61] The argument for free labor, supported by Rabasa, was that indebted labor paralyzed substantial amounts of capital that could be better employed in the interests of both workers and agriculturalists. Labor became a priority item, along with the promotion of scientific agricultural techniques, the establishment of banks, and the construction of railroads, on the agenda of the Mexican Agricultural Society of Chiapas, founded in 1893 in Tuxtla Gutiérrez.[62] It appears that different solutions emerged for Soconusco from those applied to the northern regions. Rabasa was unable to "solve" the labor problem in Soconusco during his term, mainly because of resistance from the highland elite to the transfer of "their" Indians to the coffee regions. However, a solution finally came later in the decade when a kind of compromise was negotiated between the agriculturalists of the two regions in which the debts of highland Indians were assumed by coffee planters in exchange for the transfer of seasonal labor from the highlands.[63]

As for the northern areas, Rabasa's government and those of his successors, according to Washbrook, actually reinforced existing patterns of debt servitude. Through the new government-appointed jefes políticos and municipal officials, the state lent official support and enforcement to *enganche,* a system of contract labor (a contract that often included a worker's debt to his employer). Thus, far from being a "free" system controlled by market forces, government supported enganche became in effect a recycling of older practices of extralegal peonage, adapted to the new rapidly expanding export agriculture. The mistreatment of indigenous workers under this system was particularly notorious in the *monterías* (tropical hardwood enterprises) of the Lacandón region and in the rubber plantations of Palenque.[64]

Governor Rabasa's development program for Chiapas also entailed active promotion of land speculation by Mexicans and foreigners, as well as seizing the opportunity to acquire land for himself. Soon after taking office in March 1892, Rabasa wrote Díaz that he would like to register a claim to (*denunciar*) a 2,500-hectare plot in Soconusco near the Guatemala border, following the procedure set out in the 1863 and 1883 laws. The land would be drawn from the two-thirds of a concession company survey that remained in government hands. Rabasa would pay the going rate of two pesos a hectare. He justified his request on the need to "create a modest future for my four daughters" which he said he could not do on the meager salary of a governor. His intention, he told the president, was to develop a coffee *finca,* like those that were prospering greatly in this region. Although Díaz readily granted his request, it is not known whether he actually developed the land and what became of it.[65] We do have evidence that he sold properties before returning to Mexico from exile in 1920, but not which properties. A few years later, Rabasa received a lavish dedication in a promotional book by W. W. Byam, a California broker who managed a land company in the northern Palenque region near the border with Tabasco. Byam's book urged Americans to colonize the area and raise coffee.[66] As we have noted, the same area also aroused enthusiasm for the production of rubber. Rabasa not only facilitated a contract for the major speculator Rafael Dorantes, but also acquired an adjacent division ("El Naranjo") himself. It is not clear whether this acquisition was during his governorship or later; nor do we know whether he actually developed a rubber plantation.[67] Rabasa also participated in the negotiation for a concession to construct a railroad from Tonalá to Tuxtla and Chiapa de Corso, but we know nothing of the plan's progress.[68]

On 13 January 1894, in a letter to Porfirio Díaz relating many of his accomplishments in Chiapas, Rabasa asked for the second time to be relieved of his post. The reasons he gave were that his wife's health was suffering in Chiapas and that he wanted to provide education for his daughters.[69] There is no reason to doubt the sincerity of these reasons. We can imagine that throughout his brief governorship Rabasa was torn between his strong attachment to his native state and the attractions and opportunities for himself and his family in Mexico City. These he had already experienced from 1885 to 1891. This time Díaz granted his request readily, but insisted that he recommend a substitute to fill out his term. Rabasa's choice was Fausto Moguel, a relative, who was serving as state treasurer. Moguel took office on 27 February and assured Díaz that he would carry on Rabasa's "regenerative plan . . . that will be the basis of the state's future prosperity."[70] Although Rabasa was clearly a governor of great energy, determined to transform Mexico's most remote state into "a laboratory of modernization," he undoubtedly came to realize the tremendous obstacles to be overcome. This had been his emphasis in his first speech to the legislature. This speech, he had said, would be more than "an empty formality"; better that "the governors of the people make known what is defective in order to correct it, than what is good in order to applaud it."[71] It is unlikely that Rabasa had directly sought the post, but rather that Porfirio Díaz sought him to rescue the state from its backwardness, perpetual conflict, and recent financial scandals.

Thus Emilio Rabasa left Chiapas in February 1894, never to return in an official capacity. His interest in his native state remained strong, and in the years between 1894 and 1911 the Rabasa legacy prevailed, despite opposition from the displaced elite of San Cristóbal. At age thirty-seven, Emilio Rabasa was prepared to re-enter the national scene. Before returning to Chiapas, Rabasa had become a journalist, a major novelist, and a recognized jurist. He returned to Mexico City prepared to pursue once again his intellectual and legal pursuits, even though he had abandoned literature by 1891. However, he did not withdraw from politics, for on his return in 1894 Díaz arranged his election as Senator from the state of Sinaloa, a post he was to hold until 1913.

During his short term as governor of Chiapas, Rabasa successfully applied the principles of Porfirian scientific politics to the nation's most remote and undeveloped state. As we have noted, his program of modernization won the praise of the científico press of the capital. It was based on the establishment of strong government and centralized administration, the reduction of local *caciquismo,* an ambitious program of public works and communications, and a transfer of power from the traditional quasi-feudal landowners of the highlands to the economically progressive commercial and agricultural elite of the central valley and coastal plain. The program also involved opening up lands to Mexicans and foreigners in the undeveloped northern region of Chiapas, a program from which he derived personal benefit. Unlike the Científicos of Mexico City, Rabasa made no effort to challenge the personal authoritarianism of Porfirio Díaz, though he came in time to be a leading proponent of their constitutionalism of 1893. Nor did he display the independence of other Porfirian governors such as Teodoro Dehesa of Veracruz or Bernardo Reyes of Nuevo León. He remained in constant touch with the president and sought his approval for all he undertook. Díaz undoubtedly regarded him as a model governor, but one who was too much the national intellectual to remain confined to remote Chiapas. Although Rabasa and his successors made Chiapas in political and economic terms into what has been called "a laboratory of modernization," literally bringing Chiapas into the nation, the long-standing social reality of the state was reinforced and actually aggravated.[72] Rabasa did show some sympathy for the plight of the oppressed indigenous majority near San Cristóbal; but as a Porfirian liberal, his concern for economic development, as revealed in his attack on communal property and his effort to create a labor force for the expanding coffee region of Soconusco and the plantation areas of the north took precedence over social reform. It might even be argued that in Emilio Rabasa's application of the principles of scientific politics in Chiapas, we can find the remote origins of the rebellion a century later.

CHAPTER THREE

Senator, Juridical Theorist, and Constitutional Historian (1894–1912)

In early 1894 Emilio Rabasa returned to Mexico City and resumed a multifaceted career on the national stage. During the next eighteen years he established a reputation as the nation's leading authority on constitutional law, a subject he also taught at the Escuela Nacional de Jurisprudencia, and as a noted interpreter of Mexico's political institutions. Through his two books, *El Artículo 14* (1906) and particularly *La Constitución y la dictadura* (1912), Rabasa became a major intellectual, a true national *pensador*. But his activities were certainly not limited to writing; in 1895 he opened a law office with Nicanor Gurría Urgel, a relationship that lasted until his death.[1] In addition, Emilio Rabasa served as Senator from September 1894 to October 1913 when the Senate dissolved itself. These years were critical for his career and intellectual accomplishment, but also for his family and for the nation. The two youngest of his seven children, Oscar and Ruth, were born in 1896 and 1898, and his wife Mercedes died in 1910 from a gastric disorder. This middle period of Rabasa's life also saw the culmination of the regime of Porfirio Díaz, the development of major internal tensions, and finally the regime's collapse in 1911.

In his legal work, Emilio Rabasa was appointed by Porfirio Díaz to be the judicial arbiter in at least three prominent cases. The first case was in 1899, a boundary issue between the states of Puebla and Tlaxcala; the second and third were complex property disputes, one in 1903 between an indigenous community and a hacienda in Veracruz, the other in 1906 between two landowners in the Valle de Santiago of the State of Guanajuato. We do not know the outcome of the first case, since we have only a legal plea (*alegato*), not the judicial decision.[2] In the second case Rabasa ruled in favor of the hacienda owners, who had

Rabasa Family ca. 1908. Top Row: Concepción, Isabel, Mercedes, Manuela; Bottom Row: Emilio Jr., Mercedes Llanes, Ruth, Emilio, Oscar. Courtesy of RVR.

been granted a claim by the Ministry of Development in 1895, which the indigenous community argued was an encroachment on its traditional property.[3] In the third case, Rabasa decided in favor of the plaintiffs (*actores*), heirs to a hacienda that had passed from the Augustinian community of Querétaro to Dr. Nicolás García León in 1856, and then was much divided over the years. Rabasa ruled that the Jefe de Zona Militar of León had taken the property by force illegally (for supposed nonpayment of taxes), and that the State of Guanajuato had then sold it illegally to Sr. Rodríguez in 1894. Rabasa's forty-one-page ruling in this latter case revealed especially impressive judicial analysis and mastery of complicated facts.[4]

In politics it is clear that Emilio Rabasa had his eye on the Senate from April 1892, when he first requested that Porfirio Díaz relieve him of the governorship of Chiapas. As noted in Chapter 1, the Senate itself was reestablished in 1874, the most successful of the constitutional reform efforts put forth by Benito Juárez's minister Sebastián Lerdo de Tejada in 1867. It epitomized Lerdo's complementary concepts of "good administration" and "constitutional balance," which opposed the unicameral legislature enacted in the Constitution of 1857. Lerdo argued that while a convention-type legislature, reminiscent of the French Revolution, might have been necessary to carry out basic social reforms, the present priority was to "consolidate our institutions." After 1867, the government recognized that mounting regional and military challenges made imperative some means of strengthening control short of a general suspension of guarantees and establishment of martial law by executive decree. In March 1870 President Juarez emphasized recent "disgraceful upheavals" in Zacatecas and San Luis Potosí. Direct and equal representation by the states in a second chamber, he added, could give them more authority in creating legislation and thus allow them to participate more effectively in curbing local disorder. The re-creation of a Senate, therefore, was frankly presented as a means of "consolidation." Although the Senate theoretically represented the states, in effect it became closely aligned with central authority. For example, the Senate was given the power to declare, upon the "disappearance" of a constitutional state government, that the president (with Senate approval) could name a provisional governor, who would in turn initiate new elections. After several years of debate, Congress passed the final measure reestablishing the Senate on 9 April 1874, and the new body convened in September 1875.[5]

The Tuxtepec revolutionaries of 1876 called for the suppression of the Senate, since they identified it with President Lerdo, whom they overthrew. However, Porfirio Díaz, on becoming president, rejected that provision of the revolutionary program. In fact, the Senate was strongly supported by the advocates of scientific politics in *La Libertad* of 1878. By the 1890s, the Senate had lost much of its function as an institution of "consolidation" and constitutional balance, in part because of the decline of political contention between the states and the federal government. There came to be a general coalescence of interests between the regional elites and the president (especially after the economic crisis of 1892), because of the acceleration of economic growth and investment, the granting of concessions, and the alienation of public lands. By 1900 yet another change was taking place, namely the decline of an aged cohort of legislators, many of whom had been military companions of Porfirio Díaz, and their replacement by younger civilians, such as Emilio Rabasa.[6]

In the evolution of the Senate by the late 1890s, there were also a growing number of senators who were, like Rabasa, ex-governors. María Luna suggests that the Senate was attractive to ex-governors because it provided them an effective way to continue to exert influence in their states. Again, Rabasa fits this pattern.[7] Paradoxically, senators could exert this influence even if, as in the case of Rabasa, they represented a state other than their own. There had been much debate prior to the

reestablishment of the Senate over the residency (*de vecindad*) requirement. The majority opinion prevailed, using the incongruous argument
that the Senate in fact represented the nation. As Luna says, the fact
that Rabasa represented Sinaloa, "in constitutional terms is an absurd-
ity."[8] Be this as it may, the Senate during Rabasa's tenure, at least until
1911, had lost whatever political vigor and independence it had in the
1870s. Though Rabasa's actions in the Senate before 1911 were few, the
position did help him to remain influential in Chiapas and to hone his
political and juridical thought with the occasional constitutional issue
that came before the legislative body.

President Díaz customarily addressed the Senate at the beginning of
each session, focusing particularly on material improvements, a speech
that was followed by a vapid response from the then president of the
Senate. A typical one was that of 1901: "You come before us once again
to relate the laudable result of your efforts to guide the country on the
path of order and progress in its social and economic evolution."[9] Much
of the business of the Senate during Rabasa's prerevolutionary years involved the approval of railroad, mining, and industrial contracts awarded
to prominent Mexicans and foreigners. For example, in May 1899
Rosendo Pineda (himself a senator) won a contract for La Industrial,
SA, a factory producing rope (*cordelería*) and riding gear (*caballería*),
and Joaquín Casasús (a Científico) for a packing-house (*casa empaca-
dora*). In December 1899, John B. Body, representative of Pearson and
Son Ltd, won a contract to complete port works in Salina Cruz and
Coatzacoalcos and another in May 1904 relating to the Tehuantepec
Railroad (Ferrocarril Nacional de Tehuantepec).[10] Such contracts before
the Senate were usually approved unanimously without dissent. Rabasa
regularly served on the constitutional committee (Comisión de Puntos
Constitucionales); much of its business was to approve (again usually
without dissent) diplomatic posts for Mexicans abroad and for foreign
diplomats in Mexico, as well as decorations awarded to Mexicans by
foreign governments.[11] Of more substance were the infrequent proposals
to amend the Constitution, in which Rabasa was usually a central participant, often chair of the committee. A good example is the amendment
of 1908 to Article 102, pertaining to the defense of individual rights, the
juicio de amparo. This amendment was directly related to Rabasa's first
major juridical study, *El Artículo 14*. Let us turn first to that study, published in 1906, and then to the constitutional amendment of 1908.

In one sense *El Artículo 14* was a narrowly focused and technical
study, far more so than his three major works to follow, yet it was in another sense much broader. It not only uncovered a fundamental problem
in Mexico's system of judicial review (juicio de amparo), but it also re-

vealed basic assumptions in Emilio Rabasa's political and legal thought, as well as introducing general themes to be pursued at greater length in subsequent works. Rabasa wrote at the outset that since many had been troubled by the decline of the sovereignty of the states and by the overburdened Supreme Court, it was necessary to go to the heart of the problem, which lay in Article 14 of the Constitution. It is essential "to begin by establishing its meaning and indicating its scope."[12] The work also reveals Rabasa's style and manner of thought and composition. His son Oscar wrote proudly that this book like his others showed clear and precise intelligence, severe judgment, and penetrating analysis. *El Artículo 14,* he added, seemed to flow directly from his father's pen without changes in organization or more than a very few corrections, a tribute to "the precision of his thought."[13]

Article 14, according to Rabasa, emerged from the compression of three articles, 4, 21, and 26, of the draft Constitution of 1856, drawn from parts of three articles of the United States Constitution. Article 4 prohibited retroactive laws; Article 21 said no one could be deprived of property or rights except by appropriate judicial sentence; Article 26 said no one could be deprived of life, liberty, or property, except by judicial action, according to procedures fixed by law and exactly applied to the case at hand.[14] The resulting text of Article 14 stated: "No retroactive law shall be issued. No one can be judged or sentenced except by laws issued prior to the fact and applied exactly to it, by the tribunal that previously established the law." In explaining how and why this transformation of three articles into one took place, Rabasa pointed to two major preoccupations of the delegates. The first was the necessity to protect individuals from arbitrary actions imposed retroactively, a necessity derived from Mexico's experience since independence and particularly under the recent dictatorship of Antonio López de Santa Ana. The second preoccupation was the desire to abolish the death penalty, which Rabasa said distracted the constituyentes from the true object of debate. They were guided by the "sentimentalist philosophy" of the era, which "gave to that question an importance much greater than that of any other principle." Because of these two preoccupations—obsessions in fact—the committee ultimately abandoned draft Article 26 and unexplainably copied from Article 9, paragraph VIII of the conservative Bases Orgánicas of 1843. In short, concluded Rabasa, "our Article 14 is an imprudent improvisation that indicates a very blameworthy lack of thought; it is not of clear lineage, it is a bastard."[15]

Much of *El Artículo 14* was devoted to criticizing the constitution makers for their use of imprecise language. This defect was due in part to the philosophy of the times, but also to the fact that the delegates were caught up in a great revolution. In his first novel, Rabasa had written that a revolution, as distinct from a mere petty rebellion (*bola*), "develops around an idea, moves nations, transforms institutions and needs citizens . . . it is the daughter of world progress and the inescapable law of humanity."[16] Caught up in the passions of the moment, the delegates became fixed on the rights to be established and the limitations to be placed on power, at the expense of precision and form. Thus, the Constitution of 1857, he said, contained a contradiction between clearly and precisely expressed articles protecting individual rights and abstract, vague, and "metaphysical" declarations, to wit in Article 1: "The Mexican people acknowledge that the rights of man are the base and the object of social institutions." Such a declaration, argued Rabasa, is false "as a scientific principle" and invalid as a commitment, because the Constituent Congress was authorized to "constitute the nation, but not to establish its philosophical creed." Yet, he went on to acknowledge that the constitution makers were ultimately wise enough to put aside logic for what was practical and "purely juridical," and thus not to perpetuate the error in much of the body of the Constitution. He cited the positive example of Articles 101 and 102, which established the judicial defense of individual rights, the juicio de amparo. The initial excusable error was a kind of "tribute" paid by the constitution makers "to the philosophical and tendentious defect of the era."[17] In short, for all their brilliance and heroic patriotism, the delegates were subject to human error; thus the document they produced should be examined critically in the interests of "scientific truth" and not regarded as an immutable stone idol of the kind worshipped "among the unprogressive religions."[18]

Rabasa's critique of the imprecise language used in much of the Constitution reflected not only his innate pattern of thought, as described by his son Oscar, but also (as we have noted earlier) his adherence to positivism in the realm of the law, which was akin to scientific politics in the broader realm of political thought and practice. Rabasa's positivism was particularly apparent in his attack on the "vague and metaphysical" rights of man, set out in Article 1 of the Constitution, as opposed to specific individual guarantees, "what is practical and precisely juridical."[19] In shunning the abstractions and the "sentimentalist philosophy" of the 1850s, and seeking instead "scientific truth" in his legal analysis, Rabasa was following the path of Justo Sierra and his colleagues of *La Libertad* of 1878. He mounted a critique of the ideas of Ignacio Vallarta and José María Lozano, major jurists of the 1870s, whom he said were unduly influenced by the natural rights philosophy of Article 1. His juridical critique was akin to Sierra's political attack on the "old liberals" of 1857 and their followers.[20]

Rabasa's dedication to precise language started from the premise that "the constitution is written in a generally unsuitable and frequently incorrect language."[21] In this spirit, he devoted three entire chapters (vii–ix) to a discussion of the word *exactly* in Article 14 and its implications. The term was taken to mean *literally,* which was contrary to its use in draft Article 26, where it referred properly not to laws but to "forms," that is, judicial process (as in the "due process" clause of the U.S. Constitution).[22] In an elaborate and somewhat arcane argument, Rabasa rejected the view of Lozano and Vallarta that if *exactly* meant *literally,* Article 14 could be applied in penal cases, but not in civil cases, since such application would introduce a principle that would "subvert the social order." Vallarta's assertion, added Rabasa, was drawn from "metaphysical convictions in the law," namely that civil rights were not guaranteed in Article 14 because they were not "the rights of man," as in Article 1. His error, suggested Rabasa, really stemmed from the confusion in Article 1 between the first sentence, which announced the abstract "rights of man," and the second, which referred to "the [specific] guarantees granted by this Constitution."[23] Rabasa concluded his discussion by saying that if the adverb *exactly* could be taken to denote merely "precision and correctness," it could refer without difficulty to civil rights. He stated his position, against that of Lozano and later Vallarta, that Article 14 could be applied to civil cases by examining the historical use of the verbs *juzgar* and *sentenciar.* He argued that Article 247 of the Spanish Constitution of 1812 had applied *juzgar* to both civil and criminal cases, and that the Bases Orgánicas of 1843 had followed suit, including *sentenciar* as well.[24]

Rabasa's attack on Ignacio Vallarta is confusing and paradoxical because Vallarta, the great Chief Justice of the early Porfirian era, is generally regarded as a juridical positivist, like Rabasa himself. In fact, Rabasa later had great praise for Vallarta, who he said established the amparo procedure as a simple and straightforward defense of individual rights, freed of spurious elements. The difference between them on the question of natural versus civil rights was in large part a difference of generation: Vallarta was born in 1830 and was a delegate to the Constitutional Congress of 1856–57; Rabasa, born in 1856, came of age during the early Porfiriato. Vallarta, unlike Rabasa, was literally an "old liberal," whose juridical positivism was grafted onto the natural rights philosophy of the 1850s.[25]

Rabasa's discourse on precise language and historical word usage was only preliminary to the major argument of his book, namely that Article 14 undermined the judicial defense of individual rights established in the Constitution (the juicio de amparo) and should be eliminated from the document. As noted above, Rabasa was ambivalent toward the work of the framers of the Constitution. Though he criticized them for their frequent use of imprecise language and their occasional recourse to abstractions, he lavished praise on their formulation of Articles 101 and 102, which protected individual rights in a practical sense. In doing so, he wrote, they departed "from the hollow philosophicalism and pretentious liricism" of the French constitutions. Their source was Mariano Otero's formula, drawn in turn from the U.S. Constitution, and inserted into the Acta de Reformas of 1847.[26] In short, the constituyentes didn't realize the conflict that existed between Article 14 and Articles 101 and 102.

Article 14, according to Rabasa, undermined the proper application of the juicio de amparo in three ways. The first, as we have just noted, resulted from the confusion as to whether it could be applied properly to civil as well as to penal cases. Rabasa said there continued much dispute on this matter but that the position of Lozano and Vallarta generally prevailed. The second was that the phrase "judged and sentenced" in Article 14 essentially shifted protection for the individual from abuses by "public authority" to protection against "the abuses of bad judges."[27] The misinterpretation of the word *exactly* encouraged excessive litigation by individuals against laws that might be misapplied by lower courts, essentially cassation, a judicial procedure developed in nineteenth-century France.[28] The third way in which Article 14 undermined the juicio de amparo, a result of the first two, was the overload of cases before the Supreme Court. Rabasa said that in the year from May 1904 to May 1905 there were over 4,000 cases dealing with the juicio de amparo, an average of one every fifteen minutes. About half arose because of challenges to judicial decisions triggered by Article 14. Moreover, continued Rabasa, the number of cases was increasing by 10 percent a year, in effect making impossible the work of the Supreme Court.[29]

Rabasa's final attack on Article 14 focused on the problem of justice at the state level. In the opinion of many, he said, local judges were often venal, ignorant, or unjust, and the only remedy was federal intervention. Moreover, the argument went, the elimination of Article 14 would leave state legislatures in total freedom "to pass iniquitous laws that will thwart justice."[30] To correct the conduct of local judges, responded Rabasa, we can turn to the Civil Code, which is clear and precise as to limits on the authority of judges. As for legislatures, they can only be restrained ultimately by the progress of "public awareness," not by the articles of a written Constitution alone. He also argued that under the present system, if a case is brought directly to the Supreme Court, it comes as an isolated case and makes no impression on public opinion, "the sum of sentiments and judgment common to the aware portion of the population."[31] At this point in his argument Rabasa inserted a sentence from James Bryce in support of the "laws of Nature governing mankind," under which men prosper better than under the laws of any government.

This brief passage from Bryce led Rabasa to continue, somewhat uncharacteristically, with another lengthy paragraph from *The American Commonwealth,* noting the dominance in the United States of the doctrine of laissez-faire, especially on the state level. "Law will never be strong or respected," wrote Bryce, "unless it has the sentiment of the people behind it." If the people of a state make bad laws, they will suffer from it and ultimately mend their ways. This is, according to "the philosophers" [presumably Herbert Spencer] the way "Nature governs," as does God. Local independence and not federal intervention was at the root of the American faith in democracy, according to Bryce, a view that clearly found favor with Rabasa.[32] Rabasa went on to acknowledge the traditionally strong influence of the federal executive in state governments (which he had experienced first hand in Chiapas), but he asserted optimistically that this would change. With the progress of society, there would be a gradual "political transformation."[33] With time and education, continued Rabasa, the states will demand the reestablishment of "their judicial integrity." On this optimistic note, Rabasa reasserted his faith in the Mexican federal system, so seemingly contrary to political reality in the age of Porfirio Díaz.

In concluding his treatise, Rabasa returned to his specific subject, reiterated many of his previous arguments, and proposed that Article 14 be revised and simplified following the American precept, as put forth by the authors of draft article 26: "to demand due process in law as a guarantee of life, liberty, and property."[34] Finally, he emphasized how far Mexico was from the turbulent 1850s, and he expressed his faith "in the progressive development of free institutions." Thus Rabasa completed the first of his major works, a technical legal study, and yet one that revealed many of the general themes of his later works. His reference to the Civil Code in close juxtaposition to long quotations from Lord Bryce signaled his later confrontation with the two Western legal traditions, the Anglo American and the Continental. Like the advocates of scientific politics of 1878 and 1893, he attacked (as he also did later) the "vague and metaphysical" rights of man, "sentimentalist" philosophy, "the hollow and empty philosophicalism and the pretentious lyricism" of the French Constitutions, which guided the constituyentes of 1856. At the same time he admired much of their work. He also revealed his attraction to the optimism of Spencerian evolutionary thought, which was to pervade his more general historical and political study of 1912.

Rabasa must have soon realized that despite his learned and detailed critique of Article 14, there was little chance of eliminating it or modifying it at this time. He therefore lent his support to an amendment of Article 102, which might reduce the overload of multiple appeals to the Supreme Court on cases that should be appropriately settled at the state level.[35] On 15 June 1908 Emilio Rabasa, as Chairman of the Constitutional Committee, made his longest and most passionate speech in the prerevolutionary Senate in defense of the proposed amendment. He dismissed the arguments of Gumersindo Enríquez, who called for adding the amending phrase to Article 101. Rabasa retorted that the amendment is regulatory in nature, and thus more appropriately inserted following Article 102, which was also essentially regulatory with respect to the juicio de amparo. However, Rabasa went far beyond the technicalities, chiding veteran Senator Rafael Dondé for remaining silent in the debate, even though he had been a strong supporter of a similar measure in 1868. Most of all, Rabasa made a strong defense of federalism and the need to respect the decisions of state and local judges, some of whom he claimed were the equal of many federal magistrates. I am a partisan of federalism, he continued, "because federalism provides a base for stability, liberty, justice, and national strength." He went on to evoke the heroic efforts of the states during the wars of the 1860s: "each state defended its sovereignty and its integrity, and in doing so upheld the integrity of the Fatherland." In conclusion, Rabasa made it clear that he saw this modest amendment as only the first step, and he called on his colleagues to join him in due course to "root out of our Constitution the Article 14 that disgraces it."[36] The 1908 amendment was approved, but unfortunately his broader appeal fell on deaf ears. Let us now turn to Emilio Rabasa's work of 1912.

The origin of *La Constitución y la dictadura*, Emilio Rabasa's most famous book, has always been something of a mystery. As we know, Rabasa's reserved and even at times secretive nature led him to express publicly virtually nothing about the origins of his four books or why he set about to write them. Especially puzzling in the case of *La Constitución y la dictadura* is the fact that though published in 1912, it made only one direct reference to the Revolution that broke out in November 1910 and to the resignation and departure of Porfirio Díaz in May 1911. Was it composed earlier and the publication delayed? Daniel Cosío Villegas, based on information given him by Rabasa's son Oscar, said that Rabasa probably wrote the book in 1910, in time to give a first draft to Porfirio Díaz before he left the country, and then revised it later in 1911. This information is only partially correct.[37] Now, with the help of recently available correspondence between Finance Minister José Yves Limantour and Rabasa (correspondence that will later figure prominently in this study), more of the mystery can be expelled.

In 1917, prompted by the news that Rodolfo Reyes intended to publish a second edition of *La Constitución y la dictadura* in Spain, Rabasa
revealed after some hesitation "a private fact" *(una intimidad)* to
Limantour, his close friend and fellow exile. He said that he began the
book at the end of 1909 and that he had intended to publish it "despite
complete dictatorship and at great risk." I abandoned the project, he
continued, with a third of it written, when my wife died in May 1910,
and completed it in two months in 1912, "only at the urging of my
brother [Ramón]."[38] We also know now that Rabasa discussed his plan
for the book with Limantour, probably in 1909, and that he pursued the
discussion more concretely in April 1911, just after Limantour's brief
return to Mexico.[39]

Cosío Villegas speculated, perhaps with some justice, that the remote
origin of Rabasa's work was the famous interview of 1908, in which
Porfirio Díaz told the American journalist James Creelman that he would
not seek reelection in 1910, wishing to clear the way for a transition to
democracy. Though Rabasa made no mention of the interview at this
time, it aroused much discussion and writing on the institutional future
of Mexico.[40] A good example of this sudden outpouring was *¿Hacía
Donde Vamos?* (1908) by Querido Moheno, lawyer, journalist, and national deputy who had opposed Porfirio Díaz as a student in 1893. The
president's call in the interview for the formation of true political parties prompted Moheno to engage in a lengthy and diffuse discussion. It
ranged widely from the total dependence of the country on Porfirio Díaz
(and his imitators on the local level) and the absence of a qualified successor, to the difficulties of establishing "a free and active public opinion," the fallacies of universal suffrage, and the weakness of federalism.
His essay touched on several of the problems raised four years later by
Emilio Rabasa, but *La Constitución y la dictadura* was a stronger work
than Moheno's *¿Hacía Donde Vamos?* in part because of Rabasa's decision to omit mention of the events of the day.[41]

In writing to Limantour in April 1911, Rabasa laid out the plan for
his book, by way of reminding Limantour what they had discussed two
years earlier. He emphasized that his conclusions would be the constitutional reforms he judged indispensable to Mexico's democratic evolution. He said it was an error to believe that "electoral freedom brought
about by the effective vote" is the panacea for all our problems (a clear
reference to Francisco I. Madero's program, "effective suffrage, no reelection"). On the contrary, he continued, instituting the "effective vote"
without altering the present imbalance of the three branches of government would only lead to anarchy. He then presented to Limantour what
came to be the central argument of the book, namely that because of the

extreme weakness of the executive, "the dictatorship [of Porfirio Díaz] has become a necessity arising from the Constitution and supported by the aware population," without precedent in America for its popularity and its "productivity." Moreover, he added," your superb work would not have been possible in another regime." At this point, he added, we need a stable government in order to reform the Constitution and "to get to democratic practices that assure institutional peace." He ended the letter to Limantour by saying he would present his ideas in more concrete detail when they met.[42] Thus Rabasa completed his book in the midst of the dramatic events of late 1911 and early 1912—the resignation and departure of Díaz and Limantour, the triumphant arrival of Madero in Mexico City, the interim regime of Francisco León de la Barra, and the election of Madero as president of the Republic. In characteristically serene fashion, Rabasa stuck to his plan, except for presenting concrete proposals for constitutional reform, and pursued his argument as if he had completed the book when he had first intended.

A persistent theme that runs throughout the book is the discrepancy in Mexico between the "social" and the "written" constitution. "We have expected everything from the written law, and the written law has demonstrated its incurable impotence."[43] This had been one of the principal themes advanced by Justo Sierra and his colleagues writing in *La Libertad* of 1878, which Emilio Rabasa was now carrying forward into the twentieth century. Little by little, wrote Rabasa, the political constitution, which contains much that is "artificial and mathematical," gives way to the social constitution, which is formed by the progress of general ideas, changed necessities of life, and the forces of natural growth.[44] Yet Rabasa of course did not reject the role of law; it was for him clearly an element that contributed to the organization and betterment of a society, as long as it grew naturally from that society. He also spoke of "moral progress," a "modification of the soul of a people," which only came slowly. Any law that violates this principle "remains unapplied, absolutely null and void."[45] Here Rabasa was drawing on the ideas of Gustave Le Bon, the most widely read popularizer of European evolutionary and racial theories at the turn of the twentieth century. Le Bon emphasized the "soul of races" as fundamental to their mental constitution. Though Rabasa (and other Mexicans) adopted Le Bon's racial terminology less explicitly than did many Latin American intellectuals, he like Le Bon often used the terms *race* and *people* interchangeably.[46] Rabasa was also expressing one of the principal tenets of historical constitutionalism, namely that a successful constitution must emanate from and reflect the society to which it is applied. His model was the single constitution that had guided the entire evolution of the North American government.

Rabasa emphasized that he was not presenting a general critique of the Constitution of 1857, but only an analysis of the defects that "make its observance impossible." Unfortunately, he said, it has been difficult to identify the defects because of the immense prestige the Constitution has acquired. "It was loved as a symbol, but unknown as a law."[47] The prestige of the Constitution was such that after 1867 all rebellions against established governments could be carried out in the name of the Constitution. The result was that in the popular mind there had developed "the conviction that the Constitution is sacrosanct, that it upholds the rights that all bad governments violate," thus giving legitimacy to rebellion. Moreover, Rabasa argued that the Constitution was sacrosanct in part because it became confused in the mind of subsequent generations with the Reforma, that is, with what he called the "true liberal revolution," led by Benito Juárez against the power of the Church. Rabasa always tried to distinguish between the Reforma and the Constitution. Despite his persistent criticism of many aspects of the Constitution and ultimately his call (as we have seen) for its amendment, he never questioned the "Juárez laws."[48] He was in that sense a liberal and remained so throughout his life, despite his opposition to the Revolution of 1910 and its aftermath.

Pursuing his critique of the Constitution, Rabasa expanded the argument he had made in *Artículo 14,* namely that "what is bad and unworkable [in the Constitution]" was based on discredited eighteenth-century theories. Already by 1857, he continued, general science was following "positive concepts"; and the science of government "was seeking its foundation in observation and experience."[49] The principal discredited theory Rabasa mentioned was popular sovereignty, or at least the application often made of it. He acknowledged at the outset that countries breaking from colonial rule necessarily had based their governments on popular sovereignty, or government by the people. However, he said that confusion has arisen between three different connotations of the "people," namely: "the totality of society"; all individuals capable of exercising political rights; and the "lower classes" (as opposed to "the enlightened and well-off part of society"). This confusion has given rise to false theories that privilege "the ignorant masses" and encourage demagoguery.[50] Though Rabasa was explicitly referring to the ideas that guided the formation of the Constitution of 1857, he undoubtedly also had his eye on the social upheaval he was living through. In another context, Rabasa identified the two "old Jacobin principles" of 1856, "infallible and incorruptible will of the people" and the representation of this "will of the people" in a single-chamber legislature.[51] He later pointed to popular election of judges of the Supreme Court as another of the

"French theories" that attracted the constituyentes. Although such leaders as Ponciano Arriaga, José María Mata, and Melchor Ocampo knew the U.S. Constitution well, they were the exceptions. Most looked to France and particularly to the immediate precedent of the Constituent Assembly of 1848 and were moved by its talented orators.[52]

Rabasa frequently used the term *jacobin* in his critique of the formation of the Constitution of 1857. As noted in Chapter 1, between 1878 and 1893 *jacobin* came to replace *metaphysical* as an epithet used by the advocates of scientific politics and historical constitutionalism in attacking the "old liberals" (or "Jacobins") of 1857. The term had become embedded in Mexican political rhetoric by 1912. The use of the term as a political epithet reveals the influence of the French positivist historian and theorist Hippolyte Taine. Taine's passionate attack on France's revolutionary tradition, written in reaction to the Republic of 1848 and particularly to the Commune of 1871, had appeared between 1876 and 1891, paralleling the rise of scientific politics in Mexico. The first two volumes of *Les Origines de la France contemporaine* attracted some attention from the *La Libertad* group in the late 1870s; but it was clearly Taine's trenchant indictment of the Jacobin mentality, first published in 1881, that brought the term to the debate of 1893 and later to Rabasa's work. For Taine, "Jacobin psychology" was the bane of French politics. Its indestructible roots, he wrote, are "exaggerated pride" and "dogmatic reasoning" that exist beneath the surface of society. When social bonds dissolve (as in France in 1790), Jacobins spring up "like mushrooms in rotting compost." Their principles are the simplistic axioms of "political geometry," espoused by the young and the unsuccessful and then imposed on a complex society by the "philosophe legislator." But, added Taine decisively, they are imposed in vain, because society "is not the work of logic, but of history."[53] Although Taine was not a constitutional theorist like Benjamin Constant and Edouard de Laboulaye, his political position and his critique of the revolutionary tradition, presented with great literary flair, gave strong reinforcement to Mexican historical constitutionalism in the age of positivism.[54]

Rabasa began his work with an epigraph from Walter Bagehot, the British historian and political philosopher: "Political philosophy must analyze political history." This phrase from the epigraph may provide the clue to Rabasa's method, particularly in the second section of his book, which consisted of a thorough analysis of Mexican political institutions within a comparative French, British, and North American context. This analysis provided the base for the principal argument of *La Constitución y la dictadura,* which we will see shortly.[55] Rabasa's discussion began with the fundamental question of elections. His customary target was universal suffrage, established in 1857 and now being promoted as "effective election" and "freedom of suffrage" by Francisco I. Madero. Although Rabasa did not mention Madero, the association is unmistakable. Mexico is a society of political adolescents, he argued, untutored and largely illiterate voters who become victims of "unsettling elements." These elements spring up wherever there is universal suffrage—urban bosses or Southern politicians in the United States, landowners in England, factory owners in France, state governors in Mexico—and they obstruct any genuine expression of "conscious will in popular elections." Mexico, he continued, has the added problem of the indirect vote, a problem (as we shall see in Chapter 4) Rabasa was confronting at this very moment in the Senate. Rabasa went on to treat what he regarded as two related issues in all democracies, political parties and the succession to executive power. For the first issue, he drew from the analysis of James Bryce for the United States, and for the second, from Joseph Barthélemy, a French theorist on the role of the executive, whose view was broadly comparative. Bringing the discussion back to Mexico, Rabasa maintained that without some restriction of suffrage to make elections truly effective, the alternation between dictatorship and revolution was inevitable.[56]

As we might expect, Rabasa's analysis focused principally on "the supremacy of the legislative power," the weapons at its disposal to maintain this supremacy, and on the constitutional weakness of the executive in the Mexican system. He also emphasized the potential role of the judiciary as the "balancing body," a subject we will explore in detail in Chapter 7. Under Mexico's constitution, the president was severely limited, despite the presidential form of government Mexico had adopted since independence. After 1857, the Chamber of Deputies exerted power over appointments, it could mount an "accusatory tribunal" (analogous to impeachment), and it rejected the presidential veto, seeing it as a "humiliation of the legislative power," the quintessential democratic institution. The reinstituted Senate of 1874 was intended to provide some balance, but in effect the lower body continued to dominate.

To illuminate the problems of the Mexican system, Rabasa instinctively turned to comparison, drawing from prominent constitutionalist scholars, Walter Bagehot for England, Woodrow Wilson and James Bryce for the United States, and Joseph Barthélemy for France. These analysts all pointed up the "aggressive" and "despotic" tendencies of popular assemblies in the face of executive authority. Wilson's study particularly examined the dominance of Congress in the United States following the Civil War.[57] One U.S. example noted by Rabasa was the "Tenure of Office Act," designed by Congress in 1867 to limit President

Andrew Johnson's authority to remove appointees confirmed by the Senate. The law remained as a limitation on presidential authority until it was repealed in 1886. Drawing from Bryce, Rabasa also discussed the U.S. "spoils system" and the struggle to establish civil service reform.[58] Rabasa saw the presidential veto as a simple though limited instrument to resist "congressionalism," and he found support from Barthélemy, whom he quoted twice. Through the veto, wrote Barthélemy, "the President becomes the guardian of the people's rights . . . [and] he safeguards them against the spirit of faction" and other congressional vices contrary to the public good.[59] For Rabasa, the veto was a simple negative that could be overridden by a two-thirds vote, not the threat to legislative authority envisioned by the constituyentes of 1857.

As noted above, one of Rabasa's principles was that the written constitution gives way over time to the "real" or "social" constitution. One example he cited in his comparative analysis was the change in the United States from the effective sovereignty of the states upheld by Thomas Jefferson to the effective sovereignty of the nation as a result of the Civil War. Another was the shift in France from the quasi-monarchical Constitution of 1875 to "a near suppression of the executive by the unlimited sovereignty of the popular assembly." A third example was the change in Great Britain's unwritten constitution from the dominance of the aristocracy over a century to "a broad democracy." This distinction between the "literary" and the "real" constitution that had been part of the positivist critique launched by Justo Sierra and his colleagues now also appeared in the works of Wilson and Bagehot. Rabasa, doubly influenced, identified dictatorship as a natural product of the social constitution in Mexico, emerging in reaction to parliamentary supremacy that was central to the written Constitution of 1857.

The principal argument of *La Constitucion y la dictadura* grew from Rabasa's extensive critique of the Constitution. Since it is impossible, he wrote, to govern while adhering to the ideals put forth in the Constitution, Mexico's leaders were forced to resort to de facto or unconstitutional rule, that is, dictatorship. Instead of being the victim of arbitrary rule, the Constitution has been its "principal author." As a good positivist, Rabasa made his point with the help of analogies from science. Material phenomena, he said, cannot resist the laws of physics. Mere human laws cannot resist the higher laws of nature, just as "the fragile matrass cannot resist the chemical combination that shatters it." Moreover, dictatorship since 1857 "is not an infraction of sociological laws, but its inevitable fulfillment." It had served to satisfy the necessities of national development, which constitutional government was powerless to do.[60] This development entailed two stages, the first being that of political and social formation, guided by the "heroic audacity" of the dictator Benito Juárez. The dictatorship of Juárez led naturally to the second stage, that of growth, which brought forth the dictatorship of Porfirio Díaz. It should be noted that Rabasa also singled out Ignacio Comonfort, who like Juárez and Díaz after him, realized that "government is impossible with the Constitution of 1857."[61]

Rabasa admired Comonfort, but used him as a foil for his treatment of Juárez. Comonfort, who emerged as leader following the Revolution of Ayutla of 1854, with its limited objectives of overthrowing Antonio López de Santa Ana and establishing a constitutional convention, was a "soldier of valor and a worthy citizen . . . to the fullest degree."[62] Instead of governing outside the Constitution, Comonfort attempted to change it. His goal was to "reconcile liberty and order" ("his favorite expression") by bringing into balance the powers of government. He called in vain for a strengthened executive through the power of the veto and for the irremovability of judges. This effort won Rabasa's praise. Comonfort's weakness in Rabasa's eyes was his moderation on the great issue of the day, the church. Comonfort did not realize the consequences of the revolution that had begun in 1854, and he sought to reconcile Liberals and Conservatives. When faced with the Plan of Tacubaya in 1858, the clerical and Conservative rebellion against the Constitution, he resigned the presidency. In normal times Comonfort might have been "the greatest of Mexican presidents." But the times were not normal. Rabasa concluded with a passage from Gustave Le Bon: "In politics the truly great men are those who anticipate events prepared by the past and who point out the paths to be followed." In short, for Rabasa, Comonfort was not a great man but something more modest, but no less respectable, "a great citizen."[63]

The great man was Juárez. Unlike Comonfort, Juárez sensed the movement of events and the necessity to dominate and direct them. As an "eradicator" and "revolutionary," he not only joined battle against the Conservatives, but he pushed the struggle to extremes, "putting forth in his laws, even above the Constitution, all the principles of the liberal creed." His calling was to bring about social and political transformation in order to "establish the government on the new consciousness." Juárez never governed within the Constitution, but not because of his preference for dictatorship. He did so because of his conviction that under the Constitution of 1857 the executive was at the mercy of Congress and the governors. This situation would not have allowed him to carry through the work of the Reforma and the struggle against the French Intervention and the Empire of Maximilian. Rabasa concluded that it was not possible to assume more power than did Juárez between 1863 and 1867. His government was one of "national cohesion," and Juárez won the applause of the nation, in life and in death.[64]

Under Porfirio Díaz, asserted Rabasa, Mexico lived under the most beneficent and fruitful dictatorship that America had ever seen. Díaz was a soldier with the "temperament of an organizer," who mounted two revolutions (1871 and 1876) in order to establish peace and impose order. He realized, as did Juárez and Sebastián Lerdo de Tejada, that Comonfort was correct "to declare as impossible the balance of powers established by the Constitution."[65] His imposition of order unleashed long forgotten habits of work and exploited heretofore-unknown wealth. Díaz, "the necessary man," carried the nation beyond mere political struggle, characteristic of "anarchical states" to the economic principles upheld by "civilized peoples." Internally, he put in place "the organization that peoples had never had" and with which they could live, breathe, and prosper under the protection of public authority. Externally, he established financial credit by producing wealth and political confidence through peace.[66]

In the midst of this lavish praise for the work of Porfirio Díaz, Rabasa introduced a surprising note, undoubtedly drawn from scarcely mentioned contemporary events, which launched the final message of *La Constitución y la dictadura*. While crediting Díaz with establishing unity among the peoples of the Republic, he said that from this unity "must come forth democratic life." He went on to introduce by analogy "Taine's profound observation," which he said could apply generally to "all institutions whose role has ended." In the history of France the Capetian kings had a long and illustrious reign, in war, in their alliance with the commons against feudal lords, and in the dispensing of royal justice. But when this beneficence declined, the question arose—what is the king?—and divine right took on the appearance of despotism. When royal privileges were no longer useful, "the alliance broke apart and the people rejected them and withdrew their support." Turning to Mexico, Rabasa said that since the Mexican nation has been formed by the great work of dictatorship since the mid-nineteenth century, "the dictators have completed their work." There will continue to be accidental dictatorships, he continued, "but as a regime, the historical era in which it was to reign has inescapably died."[67] Now it is urgent "to divest it [dictatorship] of the necessary privileges it had." The Constitution must be made to guarantee the stability of a useful, active, and strong government.

Thus Rabasa's closing thought was that with the passing of the era of dictatorship, "the constitutional era must follow." For Rabasa, the clear challenge in 1912 must be to reform the Constitution; "cleansed of its errors, it will make possible popular intervention in the national regime."

Yet he emphasized that he was not suggesting a "an illusionary democracy" (perhaps of the kind that Francisco I. Madero was proclaiming as he wrote), but rather "a democratic oligarchy." As noted earlier, Rabasa never spelled out in 1912 specific reforms of the Constitution, probably because Porfirio Díaz had already left the country when he was completing the book. However, suggestions emerge throughout the text. One oft-mentioned reform was to strengthen the executive by giving him the power of the veto. This reform sought by Ignacio Comonfort won Rabasa's praise, and he emphasized its advantages in his critique of parliamentary supremacy. Another reform was to improve the electoral system by restricting suffrage, at least to those who could read and write. A third, which Rabasa mentioned frequently, was to secure the independence of the Supreme Court by making judges irremovable, as opposed to being subject to popular election and thus manipulation by the executive.[68] These were all reforms that the advocates of scientific politics and historical constitutionalism had proposed from 1878 to 1893 and that Rabasa was now carrying forward. His concept of "democratic oligarchy" was not rigid, but gave space for those popular elements that were able to increase gradually their influence in national affairs. This serene gradualist vision, unrealistic as it was in the midst of popular revolution, emerged in the final passage of the book, namely that the governing class would grow "automatically and freely through the accumulation of wealth, the spread of education, and the extension of morality."[69]

I have argued that Emilio Rabasa's constitutional thought was historical or traditional, in contrast to the doctrinaire constitutionalism of those who drew up the 1857 document and their adherents. This constitutional and political thought, as revealed in *El Artículo 14* and particularly in *La Constitución y la dictadura* brought into the twentieth century the ideas of Justo Sierra and his colleagues in the newspaper *La Libertad* of 1878–80, reiterated in the great debate of 1893. I have also argued that this current of historical constitutionalism drew its inspiration from France, based on the critique of the popular democracy of the great Revolution, as put forth by Benjamin Constant, Alexis de Tocqueville, Edouard de Laboulaye, and on the attack on jacobinism by Hippolyte Taine. This constitutionalism became fused in Mexico with the doctrine of scientific politics, drawn from the positivism of Henri de Saint Simon and Auguste Comte, and permeated by the evolutionary social philosophy of Herbert Spencer. The key political element in this fusion of scientific politics and historical constitutionalism was the role of the state, translated into constitutional terms as the relationship between the three branches of government. We have seen that Rabasa was guided by the administrative dimension of scientific politics as the modernizing governor of the State of Chiapas and that he regarded Porfirio Díaz as the necessary dictator to promote progress on the national level. However, by 1912 his constitutionalist premises reappeared in the final pages of *La Constitución y la dictadura,* as he looked hopefully beyond dictatorship to the emergence of a "democratic oligarchy."

As Rabasa developed his political thought, he added to the ideas inherited from his nineteenth-century predecessors a broader comparative perspective, moving beyond France and Spain and the traditional French interpreters of Anglo American politics to theorists and historians from Great Britain and the United States themselves. In the two works we have just examined, James Bryce, a latter-day Tocqueville, became an important source for Rabasa's analysis of U.S. institutions. He also turned to Woodrow Wilson and through him to William Bagehot. We will also see in a later chapter how Rabasa turned to North American jurists to deepen his comparative understanding of the Mexican Supreme Court. However, despite this expanded perspective, Rabasa did not abandon the view from France; in this chapter we have noted for example, his frequent reference to Joseph Bartélemy's important comparative work on the role of executive authority in modern republics. In short, by 1912 Emilio Rabasa was now at home in English as well as in French, which allowed him to perfect his comparative analysis of Mexican institutions.

In July 1912, José Y. Limantour, with whom Rabasa had discussed his plan for *La Constitución y la dictadura* as early as 1909, reported from his exile in Paris that he had just read the book and that he greatly admired it. It is filled with "exact observations, judgments that are on the mark, and evidence that shows profound erudition." In the midst of the storm that threatens our country, he continued, your book is "the only sensible voice that gives us light and hope." In August, Limantour wrote that he had read it for the third time, and in November, he said he had a few objections and reservations on minor points. Rabasa was obviously delighted with Limantour's effusive words and responded that he had received many congratulations, admitting that the moral impact of the book had surpassed his greatest desires.[70] However, Emilio Rabasa had little opportunity to bask in his success. As a senator, practicing lawyer, and law professor, he was immediately forced into the maelstrom of the Mexican Revolution. Let us now turn to this confrontation.

CHAPTER FOUR

Confronting the Revolution (1911–1914)

There is little indication that Emilio Rabasa experienced any direct encounter with the Revolution until the resignation of Porfirio Díaz and
José Yves Limantour on 25 May 1911 and their departure to Europe
soon after. The outbreak of hostilities in November 1910 was principally in the north, where Francisco I. Madero and Pascual Orozco
led rebellions, but they soon spread to other regions, especially in the
state of Morelos led by Emiliano Zapata. The south and southeast of
the country were less affected. Chiapas, for example, where Emilio's
brother Ramón was governor, did not experience upheaval until the departure of Díaz. Mexico City also remained calm. Rabasa was clearly
preoccupied with family matters—the illness of his wife Mercedes and
her death in May 1910. We have seen that with her death he abandoned
his *La Constitución y la dictadura,* not to resume writing until late in
1911. But he did remain in the Senate during this period. The Treaty of
Ciudad Juárez, signed on 21 May 1911 by Francisco S. Carvajal, representing the government of Porfirio Díaz, and by Madero, Francisco
Vázquez Gómez, and José María Pino Suárez for the revolutionary forces,
provided only for the resignation of Díaz and his vice-president, Ramón
Corral. It left the legislature intact.[1] However, the change of regimes in
Mexico City soon brought Rabasa again into politics, while maintaining his customary low profile.

Emilio Rabasa's reputation as a major intellectual who commanded
great respect but whose public career achieved little notoriety made
his relation to the Científicos ambiguous. As we have noted, if he had
not been governor of Chiapas, he would likely have formed part of the
Unión Nacional Liberal in 1892, been a party to the debate of 1893 over
the irremovability of judges (and indirectly over limitation on the personal power of Porfirio Díaz), and have been counted among the original Científicos. He had been a schoolmate in Oaxaca of Rosendo Pineda

and Emilio Pimentel; he was on intimate terms with Limantour; he was a close friend and colleague of the brothers Pablo and Miguel Macedo. In addition, he was a member of the Second Convention of the National Liberal Union in 1903, though we have no record of his participation in its activities.[2] Rabasa was respected and favored by Porfirio Díaz. Moreover, Luis Cabrera, the revolutionary journalist and intellectual, in his inflammatory attack on the Científicos beginning in 1909, identified Rabasa as one of the lawyers who made up "the body" of the group.[3] Cabrera, while recognizing the origin of the group in 1892, expanded the label to include some fifty individuals who were men of high intelligence and business acumen, close to the center of governmental power, and who also benefited personally from domestic and foreign economic concessions. In Cabrera's view, one that had great influence on later revolutionary rhetoric, the Científicos were capitalist exploiters of the Mexican public. Although Rabasa was wealthy from property holdings in Chiapas, and though he later developed an important tie to North American interests, his wealth and his connections in the world of business and finance were modest by comparison with those of Limantour, the Macedos, Joaquín Casasús, and others. Nonetheless, he came to be included among the antirevolutionary Científicos and "reactionaries."

The fall of the Díaz regime threw the Científicos into disarray. Because the Treaty of Ciudad Juárez and the negotiations that led up to it provided for a peaceful and "constitutional" governmental transition, the response of individual Científicos to the change varied greatly. Some went immediately into exile, such as Rosendo Pineda, Roberto Núñez, and of course Limantour; Pablo Macedo and Vice-President Ramón Corral, who happened to be in Europe in May 1911, stayed there. Others, such as Miguel Macedo, remained in Mexico but disengaged themselves from politics or from business and financial boards that had ties to government. A few were actually drawn into the transitional regime of Francisco León de la Barra from May to November 1911. Many legislators like Rabasa kept their positions, though some were displaced in the new legislature, the twenty-sixth, which convened in September 1912.

The disarray of the Científicos was clearly revealed in the "Archivo de la reacción," the pirated private correspondence of Pablo Macedo, which covered the immediate post-Díaz year from June 1911 to June 1912. Miguel Macedo wrote to his brother that Limantour was the "true author of the disaster," since he gave away too much in his peace negotiations with the Maderos; Pineda and Macedo referred to him derisively as the "Lord." Roberto Núñez called Joaquín Casasús (who remained in Mexico) a "traitor" for continuing to represent the Waters-Pierce Oil Co. and the Southern Pacific Railroad, both of which presumably had supported the Revolution.[4] Pablo Macedo's correspondents were disappointed in the administration of fellow Científico León de la Barra, because he was weak in facing up to the *maderistas,* more a "rabbit" than a "lion (*león*)." Emilio Rabasa was mentioned only once in these letters, even though he was a friend and close colleague of most of the correspondents, further evidence of his determination to remain out of the spotlight.[5] As we will see in Chapter 5, the appearance of the "Archivo de la Reacción" in 1917 led to a significant and lengthy correspondence between the exiles Rabasa and Limantour.

The somnolent Senate awakened to new life with the departure of Díaz and the triumph of the *maderista* revolution. Three issues that particularly involved Rabasa were typical of this new activity. The first centered on the conflict that developed in several states between regions or between governor and legislature. Under the Constitution, as we have noted, the Senate had the power to intervene in case of conflict or to declare the "disappearance" of the constitutional powers of a state, and to recommend a provisional governor (Art. 72, B, v & vi). The second issue was the reform of Articles 78 and 109 of the Constitution, forbidding reelection of the president, vice-president, and governors. The third, and most significant issue involving Rabasa, was the reform of Articles 55, 58 (A), and 76 providing for direct election of the president, vice-president, senators, and deputies.

Of the several cases of governmental conflict within the states beginning in 1911, the one that naturally enough most engaged Emilio Rabasa was that of Chiapas. After Rabasa left the governorship of Chiapas in 1894, the state had remained firmly and peacefully in the hands of the *tuxtleco* elite of the Central Valley, with governors dedicated to carrying forward Rabasa's development agenda, culminating in the regime of Emilio's older brother Ramón from 1906 to 1910. However, Ramón Rabasa's reelection in 1911 ran afoul of Madero's antireelectionist cause; accepting the implications of the vague Treaty of Ciudad Juárez, Rabasa resigned on 27 April 1911.[6] The fall of Díaz and the governor's resignation rekindled the latent conflict between San Cristóbal and Tuxtla Gutiérrez, between cristobalenses and *rabasistas,* a conflict that was further complicated by differences between Madero and the interim government of León de la Barra over the course to follow in Chiapas. Four governors came and went in the following months, and cristobalense rebels took advantage of the confusion to launch attacks on Tuxtla in hopes of returning the seat of government to San Cristóbal. They often tried to disguise their effort as maderista, with little success. The rebels also abetted an uprising of Chamula Indians against the government, raising traditional fears of "caste war."[7]

Encouraged by President León de la Barra, the Senate in Mexico City finally took up the issue, and on 5 October 1911 an investigating committee reported that constitutional order had not "disappeared" and that the Executive should move energetically to squash a rebellion "which can turn into a caste war."[8] Though Emilio Rabasa did not officially take part in this investigation, his influence was evident, for the next day the Senate Committee that he chaired endorsed the recommendations of the investigators, to the applause of fellow senators. Victor Manuel Castillo, Rabasa's relative and long-time colleague, spoke at length in favor of the measure, attacking "sick elements" from San Cristóbal who had referred to "the Rabasa-Castillo faction."[9] León de la Barra ordered federal forces to cooperate with the state government, and the cristobalense and Chamula rebellion was crushed, including brutal treatment of ten Chamula prisoners by some "Sons of Tuxtla." As Thomas Benjamin put it, the 1911 conflict "was the last major political expression of a long [nineteenth-century] regional struggle."[10] Emilio Rabasa played no small part in this struggle, securing permanently the dominance of the Central Valley.

Rabasa's continuing influence in Chiapas, at least until 1912, was also apparent in the final settlement of the border between Chiapas and Tabasco. Rabasa submitted a lengthy juridical brief on the issue of state boundaries, which presumably guided the settlement. He concluded that governors, authorized by state legislatures, should negotiate the question, in the presence of an arbiter, as in international matters. Rabasa's personal interests in land along the border and those of Policarpo Valenzuela, governor of Tabasco, may also have played a role in the amicable settlement.[11] Nonetheless, Emilio Rabasa's influence in Chiapas declined with the onset of the Madero regime, one reason for Rabasa's growing opposition to Madero in the course of the year 1912.[12] Rabasa also took part in Senate sessions that dealt with characteristic conflicts of the Madero era between legislators and governors of the state of Jalisco in May 1912 and of Tlaxcala in January 1913. In these cases the Senate, including Rabasa, supported the governors against rebellious legislators.[13]

The measure to reform Articles 78 and 109 of the Constitution, sent to the Senate from the Chamber of Deputies, was brought to the floor by Rabasa's constitutional committee on 1 May 1911, only a few days after Porfirio Díaz resigned.[14] Though Senate approval was not unanimous, it was hardly a measure to elicit much controversy. "No-reelection" was a cornerstone of Francisco I. Madero's victorious revolutionary movement. President Díaz himself had paved the way for it in the Creelman interview of 1908 (and later reneged). In a last ditch effort to stave off revolution, he had called for the reform in his address to Congress on

1 April 1911 (after he had already been reelected in 1910).[15] Support for the reform had been implicit (if not stated) in the programs of the two conventions of the National Liberal Union of 1892 and 1903. In short, no-reelection had support across the political spectrum, from *porfiristas* and Científicos as well as from revolutionaries.

In the Senate debate, Francisco González Mena reflected that yesterday we were all reelectionists, today we are all anti-reelectionists. Why? Because "the searching eye of the great statesman lost at that moment its extraordinary penetration." Díaz was unable to discern that popular feeling was not sincere, and his reelection turned out to be a farce. The measure should be approved, concluded González Mena, to eliminate the "internal war" that is undercutting [material?] gains made during the period of peace.[16] The only real opposition to the measure came from Senator Juan García Peña, who objected to the word "never." He agreed with the committee view that the reform satisfied the necessity of the moment, but argued nonetheless that the people should have the right to reelect officials if circumstances were to change. The measure, he said, should be transitory. The amendment of Article 78, that the president and vice-president would serve for six years and *never* be reelected, passed the Senate by a vote of 37 to 6. Article 109, which applied the same conditions to state governors, passed by a similar margin.[17] Both became official on 7 November 1911, a day after President Madero took office. The reform undoubtedly gave support to the optimistic conclusion of Rabasa's *La Constitución y la dictadura,* namely that the era of dictatorship was over and that the "constitutional stage" must follow.

Rabasa's most significant contribution to the work of the Senate in 1911 pertained to the amendment of Articles 55, 56 (A), and 76, providing for direct rather than the present indirect election of officials. Although the measure emerged simultaneously in the Chamber of Deputies and the Senate, the key document was the substantial "initiative" presented by Emilio Rabasa and Miguel S. Macedo on 9 October 1911.[18] The authors acknowledged at the outset that "the directions" of national life resulting from the "recent political change" had revived many long-ignored political problems, the most important of which was how to "make democracy practical." The initiative was a curious combination of Rabasa's standard indictment of abstract theory, the illusions created by jacobin revolutionary enthusiasm, and a proposal to further democratize the electoral process. Free and effective suffrage, argued the authors, "is not, as popular belief would have it, the marvelous panacea that would cure our political ills." The causes that lead from dictatorship to revolution, they said, are deep and complex, but at the same time "true free suffrage is doubtless the essential foundation of all our liberties." Because of Mexico's heterogeneous and culturally uneven populace, the citizen needs to vote directly, without the imposition of "a secondary elector."

The seeming incongruity of the proposal is partly removed if we re-examine Rabasa's chapter "La Elección" in his *La Constitución y la dictadura,* presumably written in late 1911, that is, at the same time as the Senate proposal. As noted earlier, Rabasa made no concrete re-form proposals in the book, though he had initially intended to do so. Nonetheless, the chapter presented a similar, if more extensive, argu-ment, pointing up the contradictions between theory and practice in the Constitution of 1857, between universal (male) suffrage and the re-stricted suffrage of the indirect vote. The constituyentes chose, asserted Rabasa, theoretical democracy as opposed to realizable democracy, rights as opposed to function. This restriction was imposed because universal suffrage "encourages in all countries the appearance of disrupting ele-ments that obstruct the genuine expression of concrete will in popu-lar elections." Referring implicitly to the overthrow of Porfirio Díaz, Rabasa concluded that it was necessary to persuade conservative forces of the value of free elections, and that personal power was not the only way to keep order. Only then could conservatives "balance the forces in play," allowing Mexico to enter "the normal life of free peoples."[19] Was this not another expression of his vision for a "democratic oligarchy?"

The reform measure to institute direct election, supported by the ini-tiative of Rabasa and Macedo, came before the Senate on 26 October 1911.[20] The constitutional committee agreed with the initiative and added that public apathy and fraud result from the indirect vote. Because a citi-zen is voting for a secondary elector, he often does not vote. The opposi-tion to the measure came from Aurelio Valdivieso and Alfonso Alfaro. Valdivieso said that the long suppressed "indigenous race," whose "in-tellectuality has come to be worth almost nothing," cannot be expected to vote.[21] He also raised the question of those of "the feminine sex," many of whom are intelligent. Would not this measure lead to the vote for women? (He later protested that he did *not* favor it!). Alfaro de-fended the constituyentes of the mid-nineteenth century, who he said in-stituted the indirect vote because they feared that "the privileged classes would mislead the spirit of the people," and he quoted a passage from Francisco Zarco to support his point. He also argued for a literacy re-quirement that would help prepare potential citizens. On the question of the Indian, Miguel Macedo responded that the Indian of today was not the Indian of 1823, that the growth of communications, the railroad, and industry had done much to awaken the Indians. Our measure, he added, is yet another way to "awaken the Indian from his deadly apathy."[22] The measure passed, with only Alfaro and Valdivieso in dissent, and it was taken to the Chamber of Deputies by a delegation of senators, including Rabasa and Macedo. On 15 April 1912 the reform was made official and sent to President Madero.[23]

Despite the extensive argument of Rabasa and Macedo, we are left with the puzzle as to why they promoted a measure that seemed contrary to their general political and social philosophy and to their rejection of revolutionary democracy. And by extension, why was such a measure accepted (with minimal opposition) by what was still a Porfirian Senate (and Chamber of Deputies)? Were the senators momentarily swept up in the tide of democratic enthusiasm? I think we can give some credence to Rabasa's argument, particularly when supported by the often-overlooked chapter on elections in *La Constitución y la dictadura*. Indirect elections had obviously led to public apathy, fraud, and manipulation, which Rabasa and others recognized. Even Porfirio Díaz, in his speech of 1 April 1911, had called for electoral reform, though in nonspecific terms. Assuming that we can understand Rabasa's and Macedo's support for direct elections, why did they not advocate a literacy requirement for potential voters, like their colleague Alfaro? Macedo himself provided the answer in the course of the debate. While admitting frankly that he and Rabasa favored the restricted vote, "we believe that at this moment, immediately after the triumph of the revolution that flew the banner of effective suffrage and has awakened the populist yearnings and impulses of the entire nation, it is politically inopportune to raise that question."[24] They knew that if they had imposed restrictions on the direct vote, "we would have sent it to an inevitable defeat." In short, for them philosophy gave way to practical considerations.

However, there is another possible explanation, suggested by Josefina Mac Gregor, for the embrace by the legislators of the direct vote, namely that it allowed them to more readily resist executive action.[25] Ironically, what seems at first glance support for the revolutionary government and its principles may have been in reality a way of slowing their progress. Thus, while accepting the Revolution, the Legislative Power (which generally opposed revolutions) "ended up making Madero the victim of his own democratic yearnings." Seen in this way, perhaps the episode is a dimension of the parliamentarianism that emerged briefly from 1911 to 1913.[26] Be this as it may, democratic direct elections became permanently fixed in Mexico in 1912, thanks in part to the efforts of Emilio Rabasa and Miguel S. Macedo, Científicos who were later often labeled "reactionaries."

The assertion of parliamentary independence vis-a-vis the Executive reached its peak in the twenty-sixth legislature, reinforced by its pride at having been elected directly under the new constitutional amendment. Elections took place on 30 June 1912 for sessions to convene beginning in September. Whereas the entire Chamber of Deputies was renewed, only half of the Senate was affected by the elections, that is, half of the senators had been elected during the Porfiriato. Thus the resistance to President Madero was naturally stronger in the Senate. Rabasa ultimately joined this congressional opposition to the president, even though he had traditionally opposed in principle parliamentary supremacy (*congresismo*).[27] Emilio Rabasa's open opposition to the regime began in July 1912 with the student rebellion against Luis Cabrera, the new director of the Escuela Nacional de Jurisprudencia, and the subsequent founding of the Escuela Libre de Derecho. We will turn to this important episode shortly.

Although Científicos and porfiristas had been divided in their response to the interim regime of León de la Barra, their opposition to President Madero gradually hardened, especially with the increase of rebellions against the regime, beginning in late 1911. For example, news of these rebellions filled the letters written from home and abroad to Pablo Macedo. The correspondents were uniformly alarmed by the spread of *zapatismo,* but they were more ambivalent toward the rebellion of Bernardo Reyes, until it collapsed at the end of 1911. When Pascual Orozco turned against Madero in March 1912, Roberto Núñez expressed considerable interest.[28] Rosendo Pineda wrote from the United States that the only hope of stability was the overthrow of Madero by any means.[29] Of the few Científicos who accepted the regime, Justo Sierra was the most notable. However, his appointment as Ambassador to Spain was brief, for he was ill and died in Madrid on 13 September 1912. Miguel Macedo noted that Enrique Creel, Joaquín Casasús, and Emilio Pimentel received lucrative contracts facilitated by the Maderos, but they were exceptions.[30] The letters to Pablo Macedo end in June 1912, but the hostility of the correspondents to the Madero regime would most certainly have increased with the events of late 1912 and early 1913. These events included the rebellion, defeat, and imprisonment in Mexico City of Félix Díaz, Porfirio's nephew; the increasing opposition to Madero by the Mexico City press and by the U.S. Ambassador Henry Lane Wilson; the conspiracy led by General Manuel Mondragón on 9 February 1913 to free the two prisoners, Félix Díaz and Bernardo Reyes, and to take over the government; and finally the chaotic *decena trágica* in Mexico City, when rebels fought remaining Madero loyalists.

On 16 February and again on 18 February, a Senate delegation, including Emilio Rabasa, tried to persuade Madero to resign. Unsuccessful in their attempt, they met with General Victoriano Huerta, who then with other rebels forced the resignation of the president and vice-president. The next day Huerta was declared interim president with approval of the Senate. When the senators called on Madero to resign, he is said to have refused in part because they were "senators named by General Díaz, not elected by the people"[31] It is ironic that Madero would have said this in the presence of the author of the initiative for direct election of legislators. We have no record of Rabasa's reaction to the assassination on 24 February of Madero and Vice-President José María Pino Suárez. For example, Rabasa did not respond to Limantour's impassioned and philosophical reflection on the dramatic events in Mexico, news of which Limantour and others in Paris were seizing upon eagerly in bits and pieces. I would like to be optimistic about the future, he wrote, but the only thing sure is "our state of nervous agitation." He imagined the fascinating observations his friend would be making "which confirm the critical judgment of our laws and political practices contained in your beautiful book *La Constitución y la dictadura*!"[32] Rabasa clearly accepted the Huerta presidency and remained in the Senate until it dissolved itself on 10 October 1913, following Huerta's dissolution of the Chamber of Deputies.

Prior to October, Rabasa generally supported the government in several conflicts between Huerta and rebellions in the states. When Governor Venustiano Carranza of Coahuila rejected the Huerta presidency, the Senate, including Rabasa, declared the "disappearance" of the powers of the state and the appointment of a provisional governor. However, Rabasa opposed the imposition of General Juvencio Robles as governor of Morelos. In the pacification of Morelos, he asserted, the government "has to apply the law and nothing more than the law."[33] However, in September Rabasa approved the appointment of General Joaquín Maas as provisional governor of Coahuila, and he supported his vote with a legalistic comment on Mexican practice in provisional appointments compared with that of the United States.[34] Despite his efforts to apply the Constitution, it appeared that in the face of Huerta's increasingly arbitrary dictatorship, Emilio Rabasa looked more to the benefits of "pacification" in the face of chaos than to the letter of the law. Rabasa kept his reaction to the dramatic and horrendous events of these years to himself. He had done so in the case of Madero's assassination; he did so again with the disappearance of fellow senator and *chiapaneco*, Belisario Domínguez. Beginning in March 1913, Domínguez mounted an increasingly vocal denunciation of Huerta and finally fell, it was learned later, to the dictator's assassins on 7 October. Though the furor over the disappearance of Domínguez led to the dissolution of both chambers of the legislature, we find no record of Rabasa's reaction to the events, even in correspondence with Limantour. He steadfastly refused to proclaim his views publicly, even in the case of a colleague as principled and courageous as Belisario Domínguez.[35]

The major educational event of the Madero presidency was the founding of the Escuela Libre de Derecho (ELD) in July 1912. The new institution grew out of a student strike protesting efforts by the Madero government to "reform" the Escuela Nacional de Jurisprudencia (ENJ), that is, to impose tighter control, thus correcting the presumed overly lax system of Pablo Macedo, a leading Científico and director of the school since 1904. The Macedo regime in the ENJ was characterized by a system of order and discipline based on administrative tolerance and student honor. It was also characterized by a positivist curriculum, which, following ideas of Gabino Barreda, sought to broaden legal training to prepare students for the scientific, administrative, and economic realities of the modern world. Macedo's direction engendered strong fellow feeling among students and faculty, and his vision was elitist. The school's explicit mission was to train the country's political and economic leaders. By all accounts, the students were deeply attached to their benign director and regretted his resignation, which coincided with the arrival of Madero in Mexico City in mid 1911.[36]

Relations between the government and the university students had already been soured by an episode in January 1912. The Argentine intellectual, Manuel Ugarte, arrived in Mexico City, invited by the Ateneo de la Juventud to lecture on literary topics. When at the last minute he decided to speak on the threat of the United States to Latin America, the government objected for diplomatic reasons. Three thousand students protested in favor of the Latin American spirit; the lectures took place, causing great embarrassment to the government and the resignation of the minister of Foreign Relations, Manuel Calero, publicly accused of being pro-Yankee.[37] On the heels of this episode came the student strike in the ENJ, sparked by the appointment in April 1912 of Luis Cabrera, the leading maderista intellectual and anti-Científico spokesman, as director of the ENJ. Cabrera was appointed by Vice-President José María Pino Suárez, in his secondary role as minister of Public Instruction; and the appointment brought the immediate resignation of Jorge Vera Estañol, a popular law professor who had served as Díaz's last minister of Public Instruction. Pino Suárez openly acknowledged that the appointment of Cabrera was political, an attempt to liquidate the old regime in the nation's most important professional school. The striking students, soon to be expelled, sought professorial support, and within two months the idea of a "free" school was a reality.[38]

Left to Right: Agustín Rodríguez, Emilio Rabasa, Miguel S. Macedo, February 1913. Courtesy of ELD.

Emilio Rabasa was perhaps the central figure in the ELD of 1912; he was a member of its first Junta Directiva, author of its initial statute, and professor of Constitutional Law. Among the professorial founders were men we have encountered, Francisco León de la Barra, Jorge Vera Estañol, and Miguel S. Macedo. The justification for the school rested on the guarantee of *libertad de enseñanza,* as stated in Article 3 of the Constitution of 1857 and presented by Rabasa as "independence with respect to the government . . . detached from any political objective or religious creed." The founders always emphasized this basic idea, perhaps in part to avoid further conflicts with the Madero administration. Nonetheless, the "científico," antimaderista, and ultimately huertista orientation of the institution was clear. In short, the ELD was a product of the major internal political conflicts of the Madero presidency.[39]

A major challenge for the new school was to gain official recognition for its degrees, making them equal to those granted by the ENJ. To this end, the professors of the ELD brought a proposal before the Senate, supported by the prestigious College of Lawyers. The Senate was basically sympathetic, but questions were raised about the durability of the institution. Does it have sufficient capital to survive? asked Victor Manuel

Castillo. Manuel Gutiérrez Zamora feared its life might be ephemeral, in the absence of such eminent figures as Rabasa and León de la Barra. He made special reference to the "recent monumental book that [Rabasa] has just written."[40] Though the accreditation measure passed the Senate by a vote of 35 to 3, the Committee on Public Instruction of the Chamber of Deputies rejected it. The Committee report, presented by José I. Novelo, was a lengthy and devastating critique of the ELD, a strong defense of *libertad de enseñanza* in state higher education, and of the high quality of the curriculum of the ENJ, which "is the equal in scientific advances in the most enlightened countries." If the degrees of the ELD were recognized, he said, anarchy in legal education would ensue.[41] Novelo was bound to oppose the ELD, since he was private secretary to José María Pino Suárez, an advocate of popular education, and a militant opponent of the Científicos.[42] Despite the rebuff by the Chamber of Deputies, the ELD survived, in large part because of the eminence of the founders within the juridical community. Moreover, its degrees were recognized by several states in late 1912 and early 1913. The institution generally prospered under the regime of Victoriano Huerta. Although the federal government did not give the ELD official recognition until 1930, political antagonism between the two law schools faded with the coming of Venustiano Carranza in mid-1914.[43]

In the midst of the events that culminated in the founding of the ELD, José Y. Limantour retained Emilio Rabasa as his defense attorney before the Chamber of Deputies. José Barros, a young militant and supporter of Luis Cabrera's campaign against the Científicos, had formally accused Limantour of financial misdeeds as minister of Hacienda. From Paris, Limantour rallied his friends and associates, the brothers Macedo, Luis Elguero, Joaquín Casasús, and Hugo Scherer, Jr. to manage the case, and they recommended Emilio Rabasa to be principal defense attorney. Besides his great attributes as a lawyer, they also emphasized that Rabasa for sometime had stood apart from them, and was "almost detached from active politics." Apparently, the recommendation was unnecessary, for Limantour had already officially appointed him. Limantour told Rabasa that he would be "a moral safeguard" and provide him the consolation that in difficult times "I have managed to keep good friends."[44] The charges against Limantour were essentially, first, that he had contracted a public debt in 1908 without authorization of Congress and had provided loans to third parties from this source, and second, that he had appropriated public funds for private use. Specifically, according to the charge, he had used public money to purchase property privately at a low price from Valbuena Park and then resold the property to the government of Mexico City through another person at a considerable profit. Rabasa was confident from the beginning that the Grand Jury of the Chamber would dismiss the accusation, in part because the present Minister of Hacienda had supplied two long depositions stating that it had no substance. Rabasa published a pamphlet including the ministry reports plus the text of the Barros accusation.[45] However, he did not realize that the case would linger on for two years before it was put to rest.

Rabasa remained in close touch with Limantour throughout the two years, as well as with "the friends" who were overseeing the case. The correspondence reveals Rabasa's attention to detail, his concern for strategy, his broad network of friendship and association with key deputies and judges, and his multiple efforts to exert his influence extraofficially. On 7 September 1912 Rabasa passed on to Limantour the report from the Second Section of the Grand Jury, commenting that it was generally satisfactory, but that it should have been more specific, to wit, "that there was no crime to pursue." His major concern was the unpredictability of the new (twenty-sixth) Congress, to meet beginning 16 September. His fears were borne out when Luis Cabrera was named new head of the Second Section; but then to his great relief, the case was moved to the First Section.[46] One of Rabasa's surprising associations, a member of the Gran Jurado in the new Congress, was Serapio Rendón, a dedicated maderista, whom Rabasa said showed good will toward him and who agreed to support Limantour's case in the Jury. Rendón does not agree, wrote Rabasa, with the "scandalous conduct of the deputies," and he talks to me freely and even consults me about his difficulties in the Chamber.[47] Rabasa also reported that "our" cause was gaining in the Section, because its secretary, "my compatriot" and good friend, Adolfo Grajales, supported it and was keeping him informed. Despite Limantour's anxiety and impatience, Rabasa thought it best not to try to rush the decision, since "the Chamber is very much in disorder and lacks unity," including many committee changes, clearly resulting from the *decena trágica* and the assassination of Madero in February 1913. Nonetheless, Rabasa could report on 6 March that he had persuaded three of the Sections of the Gran Jurado, and he was now taking on the fourth.[48]

Much to Rabasa's distress, Congress ended its current session on 31 May with the case still unresolved. He attributed the delay not only to the disorder of the Chamber, but more specifically to the "peculiar personality" of Pascual Luna Parra, head of the Gran Jurado. Despite his favorable inclination toward the case, Luna Parra repeatedly delayed the conclusion, according to Rabasa. Rabasa continued to lobby members of the Jurado and kept Limantour informed on seemingly every detail. In the meantime, President Huerta had named Rabasa ambassador to the

United States, pending recognition of the government by Washington. Rabasa assured Limantour that if he had to leave, he would return if necessary to deal with the case (in the absence of any international crisis). This would be necessary, he said, because of the special and often personal relations he had with the various factions in the Chamber.[49] The possibility of his departure obviously alarmed the ever-anxious Limantour, but he did acknowledge that Rabasa was the ideal choice for ambassador. He added for good measure that as demonstrated by your "famous" book and your "movements and tendencies" in recent years, "you are for me . . . the only [person] capable of directing wisely national policy." But U.S. recognition and thus the appointment were withheld, and Rabasa was able to continue his efforts.[50]

The climax of the case came in late September, when José Barros (or someone acting for him) submitted an amparo petition to a district judge, claiming that his individual rights had been violated by improper procedures followed in the committee reports favoring Limantour. The amparo led to a potentially serious conflict between the three powers of government, when the district judge ordered that the deliberations of the Gran Jurado be temporarily suspended. After much debate, including strong statements of support for the sovereignty of the legislature by Francisco de Olaguíbel, Querido Moheno, and José Natividad Macías, the Chamber of Deputies rejected the judicial order by a vote of 77 to 70. The judge then appealed to the Executive to intervene. In the meantime the Supreme Court overturned the judge's order, and the crisis was averted. The Gran Jurado proceeded with its deliberations, and finally on 30 September 1913, the last of two cables arrived in Paris: "Happily finished. Opposition weak. Congratulations."[51] The overjoyed Limantour pressed Rabasa for details—who said what in the debate, who voted for and against him. Rabasa responded that though he had pressed for a vote in the first weeks of the new session, it came sooner than expected (probably because of the judicial tangle), which demanded a sudden change of strategy. Limantour later praised Rabasa more than once for pushing an early decision prior to the "coup d'etat" by Huerta on 10 October, the dissolution by force of the Chamber of Deputies. Limantour was certain this event would have derailed the decision.[52]

However, the Barros case did not end with the vote of the Gran Jurado; the amparo itself still had to be decided by the Supreme Court. Rabasa was convinced that the amparo was ridiculous; besides, he reminded Limantour, the Chief Justice Francisco S. Carvajal, "is a friend of yours." But Rabasa could not prevent delays in the process. He reported in February 1914 that the amparo file was temporarily "lost" and that the Judge intended an "extension." Rabasa then spoke with

Adolfo de la Lama, the minister of Justice ("a good friend"), the case was expedited, and the decision finally came.[53] On 14 June Rabasa sent a telegram from Niagara Falls, Canada, where he had gone as head of the Mexican delegation to the ABC Conference: "Cordial congratulations on the Court decision. Matter finished." In his absence, Rabasa turned over the final work of the judicial case to his law partner, Nicanor Gurría Urgell, who handled it effectively. Limantour worried that the case might be annulled, given the chaotic political state of the country; but Rabasa assured him that it would not, because the Congress that resolved the matter was maderista, and because a Supreme Court decision was rarely overturned.[54] Limantour paid Rabasa 6,000 pesos for his services, which Rabasa said he accepted reluctantly, lest "you were to feel insulted." He never thought, he insisted, "to receive honoraria for defending you"; his only concern was "to serve you by reaching the resolution demanded by truth, justice, and morality." Later, at Rabasa's suggestion, Limantour paid 3,000 pesos to Nicanor Gurría Urgell.[55] Limantour wanted to sue Barros for libel, or at least to write up the case as an act of self-vindication, but Rabasa dissuaded him. In characteristic replies, Rabasa advised that in the first instance "you stand taller by not further acknowledging your accusing tormentor," in the second, "I believe it would be absolutely inopportune at this point."[56] This was not the first or last time that Emilio Rabasa managed to dispel his friend's obsession with defending his honor.

In fact, a few months earlier, Rabasa had been able to restrain Limantour in a similar fashion. In corresponding with Rabasa, Limantour enclosed a strongly worded letter he had written to Manuel Calero, asking Rabasa to send it on only if he thought it wise to do so. Apparently, Calero had broken relations with Limantour in April 1911, when (according to Calero) Limantour was responsible for advising Porfirio Díaz to appoint Jorge Vera Estañol Minister of Public Instruction rather than him. Limantour of course rejected the accusation and took offense when Calero went public and charged him with of lack of sincerity in a letter to the newspaper *El País*. Rabasa returned Limantour's letter to Calero, saying that if someone "has turned his back on me," I feel I should respond in kind, "condemn him to complete oblivion," and try to persuade myself that the person no longer exists. Couldn't you do the same? he asked his friend. Limantour thanked him for his advice and his decision not to send his letter on to Calero.[57]

Emilio Rabasa, like many Mexican intellectuals and public figures of the early twentieth century, had, as we have seen, a private law practice. We know little about this activity, except when it came into the public domain, as in the case of the Barros accusation. What we do know comes principally from the papers of William F. Buckley, Sr., the American who was Rabasa's associate and close friend from about 1910 to the 1920s. Through Buckley we see a private side of Rabasa that has been heretofore obscure. Born in 1881, William F. Buckley was a Texan who grew up in the south Texas town of San Diego, the county seat of sparsely settled Duval County. His father, an Irish immigrant, was a small sheep rancher and the county sheriff until his death in 1904. The Anglos in the county were principally in San Diego, the rest, some 90 percent, Hispanics. By the turn of the century, land was largely in Anglo hands, worked by Hispanics. Buckley grew up in an environment in which Hispanics were clearly dependent on and manipulated by Anglo political bosses.[58] From an early age Buckley acquired fluency in the Spanish language. He entered the University of Texas in 1900 and received a law degree in 1906. He worked briefly as a translator for the General Land Office of Texas, a position secured for him by Marshall Hicks, state senator from San Antonio and a friend of his father.

In 1908 Buckley went to Mexico, studied at the ENJ (where Luis Cabrera was his professor of Civil Law) and then joined a Mexican firm.[59] After what he described as a "terrible time" in Mexico City, he sensed great opportunity in the burgeoning oil industry. In 1912 he opened a law office with his two brothers, Claude and Edmund, in Tampico, the center of the great oil boom. British and American entrepreneurs sought leases from local landowners, and Buckley (aided by his knowledge of Spanish) "specialized in perfecting oil leases."[60] It was during this period that the association between William F. Buckley and Emilio Rabasa began, for in 1914 Buckley referred to Rabasa as "my consulting attorney in the City." Rabasa's business relationship with Buckley was not uncommon, for major public figures such as Pablo Santiago Martínez del Río, Joaquín Casasús, Francisco León de la Barra, and Manuel Calero worked as lawyers and representatives for oil moguls Edward Doheny and Weetman Pearson (Lord Cowdray).[61] However, by 1914, Buckley said he had worked himself "into a nervous wreck," quit the practice, turned it over to his brothers, and entered the oil business himself. He told a close friend he had "acquired some good property in Mexico [presumably Tampico] worth at least $100,000 American money." It was at this moment (May 1914) that Rabasa recruited him as counsel to the Mexican delegation at the ABC Conference in Niagara Falls, after Buckley had declined the position of assistant to the civil governor of American-occupied Veracruz.[62]

Two other nominations that never materialized preceded the appointment of Emilio Rabasa as head of the Mexican delegation to the Niagara Falls conference. As noted above, General Huerta designated him ambassador to the United States, an appointment that depended of course on U.S. recognition of the Huerta government. The outgoing administration of William Howard Taft, at the urging of U.S. Ambassador Henry Lane Wilson, was disposed to do so; but Woodrow Wilson, who took office on 4 March 1913, refused to recognize a government that had come to power by force.[63] Nonetheless, Rabasa assumed for several months that recognition would come and that he would soon be in Washington. He received Limantour's effusive congratulations and (as we have seen) assured his friend that he would return occasionally if necessary to carry through his defense of Limantour against the accusation by José Barros. In acknowledging Limantour's congratulations, Rabasa wrote that "with not much health and filled with fatigue from these two years, I am retiring to *rest* at the side of Wilson and Bryan." As the months passed and relations with the United States worsened, he admitted that "the Embassy in Washington will be a torture (*potro*) for me, but then repeated, obviously further fatigued by the turbulence of Mexican revolutionary politics and the constant turnover of Huerta's cabinet, "nevertheless I see it as a time of rest."[64] By September the ambassadorship apparently had been abandoned, for Huerta now nominated him rector of the National University, after Antonio Caso declined the post. Again Limantour sent congratulations, telling Rabasa that despite "the hatred that today is pulverizing our unfortunate society," you manage to garner "eloquent proof of the esteem and respect of all."[65] When this appointment also failed, Huerta persisted, and finally named him head of the Niagara Falls delegation.

The "fatigue" that Rabasa complained of to Limantour was in part the disillusionment of an intellectual who had envisioned in 1912 the coming of a "constitutional era" characterized by "democratic oligarchy," a vision now seemingly shattered. The revolutionary actions and pronouncements of Emilio Zapata, Pancho Villa, and Venustiano Carranza were anathema to that vision, as was the personal dictatorship of Victoriano Huerta, which undercut the potentially more congenial ideas and measures of cabinet members such as Francisco León de la Barra, Nemesio García Naranjo, Jorge Vera Estañol, and José María Lozano. Rabasa also reacted as a Mexican patriot to Woodrow Wilson's hostility toward the Huerta government, his thinly disguised support for Carranza, and the continuing threat of intervention. In fact, Rabasa would have been confused and probably shocked had he known that his friend and associate William F. Buckley in November 1913 had advocated U.S. intervention in Mexico. Buckley's argument for intervention came in a lengthy letter to Colonel Edward M. House, his friend and fellow Texan, now President Wilson' close advisor.

Buckley's letter was a freewheeling commentary on Mexican affairs—business practices, the incapacity of Mexicans for self-government (monarchy would be better), the opposition to Madero by 95 percent of the "intelligent element of the public," the need for vigorous protection of American interests, and U.S. intervention as the only solution to the Mexican "problem." Of course, he added, "intervention will mean occupation . . . and will lead to the southern boundary of the U.S. being moved further south." Buckley concluded his peroration by emphasizing proudly his fluent Spanish, his study of Mexican history and institutions when he first arrived, and his plan to live in Mexico permanently. I have come to meet, he said, "many of the best Mexicans and cultivated their friendship" referring specifically to "attorneys [like Rabasa?] who have become prominent in Mexican affairs."[66] Colonel House, to whom the letter was directed, was a large landowner and railroad entrepreneur in Texas and the major kingmaker in Texas politics until 1912. His family also had land and oil interests in Mexico. Buckley's law firm represented The Texas Oil Company in Tampico, managed by House's cousin Henry. The House and Buckley families were good friends. The House mansion was a few blocks away from the Buckley home in Austin, just south of the university. Buckley's mother moved there after the death of her husband, and William visited her frequently over the years.[67] Rabasa, in all probability, had not known of Buckley's letter to House when he recruited his friend as counsel to the Mexican delegation to Niagara Falls, but, as we will see later, Rabasa revealed an unusual tolerance for Buckley's rash interventionist tendencies.

Intervention did of course come on 22 April 1914, following a trivial incident involving the mistaken arrest and then release of American sailors who had come ashore in Tampico to purchase fuel. The American admiral off shore construed the incident as an affront to the flag and demanded a twenty-one-gun Mexican salute, which the Mexicans ultimately rejected. The Americans then occupied Veracruz, presumably to prevent the unloading of arms arriving from Europe for the Huerta government. Mexico broke diplomatic relations with the United States, and the shaky Huerta government enjoyed a brief period of patriotic support. In response to the intervention, Argentina, Brazil, and Chile offered to mediate between the two countries.[68] The offer was accepted and Huerta turned to Emilio Rabasa. After a three-hour interview with his friend Adolfo de la Lama, the minister of Hacienda, Rabasa agreed to chair the Mexican delegation to Niagara Falls.[69] Joining Rabasa were Agustín Rodríguez, a fellow founder of the ELD, and Luis Elguero, one of those whom Limantour had selected to manage the Barros case. It is significant that Huerta chose three prominent Mexicans not directly

Garden Party, Toronto, Canada, for ABC Mediators, 27 May 1914.
Left Foreground: Mercedes, Emilio, Ruth. Courtesy of RVR.

associated with his regime, evidence of his desire for a meaningful settlement.[70] Rabasa arrived in Niagara Falls with four of his seven children, whom he told Limantour he couldn't leave in Mexico "given the
present danger." He also confided to his friend that the delegation's task
would have been successful a few months ago, but now rebel victory is
"assured only after spilling some thousands more hectoliters of others'
blood." However, he continued, "We are not despairing totally, nor are
the mediators, who are totally sympathetic to us."[71]

Emilio Rabasa's charge was a frustrating one. Despite the support and
the conscientious efforts of the ABC commissioners, the Niagara Falls
Conference, which took place formally from 20 May to 9 July 1914, was
from the start destined to failure. The United States refused to accept
Huerta's initial position that the conference be limited to the international
conflict between the two countries and insisted that it include as well
the internal conflict. Venustiano Carranza's Constitutionalist forces were
rapidly gaining the upper hand, and for the United States their victory
was inevitable. John Lind, Wilson's informal envoy to Mexico, had been
pressing this point constantly for several months, and he continued to do
so to U.S. delegates during the Conference.[72] Even Rabasa had acknowledged privately to Limantour that rebel victory was certain; nonetheless,
he continued to search for an alternative solution. The negotiations were

further complicated by Wilson's refusal to accept any action or statement that suggested the legitimacy of the Huerta regime. For him, the Mexican internal conflict was purely and simply a conflict between factions. That stance forced the Mexican delegation to decide whether it should deal with representatives of "the rebels." William F. Buckley in Washington passed on to Rabasa advice from an unnamed official (probably American) that the delegation should negotiate with the Carranza party. Rabasa responded that he at first (like Buckley) had thought it not "suitable" to do so, but that "subsequent facts" made him change his mind.[73]

The ABC mediators proposed from the start that Huerta should resign in favor of a "neutral" person, chosen by election and agreed on and then recognized by the United States. Though Rabasa found the proposal vague and wired De la Lama confidentially that "we let the point go discretely as simply conversation," he ultimately accepted it. Huerta agreed to the proposal on 1 June, and much of the rest of the conference was devoted to its implementation.[74] Rabasa and the U.S. authorities disagreed sharply on the makeup of a potential "Board" that would call for elections: how much it should be weighted toward the Constitutionalists. On the other hand, the United States opposed any solution or any Mexican successor that might suggest the perpetuation of a *huertista* regime. With the Mexican delegation and the American government at loggerheads and with Constitutionalist troops at the gates of Mexico City, mediation essentially failed. Huerta did resign on 15 July, in favor of Foreign Minister Francisco J. Carvajal, formerly chief justice of the Supreme Court, but no agreement had been reached. Just prior to the official resignation, Rabasa sent a confidential memorandum to Mexico that the only way to save Mexico City from the entry of Carranza's troops was to have Carvajal resign in favor of a *cabildo abierto* (open city council meeting), which would organize a Junta de Gobierno that might be acceptable to both the United States and Carranza.[75] Perhaps this represented Rabasa's final vain effort to find in the Spanish colonial tradition an institution that could lead to a "democratic oligarchy."

The attitude of Woodrow Wilson, expressed as early as 26 May, revealed the impossibility of any agreement. Through Secretary of State William Jennings Bryan, he told the ABC Commissioners that it was "futile" to set up a provisional authority that would be neutral; it must be "avowedly and in favor of the necessary agrarian and political reforms." He continued: "Confidentially, we suggest that the Mexican representatives, being Científicos, are making a last desperate attempt to save their privileges from the reforms which the Carrancistas would certainly insist on."[76] Rabasa, for his part, was no less hostile to the Wilson administration. It is lamentable, he wrote Buckley, that "the clumsy errors committed by the highest officials of the U.S. Government are bringing both countries into a lamentable situation."[77] As for defending his "científico privileges" (a questionable appraisal of Rabasa), it is true that he showed great concern for the security of anyone involved in any way with the Huerta regime, if and when the Constitutionalists entered Mexico City. Three months after the conclusion of the Conference, Rabasa was alarmed over the arrest by the Carranza regime of Nicanor Gurría Urgell, his long-time law partner, and he asked Buckley (now back in the capital) to take care of his office and do everything possible to secure Gurría's freedom.[78] By now Rabasa was settled into exile at 440 Riverside Drive in New York with his children. The diplomatic experience left Rabasa with bitter feelings toward Woodrow Wilson (ironically, the author he cited favorably in 1912) and a permanent hostility toward Carranza's revolutionary faction.

Thus ended the period of four years that Emilio Rabasa said caused him much "fatigue." On the personal side, this fatigue undoubtedly came from the tragedy of this wife's death and the burdens of being sole parent to his seven children, four of whom he was obliged to take with him to Niagara Falls. The fatigue probably also came from the onset of an eye disease, as we will see in Chapter 5. The exceptional political turbulence of the period must have also been fatiguing, though in some ways Rabasa reached the peak of his career during these few years, his mid fifties. With the publication of *La Constitución y la dictadura* and the founding soon after of the ELD, Rabasa became recognized as perhaps the country's leading political historian, constitutional theorist, and legal educator. He was also of course an influential senator, later chosen to carry through an impossible but important diplomatic mission. At the same time, he became in 1911 a figure of the Old Regime, an increasingly antirevolutionary "científico" and a supporter of Victoriano Huerta, the "usurper." Because of the moderation of the early Revolution, and because of his own nature—his determination to maintain a low political profile—Rabasa survived and even to some extent flourished amid the turmoil. He had a broad network of friends and associates—ranging from Serapio Rendón, a dedicated maderista, to Adolfo de la Lama, a Huerta minister—on whom he could rely in defending José Yves Limantour against the accusations of José Barros. His broad network also included William F. Buckley, an American lawyer and entrepreneur whose private ideas in 1913 about Mexico and Mexicans might well have been an affront to his patriotism.

Rabasa's ideas certainly clashed with the democratic ideology of Francisco I. Madero, and in one sense Rabasa's vision of "democratic oligarchy" and a postdictatorial "constitutional stage" became outmoded by the time his magnum opus was published. And yet Rabasa showed in his initiative to institute direct elections in Mexico that he could adapt to change, granted his reasons for doing so remain unclear. But with the triumph of Venustiano Carranza and the departure of Huerta, Rabasa was no longer able to survive in Mexico, ideologically or politically; the only recourse was exile. We now turn to his New York years, which despite all obstacles, continued to be fruitful, though in some ways probably less fatiguing.

CHAPTER FIVE

The Exile Years: Politics, Journalism, and History (1914–1920)

◡

We have to admire Emilio Rabasa's ability to live a productive life in New York City from July 1914 until the spring of 1920, when he finally returned to Mexico. Though he obviously had sufficient means to rent apartments on upper Riverside Drive, he was not a man of great wealth who could like José Yves Limantour occupy a mansion adjacent to La Place de l'Étoile in Paris or spend months at fashionable resorts such as Deauville, Biarritz, or Bournemouth.[1] Rabasa was a widower with four unmarried daughters and two sons in tow. In addition, his married daughter, Manuela, her three children, and her husband, Dr. Antonio Barranco, joined the household in 1915, which necessitated one, if not two or more of the moves the Rabasa family made within the city during the exile years. Until 1917 it was a household of at least eleven individuals.[2]

Emilio Rabasa was a man of spare physique, unaccustomed to northern winters, the subject of occasional complaints. Most of all he was afflicted with an increasingly severe eye disease, which made his reading and his writing in longhand difficult. Reference to his eye problem was a regular part of his correspondence with Limantour. In September 1914 he said Limantour would probably have to "decipher" a letter he was writing in pencil, because his eyes would tolerate lead better than ink. (Indeed, Limantour had the letter copied, much to the relief of this reader.) As winter approached in 1916, Rabasa complained that "the day ends for me at 4 PM," since he couldn't work with artificial light. He said he tried to use the time to think, "but for me thinking without a pencil in my hand is only half thinking."[3] The next year he admitted to his friend that after twenty injections his eyes were no better. He later described what was undoubtedly macular degeneration, which allowed him peripheral vision, but central vision only in one eye (with

First Rabasa Apartment, 440 Riverside Drive,
New York City, 1914–15. Photo by Pablo Piccato.

strong glasses).[4] Limantour tried repeatedly to persuade Rabasa to come
to Europe for a consultation. Before leaving for Niagara Falls in 1914,
Rabasa had written that "perhaps I will come to your world to attend
to an eye affliction that much alarms me every day." However, by 1917,
on the advice of his New York doctors, he concluded that it would be
useless.[5] Despite these major obstacles during his exile years, Emilio
Rabasa completed two major works and many articles, as well as engaging actively in exile politics and some private legal work.[6]

His daughter Concepción recalled his daily routine in New York. He
began his day at 6 A.M., followed by a walk on Riverside Drive that
ended at a small office he had at the firm of Aldao Campos y Gil. There

he dealt with personal matters and continued his work for various clients, including U.S. companies and the British oil company "El Aguila" (owned by Weetman Pearson). According to Concepción, he usually spent his afternoons (when he was not writing) with friends and fellow exiles, discussing "the latest news from our beloved and much-missed Mexico." These friends included, she wrote, the Elguero brothers, Agustín Rodríguez, Ricardo Guzmán, Carlos Aguirre, and the former ELD student Ezequiel Padilla.[7]

Rabasa's voluminous correspondence with Limantour during the exile years reveals an intense interest in Mexico's chaotic internal politics, in the twists and turns of U.S. policy, and for a time in possible armed incursions by exiled leaders. Rabasa also tried to organize a campaign in the U.S. press against Venustiano Carranza, the Primer Jefe of the Revolution, a campaign that failed for lack of funds and a shift of American public interest away from Mexico to the war in Europe. It is clear that Rabasa commanded considerable respect and some influence among exile groups for his intelligence, his judgment, and his caution, while keeping himself, as usual, out of public view. In 1919 he collaborated with William F. Buckley and with Limantour (as we will

Limantour Mansion, 8 rue Presbourg, Paris, 1911–35. Photo by Jon Benfer.

see in Chapter 6) on projects to finance economic reconstruction, before returning to Mexico in 1920. However, Rabasa ultimately turned back to his greatest strength, writing, and what he wrote was the enduring legacy of his exile years.

Rabasa and Limantour began the immediate post-Huerta era exchanging speculations on what the future held, for the country and for their interests. In mid July 1914, Rabasa wrote from New York predicting that soon Carranza would enter Mexico City "with a horde," also that Wilson, the "saint of the White House," was pressing for a general amnesty, which, said Rabasa, would probably lead to "freedom for vengeance and for venting rancour." Yet, at least the departure of Huerta meant for him that the capital would not have to be forcibly taken by Carranza's troops. Rabasa was perplexed two months later by fragmentary reports of the mission of Wilson's agent Paul Fuller to Pancho Villa, resulting in Villa's proposal that there be a general amnesty, plus a meeting of military chiefs on 1 October to name an interim president. These proposals, Rabasa wrote, met with U.S. approval "because they are probably their own." Carranza of course rejected them, which led Rabasa to conclude "that Villa comes out more humane, more politic, and more skillful than Carranza." For Rabasa the question was whether Carranza would be elected president, and if so what would Wilson do with Villa, whom he appeared to be supporting.[8] Interestingly enough, William F. Buckley at the same time, in his several wide-ranging and highly opinionated letters to L. M. Garrison, U.S. secretary of war, was condemning Carranza (who held Tampico and was taxing oil wells). "We [in Tampico] are all for Villa," wrote Buckley, adding that the U.S. government should support him for the presidency.[9]

Rabasa and Limantour also speculated on the fate of exile properties, their own and those of others. Would they be returned if the rule of law were restored? Rabasa heard from Mexico that several houses had been occupied, and that people were visiting those of Casasús and Escandón as public buildings, marveling at their "beauty." Limantour, as usual, welcomed Rabasa's information and worried particularly over reports that his properties had been occupied, complaining that he couldn't get any direct information from "representatives, relatives, friends, dependents, or servants."[10] Rabasa also expressed concern, given the uncertainty of the situation, for the safety of his married daughter Manuela and his brother Ramón and family, though as noted above, Manuela was later to come to New York, given permission by a Carranza general to leave. Rabasa's house in Mexico City was ransacked and his books burned.[11] Thus, as Mexico entered the era of the Convention of

Aguascalientes and of factional conflict between the forces of Villa, Zapata, and Carranza, the two exiles, while deploring the chaos, consistently vented their principal frustration against the Primer Jefe, whom they feared would emerge as victor in the civil war.[12]

Speculation continued in 1915, but it now turned to more concrete thoughts about specific exile projects. After several months of silence, Rabasa wrote a long and detailed letter in April, reporting on intervening events and announcing his press campaign. In November 1914, a small (unnamed) "junta" sought his opinion on a plan for "an armed movement." Always cautious, Rabasa agreed that "it is necessary to do something . . . provided it is not stupid." He told the group that as long as Villa's manifesto (of 30 September) seemed to have broad support, it was imprudent to launch a campaign. "I passed," he added, "for being semi-*villista* and a bit of a coward." He then admitted to Limantour that he was left confused when the situation changed markedly after Villa entered Mexico City and Eulalio Gutiérrez (president of the Revolutionary Convention) rebelled, "publishing a manifiesto that we both would have signed." But alas, it got no national support. By February 1915, Rabasa continued to be perplexed by U.S. policy when he learned that a new Wilson representative, Duval West, was in Mexico, conferring with Villa and with Felipe Angeles. At the same time, he was drawn into what was another short-lived U.S. scheme, this time to promote Eduardo Iturbide, Huerta's governor of the Federal District. Iturbide, reported Rabasa, came to visit him in New York, but again Rabasa urged caution in the face of Iturbide's "impatient ardor."[13]

Rabasa also received a visit from Toribio Esquivel Obregón, Huerta's minister of finance who resided in Brooklyn. Esquivel sought Rabasa's support for Iturbide, on behalf of the Asamblea Mexicana Pacificadora, an exile organization in San Antonio, Texas. According to Esquivel, Rabasa dismissed the Asamblea because it was officially identified with Texas and not Mexico. He was also skeptical about the possibility of raising money for it in New York. In the face of the resistance of Rabasa and others, Esquivel Obregón finally abandoned the ephemeral Asamblea.[14] Though Rabasa expressed some sympathy for Iturbide's and other counterrevolutionary military projects, he saw the obstacles: securing arms; facing Wilson's contradictory policies; and finally, "the stigma of being a reactionary and a Científico," even in the eyes of the American people. In short, he pulled back from direct involvement, and rationalized to Limantour: "having a base in absolute disinterest, one preserves very well serenity and good sense." Rabasa apparently influenced Iturbide to turn away from violence and join him instead in legal work.[15]

Limantour and Wife María Cañas at Deauville, France, 1915. From María y Campos, *José Limantour.* Courtesy of Condumex, S. A.

María Cañas in Parlor, 8 rue Presbourg. From María y Campos, *José Limantour.* Courtesy of Condumex, S. A.

However, Emilio Rabasa's inaction was limited to engagement in military projects. The climax of his lengthy letter to Limantour was his idea, supported also by Luis Elguero, for a press campaign in the United States to counter revolutionary propaganda, particularly from the Carranza camp. Rabasa was encouraged by what he saw as a shift in public opinion from support for the revolutionary chiefs to seeing them as "bandits," incapable of forming a government. But unfortunately the Científicos were also maligned, he said, the general view being that Mexico had no "honorable class," no "decent man." The country "is unworthy of free existence," and the United States must tutor it like the Philippines "and after many years extend it out of charity a diminished autonomy." The Republicans, whom he thought would win the election of 1916, would undoubtedly carry out such a policy of intervention. We cannot, wrote Rabasa, let nature take its course; we must try to influence American opinion. Rabasa acknowledged that the idea came originally from an American friend in Chicago, a diplomat who knew Mexico well, and who was "a *pensador,* a writer, well-educated, and intelligent." He naturally detests Bryan and Wilson, added Rabasa. This friend ("whose name I can't put in a letter") wrote him, he continued, beginning in mid 1913 and later at the onset of the Niagara conference, predicting everything that happened thereafter, including the failure of the conference. He invited me to come to Chicago after the conference; and with his help as a translator, I could devote myself "to fulfilling my only possible patriotic duty, preventing intervention." At first I agreed, he told Limantour, but then decided to remain in New York, where I could be in contact with Mexicans and receive direct news from Mexico, including news about my married daughter.[16]

Rabasa proceeded to present the advantages of a campaign in the press, noting that the American public was very much influenced by what it read in newspapers; the campaign could counteract "the shamelessness of the defenders of Wilson." It could be "entirely national and thus impersonal"; and yet he added that it could support any armed movement "that might prosper" (whether it be by Iturbide, Félix Díaz, or even Eulalio Gutiérrez). "It matters little to us [which one]," he wrote, "provided it brings about the establishment of law in Mexico." By presenting the truth, such a campaign could reestablish "some dignity for the nation and much for the superior classes of Mexico." Limantour responded with enthusiasm to "the work of converting American opinion to the religion of truth and justice," but was skeptical about securing funds for the enterprise in Europe, since Mexicans there were in financial straits and potential Europeans were either absorbed in the war or believed Mexicans were incapable of establishing peace.[17] Moreover, the exchanges between Limantour and Rabasa became diverted by Limantour's perennial concern for his reputation and his desire to pursue those who maligned him. This time it was a false letter, supposedly by Limantour to the *New York Times*. Rabasa was openly sympathetic, as usual, and gave legal advice; but both he and Elguero were relieved when Limantour finally decided not to pursue the matter.[18] Both Rabasa and Limantour were frustrated by Woodrow Wilson's apparent reversal of position on Mexico. On 9 January 1915, he appeared to say, as Rabasa expressed it, "that the Mexicans have the right to cut their throats in their struggle for liberty"; then on 2 June, he seemed to announce that if Mexicans could not unite, the United States would be obliged to unify the factions, support one leader, or to intervene.[19] By mid June both correspondents sensed that Wilson intended to take the easy road and to recognize Carranza. Rabasa announced he was giving up the press project.[20]

The one tangible result of the campaign in the press was an article supposedly submitted by Rabasa with the help of Buckley to the New York *Sun* prior to giving up the campaign. (The article may or may not have been published). Entitled "Unconditional Surrender," the article detailed Venustiano Carranza's pattern of rigidity beginning in 1913, when he sought U.S. support "without conditions" in the negotiations with Wilson's envoy William Bayard Hale, continuing in 1914 when Carranza refused to send a delegate to the Niagara Falls Conference (even though Huerta had offered to resign). In November 1914, asserted Rabasa, the United States offered to hand over the port of Veracruz, only requesting that Carranza protect Mexicans taking refuge in the city during the occupation. Carranza refused, and finally U.S. troops evacuated the port "without any conditions." Most recently, concluded Rabasa, Carranza rejected the American proposal to mount a second Pan American Conference to resolve differences between the Mexican factions. In short, "UNCONDITIONAL SURRENDER, which appears to be the slogan of the First Chief, is now imposed on the American Government, and since this Government represents the American People, the submission of the former signifies the humiliation of the latter." The speculation by the exiles over Wilson's policy toward the Mexican revolutionary factions finally ended in October 1915 when Carranza received de facto recognition, first by the Pan American Nations and soon thereafter by the United States. Thus, by 1916 Rabasa was forced to turn his thoughts and actions in other directions.[21]

With the collapse of the governments of the Revolutionary Convention and the de facto U.S. recognition of Carranza in October 1915, Rabasa and Limantour's speculation concerning Mexican politics also subsided. Expectation gave way to discouragement, resignation, and a general *anticarrancismo*. However, Rabasa continued to send reports to Limantour for the next three years, information that the latter was always eager to get, since Rabasa's sources were more direct than those of his friends. One subject of interest was the raid on Columbus, New Mexico, by Pancho Villa in February 1916 and the subsequent "punitive expedition" into northern Mexico, led by General John J. Pershing. Rabasa's commentary on the episode was half satirical, half serious. He noted the ridiculous exaggeration in the U.S. press and predicted "a comparison between the tactics of Pershing and those of [General Joseph Jacques] Joffre and that . . . the defense of Columbus can become a model for the defenders of Verdun." In a later letter, Rabasa wrote that he had a great desire to write a history of the expedition, "taken from American newspapers and with opinions and commentaries by Sancho Panza." On the serious side, Rabasa noted the deprivation and suffering in the Chihuahua desert and identified the Mexican dilemma as: "either to tolerate the invasion shamefully, or to come together in support of a government of brigands to defend national honor."[22]

The only still viable military project was that of Félix Díaz, which Rabasa followed in some detail. In fact, Mexican government intelligence reported that Rabasa was actively involved as the representative of Díaz in New York. According to this source, Díaz was merely a figurehead for the "Científico Party." The Díaz military expedition, which set out from New Orleans in February 1916, was a comic opera affair, putting in unsuccessfully at several points along the gulf coast and finally making an incursion into Chiapas with modest initial success.[23] However, on 30 November Rabasa was skeptical about Diaz's prospects and predicted that "all Chiapas will be under the power of the revolution, which has a base of organization." In August 1917, Rabasa reported that Juan Albreu Almazán, Félix Díaz's second in command, had taken Tuxtla Gutiérrez, but only briefly.[24] The felicista movement continued intermittently till 1920, when Díaz surrendered and went into exile. Rabasa's name also showed up in a consular report in 1918 as the representative in New York for Manuel Peláez, a rebel in the oil region who had sporadic ties to Félix Díaz, but Rabasa did not mention him in his letters to Limantour.[25]

During this period, Emilio Rabasa continued his concern for his friends in Mexico, for their property, and for general living conditions. On 16 July, he announced that despite his better judgment the Elguero brothers, José and Luis, had left New York for Mexico. "You will understand," he told Limantour, "that their absence will produce a void for me that can't be filled."[26] He later learned that the brothers had been imprisoned on 6 August, but were released two days later. On hearing of the departure of the Elgueros, Limantour responded that he had just sent a letter to Luis and that he would give Rabasa permission to retrieve it at the Lazard office. In it, Limantour said he dealt with public and private (money?) matters with customary "frankness and openness." Rabasa obviously appreciated the gesture, a good indication of the degree of intimacy and trust that existed between the two friends.[27] Rabasa worried about the fate of Miguel Macedo, whom he hadn't heard from for two months and then learned he had been detained. In September, he related the good news that Macedo had been freed in the middle of August. The Pimentel family informed Rabasa of Emilio's temporary imprisonment and of the harsh conditions that had affected his mind.[28] But Rabasa was pleased to note that the government had returned properties of the Casasús family, those of Pedro Lascurain, of the widow of Limantour's brother Julio, and those of Doña Carmen (widow of Porfirio Díaz?). The state of the country was less encouraging. Rabasa pointed to the popular frustration over the shrinking value of the new paper money, issued by Minister of Finance Luis Cabrera, whom he and Limantour frequently ridiculed. The exodus from the countryside meant Mexico City now had a million people, said Rabasa, including my "countrymen" who have abandoned their haciendas. "The houses of Mexico are packed like cans of sardines; in my brother's that is quite small there are three families."[29]

The one unpleasant but brief intrusion into Rabasa's correspondence with Limantour involved Francisco León de la Barra, former interim president of Mexico and a close colleague of both men. León de la Barra had been a fellow founder of the ELD and had recruited Rabasa to take part in a political initiative in mid 1913. He called it a "civic league" for the purpose of guaranteeing a broad base of participation from several parties in elections supposedly to take place in October following Victoriano Huerta's "usurpation" of the presidency in February. In a speech in June, León de la Barra recommended Rabasa for president of a Provisional Junta to prepare for the elections.[30] The plan never materialized, because Huerta undercut the electoral process and was sole candidate in October. Rabasa apparently had misgivings about this episode or about other relations with León de la Barra, for when the latter sought Rabasa out in New York in April 1916, Rabasa shot off an uncharacteristic diatribe against him to Limantour. Rabasa depicted León de la Barra as "intoxicated (*enajenado*) by his exaggerated mania for personal importance," recently arrived from Washington, where he dealt with supposedly very important people. In New York "groups of bankers are having banquets for him on a daily basis." León de la Barra has irritated us all, he complained to Limantour.[31] His friend apparently much upset Rabasa by his response, suggesting that in their exile situation they must embrace "the union of all good Mexicans." Rabasa was at pains to insist that he was not a person to be governed by "petty feelings." The frank exchange, which included a serious consideration of Léon de la Barra's strengths and weaknesses, ended with Rabasa's affirmation that he was not "one of those easily offended men" who has to be handled "with kid gloves." The two were reconciled: "We must put an end finally *(dar punto y remate)* to the intrusion of Don Pancho into our correspondence."[32] He was not mentioned again.

Although Emilio Rabasa was engaged sporadically in active counterrevolutionary schemes, his true vocation could not be suppressed for long in his New York exile. He must write. When the campaign to influence American public opinion through the press failed to materialize, except for his lone article, possibly published in the New York *Sun,* Rabasa sought other channels in which to express himself and his opposition to the Revolution. W. F. Buckley had encouraged what apparently was his early intention to write a history of the Niagara Falls Conference, but there is no evidence that he undertook the project.[33] We have noted his tongue-in-cheek desire to take on the "expiatory expedition" against Pancho Villa. However, Rabasa finally rediscovered his voice in a series of articles sent under pseudonym or anonymously to the *Revista mexicana,* a weekly exile journal published by his friend Nemesio García Naranjo in San Antonio, Texas, beginning in early 1916. García Naranjo had been a member of the famous *Cuadrilátero* group, opposed in Congress to Madero in 1912–13, and later served as Huerta's minister of Public Instruction. García Naranjo insisted years later in his memoirs that Rabasa was the author of the articles, a claim verified in the Rabasa-Limantour correspondence.[34] Flashes of Rabasa the novelist appear in the articles, written in a style that may have prompted him not to attach this name. As García Naranjo commented, "the pen of Rabasa combined . . . deep seriousness and agile irony; it revealed at the same time the soaring of the eagle and the fluttering of the butterfly."[35]

The first series of four articles appeared in late 1916 as a review of *The Whole Truth About Mexico: President Wilson's Responsibility,* a polemic by Francisco Bulnes, published in New York.[36] Rabasa attacked the book unmercifully, but only in private to Limantour. The published articles were generally in a lighter, more satirical vein, though Rabasa did use the review to make interpretative comments on the Revolution— which are absent in his other works. He admitted to Limantour that he had only read pieces of Bulnes's previous books, because "I can't tolerate books by orators," even though he might like their orations. "Nonetheless, I must say," continued Rabasa, "that this one is his worst and that it is written with more recklessness and more passion." Bulnes cannot write without combating something. In vilifying Wilson, continued Rabasa, he has some praise for the Díaz regime, but for this one must pay dearly "in insults, maliciousness (*insidias*), and calumny." Rabasa had never seen Bulnes "more juvenile . . . especially when he tries to be original and caustic." Rabasa said he firmly believed that "senile degeneration" or at least "decline" had set in. Bulnes appears to have lost the genius "that was his magic on the platform."[37]

In the articles, Rabasa's principal target was Bulnes's style, not his indictment of Wilson, who Rabasa agreed had produced the errors "that have opened the way for the destructive hordes of a quiet and good nation." The severe and circumspect jurist (under cover of anonymity) seemed to take delight in satirizing the oratorical style of his fellow Científico. Bulnes "has just spoken a book, because Señor Bulnes, a congenital orator by temperament, has never succeded in writing books; he always speaks them, he orates them." He is the orator in all he does; for him "the world is simply an auditorium." He seeks applause at any cost. But in English, said Rabasa (adding a risqué touch), the Bulnes oratory has no effect; it is flat and colorless: "it comes out like the naked Miss, who according the the custom of the day, is photographed through a stiff, wet sheet, as in shadow theater (*sombra* chinesca); it is her all right, but without color, without the details that we would most want to see."

Never noted for his oratory, Rabasa as historian and constitutional jurist was the complete opposite of Bulnes. Reasoned argument, clear diction, always directed toward the careful reader, was his forte. As he said to Limantour, Bulnes "is incapable of explaining, developing, reasoning, and concluding." The reader is different from the listener, wrote Rabasa in the *Revista Mexicana;* "he doesn't get inflamed, he is in control of himself. The reader is a very dangerous animal, because he is the most rational one known."[38] Rabasa's distaste for the Bulnes oratorical style had obviously struck deep roots over many years, despite the two men's general agreement on political issues. Moreover, he added, Bulnes's procedure is similar to Wilson's, accommodating facts to his conclusion, instead of vice-versa. This theological procedure is understandable in the case of Wilson, who "has theology in his blood, but I cannot understand it in a true positivist (*positivista de ley*)."[39]

Rabasa had two basic objections to the substantive argument in *The Whole Truth about Mexico*: that for Bulnes there had been two revolutions, not one; and that he vilified the Mexican people as well as its leaders. According to Bulnes, Madero, the leader of the first revolution, was a dreamer of good faith who believed in public liberties and who attempted to "found the semi-parliamentary government that Bulnes advised." The second revolution, in Bulnes's view, was that of Carranza and Villa, based on vengeance and extermination, "fertile for evil in all its horrible forms." For Rabasa, by contrast, "the revolution is one and indivisible," essentially "demoguery arousing all the low bestial instincts." The revolution has been the same "since November 1910." Rabasa objected particularly to Bulnes's disdain for the Mexican people, that is, Indians and mestizos whom he depicted as inferior species. On the contrary, retorted Rabasa, "[the revolution] was not carried out by the people, but by a horde," a mere 1 percent of Mexicans. Rabasa ended his articles saying he felt oppressed, as if he were reading one of Zola's novels, "in which there is no agreeable personage; and one feels sick, unsociable, disgraced by life, and sorry to have read them."

Rabasa sent a copy of the book to Limantour and also said coyly, "I am going to try to send you those articles . . . that have been submitted to periodicals of S. Antonio." On receiving Limantour's congratulations to the "author of those articles," Rabasa continued the charade, responding: "my friend the author of the articles thanks you very much for your opinion and is very proud that you have found them good."[40] Limantour agreed with Rabasa's critique, "although it was very severe," but characteristically his focus was on what Bulnes said about *him*. Bulnes approved of his role in Hacienda, but supported the partisans of Bernardo Reyes who opposed Limantour in the years before 1910, a section that Rabasa found "the most malevolent and capricious of the work." Limantour, as usual, sought Rabasa's advice as to whether he should respond to "Pancho" Bulnes. Rabasa, as usual, told him to ignore the charges, saying, "I suppose there is no advantage in answering what you can't destroy."[41] Rabasa was pleased by the reception of the articles, especially by two lawyers (probably in New York) who changed completely their opinion of the book, without knowing who wrote the articles. On the other hand, Rabasa was forced to admit to Limantour in 1918 that he had heard *The Whole Truth about Mexico* was selling well in Mexico.[42]

In a subsequent series of articles entitled a "Constitutionalist gallery," Rabasa proceeded to expose the failings of five prominent members of Venustiano Carranza's government, Pastor Rouaix, Jesús Urueta, Luis Cabrera, Antonio Manero, and Fernando Iglesias Calderón.[43] As the master of constitutional law, Rabasa was undoubtedly piqued by Carranza's appropriation of the term *constitucionalista*. In the portraits, he again resorted to satirical barbs and to sarcasm, but he also used these individual portraits to mount his attack on the regime and its policies. The initial article on Rouaix set the tone for the rest. He was unable, he said, to pen portraits of "the millions of *pensadores* and intellectuals" who were guiding the triumph of the Constitutionalist Revolution.

He did not even yet have "the corrosive substance and the very black ink" for the most eminent, like Cabrera and Urueta; "the watered-down and faded ink that I have at my disposal hardly permits me to deliniate something of the moral figure of a man like Rouaix." Pardon my disrespect, Rabasa told his readers, if I deny "the good *pastor* the designation of *pensador* and statesman." Rabasa proceeded to depict Rouaix's obscure and mediocre career as student and teacher, and his 6,592 "dissertations" in 638 volumes of the *Anales de la Sociedad Antonio Alzate* on such momentous topics as "the maguey worm as food for humans, tasty and easily digestible." Among the hundreds of articles, Rabasa could not find one that pointed to the "demagogue or to the Minister of Development," who called for the division of large properties and the distribution of wealth. In fact, said Rabasa, one article of 1911 argued the opposite: "the detrimental social and economic effects of the division of large properties of the frontier states." Rabasa concluded that Rouaix was like a child, tied to his mother's apron strings until age twenty-five, who when suddenly free turned libertine. Until 3 July 1911 he was "a proper and judicious citizen," then suddenly became "what he is now, a wretch (*descamisado*)."

Rabasa's portrait of Jesús Ureta was replete with amusing anecdotes about a man who was a good actor but a total failure in school and in the world of the law, disreputable in his personal life, and one who made his way only because he was protected by his wife's uncle, Justo Sierra. After Sierra's death in 1912, with all other avenues closed to him, he fell "from bump to bump into the Constitutionalist sewer." As for Luis Cabrera, Rabasa of course held a major grudge against this supporter of Madero who excoriated the Científicos and whose actions forced the founding of the ELD. Rabasa characterized Cabrera as a "*talento de fe,*" a mediocrity whose reputation was built up by friends and then spread imperceptibly to others. In this way Cabrera, without any real qualifications, became known as an expert in finance, and thus Secretario de Hacienda in the Carranza government, dubbed by Rabasa, the "minister of paper money." His article on Antonio Manero was brief, a "self portrait" consisting mostly of quotations from Manero's writings. Rabasa was clearly disillusioned by Manero's embrace of the Constitutionalist cause, after writing in 1911 that the Científico Party of 1892 had shown the only path "that can lead the Mexican people slowly and gradually to the knowledge of democracy." For Rabasa he was seemingly a former advocate of "democratic oligarchy" who had turned opportunist.

Rabasa's final series of articles, also published separately as a pamphlet by García Naranjo, was somewhat different from the others, since its focus was on the historical accounts written by Fernando Iglesias

Calderón, though preceded by a characteristically sharp "sketch" of Iglesias himself.[44] Rabasa began by noting that Iglesias had a place in the "Constitutionalist gallery," since he had been a partisan of the revolution or "continues pretending to be one for lack of another cubby hole in which to put himself." Rabasa emphasized, however, that though the revolution rejected him and though he ultimately rejected the revolutionaries, he was basically an honorable man—not given to lucre. As a historian, Rabasa judged him a man without talent, driven by passion, vanity, and disregard for the facts. He was particularly incensed by the accusation that Jorge Vera Estañol and Francisco León de la Barra were implicated in the assassination of Madero. Rabasa went on to criticize Iglesias Calderón's lifelong obsession with the defense of his father, José María Iglesias, the Chief Justice of the Supreme Court who claimed the Presidency in 1876 on constitutional grounds. Rabasa the jurist dismissed the validity of the claim itself and the son's insistence on keeping it alive. Don Fernando's reverence for his father is admirable, concluded Rabasa, but "he publicizes it to the point of making it ridiculous." Everyone is now weary of the Iglesias affair of 1876.

In the midst of his contributions to the *Revista mexicana*, the everactive Emilio Rabasa decided to undertake another major book. In a sense this work was a logical substitute for the now abandoned press campaign, one more suited to his talent and temperament than a series of newspaper articles. He first announced the project to Limantour in April 1916 as a book "of national defense," which after several transformations finally appeared in 1920 as *La Evolución histórica de México*. He sought Limantour's approval for the project, in part because the latter willingly helped arrange a subsidy for it from Weetman Pearson, who as we have seen, had been willing to underwrite the abortive press campaign the year before. Pearson (Lord Cowdray) was the world's foremost engineering contractor, builder of modern port facilities in Veracruz and the railway in Tehuantepec, and since 1906 a major figure in Mexico's burgeoning oil industry.[45] Rabasa made it clear that the principal focus of his book was to be the recent history of Mexico; "the balance sheet of 1876–1910, which is in large part the balance sheet on Porfirio Díaz himself." He cited his *La Constitución y la dictadura,* which he claimed served as a better defense of Díaz than "all the books dedicated to exalting him."[46] Rabasa also emphasized that his book would not be directed against the revolution and that reference to it would be precise, brief, and clear. The book, he wrote Limantour, would be intended for readers in the United States, Latin America, and Europe, and it must above all be "high-minded and honorable, the only way to produce respect and gain adherents." But, he added, he could not "sign it now"; to do so would lead to loss of his property and "aggravate the wrath of the others against all of us." He planned to recruit his friend from Chicago to translate the book into English, who, he assured Limantour, was a good writer and well educated "for this country." Clearly, the work was designed to rehabilitate the reputation of Mexico abroad, as Rabasa put it, "in order that it is not put in the category of Haiti and Nicaragua."[47]

Rabasa expressed concern about the effect the subsidy might have on the book, but he insisted that "the book must be free of all moral concern that could inhibit the author"; the funds must clearly be put to the defense of national honor. "Thus I will have all moral freedom and total responsibility without which an honorable book is impossible." Limantour responded positively to Rabasa's full explanation of the project: "Your program for the book is accepted"; he should work with "no more restrictions than your conscience dictates." His only recommendation was to complete the work as soon as possible, since it could have an effect on national politics, despite Rabasa's intention to avoid much direct commentary on events after 1911. Rabasa solicited materials from Limantour, particularly those related to finance and economic development; but Limantour was unable to send very much, since he had little with him in Paris, and since he was spending most of his time in 1916 in Biarritz. He recommended that Rabasa consult the *Memorias de hacienda,* especially "the famous one" by Matías Romero of 1870, and to look for materials "in the Hispano-American library that Huntington founded in New York."[48]

Rabasa could report on 25 October that not only was he pleased "that you fully approve my program," but also that he was busy gathering materials. He agreed with Limantour that his book could not help but have some influence on Mexican politics, but that "it must not appear dedicated to a political campaign" or be seen as a book combating the Revolution. He reiterated that the work would be dedicated to "the defense of the nation [and] the punishment of its tyrants." These two objectives are inseparable, "but the effect of the attack will be greater if it is incidental to the major objective." He could also report that he had received notice from Herbert Carr, Lord Cowdray's agent in New York, that $2,500 was awaiting him at Lazard Freres. At the end of November he announced that he had completed the first part, ending in 1876. The second part would treat the regime of Porfirio Díaz, the third the Revolution, and the fourth "the so-called problems" and "the lies that have dishonored Mexico."[49] In March 1917 Rabasa wrote that he was moving slowly, in part because of a treatment for his eyes that forced him to be bed-ridden for two weeks. He had wanted to send Limantour some early chapters, but hesitated for fear they might get lost. By July he announced that the work was completed and that he regretted not being able to go over it with his friend. Rabasa was proud that he had been able to maintain serenity, for "only the serene work gains certainty . . . and only the book that convinces survives." He added that many people think I have no passions, but "only I know the work and the sacrifice it costs me to repress them so they don't harm my basic intention."[50]

The actual publication of the volume suffered much delay. The original plan, as noted above, was to publish it in three languages, Lord Cowdray paying for the translations. However, by September 1917 problems set in. Limantour wrote from Biarritz that it was difficult to communicate with the backers because of continued delay in the mail, sometimes by a month and a half. More significant, however, was their growing opinion that it would be more prudent to delay the anonymous publication, lest the author be identified, resulting in retaliation by the Carranza government. As Limantour put it, "it would not be possible to prevent our persecutors from finding out who are the true author and his sympathizers." Rabasa, who was always cautious, agreed with the advice, in part because the decision was not really his to make. He responded to Limantour that people would certainly guess the identity of the author, by the fact that it was written in New York, and by the style of this work compared to others by him. "It would be a matter of simply putting two and two together." However, if the book was to be published in translation, Rabasa suggested that the name attached to it be that of his American friend in Chicago.[51]

In any case, Rabasa was anxious to publish the work in Spanish, even if the translations were delayed. The translation project continued to languish, probably because by November 1917 Limantour had received "El Archivo de la reacción" (see below and Chapter 4) and was obsessed with its revelations. His obsession inevitably drew in Rabasa, who tried to reassure and calm his companion. Finally, on 9 March 1918 and definitively a year later, Emilo Rabasa decided to go ahead with the publication of *La Evolución histórica de México* in Spanish, eliminating chapters he had included on the Revolution and expanding the rest, including a final defense of the Díaz regime and with special emphasis on Limantour's role in finance. Thus revised, Rabasa said he could publish the book under his own name. Limantour agreed with and applauded his decision.[52] On 11 July 1919 Rabasa repeated once again his desire to maintain serenity, to avoid combat, and to adhere to his principal purpose: "to defend the old regime [which is] the best defense of the nation." The book was finally published by Bouret in Mexico City and Paris the next year, but the French translation not until 1924.[53] The English translation never appeared. However, the long and frustrating process toward publication and the constant struggle against his eye disease apparently did not immobilize Rabasa; as we will see in Chapter 7, he completed and published in 1919 yet another work, the juridical masterpiece *El Juicio constitucional*.

The exchange between Emilio Rabasa and José Yves Limantour provides an accurate picture of the book's content and interpretation. Rabasa wrote in the preface that the book's purpose was "to combat ignorance abroad about his country, to substitute truth for vulgar prejudices . . . that are given substance by the disorders of the country." He maintained his customary serenity, as he said he would, and in defending the Porfirian regime and its accomplishments, he did examine critically Don Porfirio's increasing exercise of personal government and his disinclination to relinquish power. In fact, Rabasa's treatment of the economic and financial administration of the country under the leadership of Limantour is far more positive than his treatment of politics under Díaz. Also, as stated to Limantour, he omitted substantive discussion of the Revolution, ending his history with the departure of Díaz. He insisted that the Revolution could not be justified by an accusation against what preceded it, but rather must be explained by the forces that produced it. "To condemn the period of General Díaz," he asserted, "is to take from the Mexican nation all means of vindication and even its right to life."[54] The final section of the book, which we will examine in the next chapter, was devoted to "the national problems" or as he put it, "the so-called problems." In this important section, Rabasa clearly showed himself to be at odds with the social agenda of the Revolution. It is also true, as he predicted, that the measured and nonpolemical tone of the book added to its credibility and durability. However, the lack of an English edition meant that Rabasa obviously failed to combat prejudice toward Mexico in the United States, his incentive for undertaking the work in the first place.

Since Rabasa's objective was "the defense of the nation," his history essentially began at Independence. Like Simon Bolívar, he emphasized that the Latin American nations emerged, unlike the United States, without experience in self-government, "not even a [local] despotism to which they were subjected." No people have been "superior to their history," he maintained; miracles are never factors in the evolution of peoples. Moreover, Mexico's inability to overcome its history cannot be attributed to "ethnic inferiority or moral perversity."[55] In his view there had been only had two stages, the stage of formation and the stage of growth, or as he entitled the first two sections of his book, "the violent transformations" and "peaceful evolution." Like Justo Sierra, Rabasa viewed the pre-Reforma era as anarchical, from seeds sown during the decade-long struggle for independence. As in his *La Constitución y la dictadura*, the climax of this first stage was the Reforma, which he applauded, and the Constitution of 1857, which he assailed. The liberal revolution "forged a nationality," ultimately propagating liberal ideas among the lower classes, which represented "a profound transformation in the spirit of the people."[56]

Rabasa's critique of the Constitution of 1857 followed the familiar lines of *La Constitución y la dictadura*, but included a nuance not present in 1912. As in the earlier volume, universal suffrage was Rabasa's particular target. No country, he argued, not even England, France, or the United States, went as far as did Mexico, thrusting universal suffrage on an unprepared, mostly ignorant populace. Universal suffrage produced anarchy and dictatorship, and it necessarily led to fraudulent elections, which even the institution of the direct (as opposed to indirect) vote in 1912 could not correct. In a given district, he said, there were often more "wise dogs" than "citizens aware of their rights." Rabasa asserted further that the "lower classes," which had shed blood to uphold the nation, would not have demanded the vote.[57] Again, as in 1912, he attributed universal suffrage to the "populist spirit" or jacobinism that guided the constituyentes of 1856. However, he was now less hostile to theory than he was earlier. Among Latin peoples addicted to "the ideal," theories translated into programs have had "much more value than is scornfully attributed to them." They have been, he asserted, "the soul of the most profound transformations and the most intense struggles." Yet Rabasa admitted that unfortunately the Jacobin spirit that established universal suffrage became entrenched with the triumph of the Reforma and the restoration of the Republic in 1867. The result was that presidents Benito Juárez and Sebastián Lerdo de Tejada were unable to modify the Constitution to stabilize the government and thus avoid the revolts by Porfirio Díaz, unsuccessful in 1872 and successful in 1876.[58]

The heart of Rabasa's *Evolución histórica* was of course the portrayal of the regime of Porfirio Díaz, its rise, its accomplishments and problems, and its collapse. As he had told Limantour, the defense of the nation in the face of foreign ignorance and denigration would necessarily be tied to an assessment of the Díaz regime. Porfirio Díaz, he wrote, came to power as a soldier and a revolutionary and thus could only conceive of a government founded on authority. He was able to exert this authority in his first term from 1876 to 1880, despite the political insecurity of the new government; "the President's inspired tendency toward order and progress" soon revealed "a new spirit in the country's government."[59] Following the interregnum under Manuel González, whom Rabasa criticized as an administrator but praised for freely relinquishing

power in 1884, Díaz instituted "personal government," which characterized his regime till 1911. This government was a de facto dictatorship,
but always "careful to respect constitutional *forms.*" As a dictatorship,
it was basically benign, maintained Rabasa, and to put Porfirio Díaz in
the same category as tyrants like Dr. Francia of Paraguay, Juan Manuel
Rosas of Argentina, or Guzmán Blanco of Venezuela "is not only unjust
but also stupid."[60]

Mexico's international reputation during the era of Porfirio Díaz was
built on political stability, but even more on the nation's economic development and financial management. Thus Rabasa sought details (with
limited success) from Limantour in these areas before beginning to write
and emphasized them in his account. The rapid expansion of railroads,
telegraph lines, postal service, banking institutions, foreign investment,
trade, and particularly finance appeared prominently in his characterization of the regime. Rabasa highlighted the work of the three major
ministers, Matías Romero ("an enemy of theories"), Manuel Dublán,
and especially Limantour himself. An indication of the importance he
gave to finance appears in his classic portrait of "a minister of finance,"
inserted in his discussion of Romero, but probably referring more to
Limantour: "No one is less likely to be popular than a minister of finance . . . Since finance is money, everyone thinks he could give it, and
no one believes that he doesn't take it for himself. A severe and resigned
or haughty patriotism is the minister's indispensable quality"[61] Rabasa's
focus was on the work of Limantour, as he told his friend it would be.
He depicted the economic crisis that brought Limantour to office in 1893
and his major work of reconstructing the nation's finances. Despite criticism, Limantour immediately instituted a program of austerity "with
an effectiveness never before seen and he gave to the organization . . .
of finance, order, method, and morality." His multiple efforts brought
praise from foreigners for the first time, and "the [Mexican] traveler felt
pride in his nationality."[62] Rabasa's admiration for Limantour's financial administration was undoubtedly based on his own experience as
governor of Chiapas, in which he attempted to apply the principles of
scientific politics.

It is significant that Rabasa introduced in his chapter "the organization of finance" a discussion of the National Liberal Union Convention
of 1892 and Justo Sierra's famous manifesto, which called for the reelection of Díaz and spelled out the agenda of the Científicos. The manifesto, as Rabasa pointed out, included a series of administrative and
fiscal reforms (soon to be carried out by the new Secretario de Hacienda
and principal Científico, Jose Y. Limantour), and plans for economic
development. But the manifesto also called for the irremovability of

judges and a provision for a vice-president. This manifesto of course led to the great debate of 1893 over the constitutional amendment to make judges permanent, the debate in which, said Rabasa, "the reformers were called *científicos*," and their adversaries "*jacobinos*." The reformers called them jacobins because they invoked "absolute theoretical principles" that supported autocracy "in the name of pure liberties."[63] Rabasa argued that although the manifesto and the reform agenda were directed to the nation, they were really meant for Díaz himself. The political agenda of the Científicos was always toward the limitation of absolute power, that is, the "personal government" of Porfirio Díaz. Their objective, continued Rabasa, was to transform the country from a dictatorship into an oligarchy, "with the democratic tendency of oligarchies that are not founded on castes."[64] Here Rabasa was taking up again the final argument of *La Constitución y la dictadura*: the era of dictatorship is over; the constitutional stage must follow.

Rabasa's models were the three South American governments (presumably Argentina, Chile, and Uruguay), which he said had now achieved constitutional regimes, and would evolve slowly "through the broadening of the governing classes, toward a regime every day more popular and secure."[65] Unfortunately, continued Rabasa, the president paid little attention to the political agenda of the Científicos, forcing the Senate not to act on the constitutional reform. His focus instead was on "material transformation of the country." Rabasa's assessment of the regime was clearly ambivalent. He recognized not only the material gains, but also the peace and security that came from the suppression of local and regional caciques, a process Rabasa himself took part in as governor of Chiapas.[66] In this sense, Díaz was "the necessary man." Don Porfirio was able to "dominate the present, to win it over," and do it peacefully. Thus he was "a great governor," undoubtedly, as Rabasa had said before, "the greatest . . . of Latin America." And yet Díaz in the last analysis was "much more governor than statesman."[67] He had no vision of the future. This lack of vision led of course to his downfall.

Symptomatic of the president's lack of vision, according to Rabasa, was his interview with James Creelman, the American journalist, in January 1908. As noted earlier, the episode may well have triggered Rabasa's decision to undertake *La Constitución y la dictadura*, his most important work. He devoted an entire chapter of *La Evolución histórica* to the interview and its aftermath, though he had made no reference to it in the 1912 volume.[68] Uncharacteristically, Rabasa quoted at length from the document, which appeared in *El Imparcial* almost simultaneously with its publication in English. Rabasa criticized severely Don Porfirio's decision to choose the foreign rather than the national media to announce that he would not seek reelection in 1910. As Rabasa put it, "the nation had to read its own destiny in English translation."[69] The whole episode was unfortunately timed, he asserted; the president's language appeared harsh, when he meant it to sound paternal. The public was confused: did Díaz mean what he said or not? Either way it led to unfortunate results. Speculation abounded, "no longer in private conversations, but in the form of publicity and popular propaganda." Since, according to Rabasa, it came to be generally assumed that Díaz would be reelected, attention focused on the need for a free election for the vice-presidency; and parties formed around Bernardo Reyes, Governor of Nuevo León, and the Científicos, who were thought to support the current Vice-President Ramón Corral. When Díaz opted for Corral, open opposition emerged against "imposition." Amid this political turmoil, there arose the conviction, which Rabasa apparently shared, that "without the Creelman interview, there wouldn't have been revolution in Mexico, a least for several years."[70]

The most significant consequence of the Creelman interview, according to Rabasa, was the appearance of *La Sucesión presidencial en 1910*, completed by Francisco I. Madero in October 1908. Rabasa judged the book to be unsophisticated and poorly written, but also revealing "courage and good faith" and generally moderate in its tone and in its proposals. He found it incongruous that this nonviolent man who lavished praise on Díaz and then incited revolution, took up arms himself, and "initiated the demoralization and spontaneous destruction of the country."[71] Madero, said Rabasa, failed to consider the impact of his book in the post-Creelman environment. He was a dreamer and lacked "foresight." Madero did not call for the removal of Díaz, but only for a vice-president to be elected popularly; however his antireelectionist party went further and nominated him for president. Madero, continued Rabasa, only envisioned a political revolution; the ideas of "ignorant socialism" and "demagogic anarchism" came later, influenced by men more intelligent than Madero, "but much less honorable." Madero's triumph was in large part due to the revolutionary press, which Rabasa (citing Gustave Le Bon) identified as "the vehicle of contagion in a widespread multitude."[72] Such a revolutionary struggle soon becomes unequal because the government has to be moderate in the means it employs, while "the revolutionary can do what best suits him." Rabasa concluded that the regime of Don Porfirio ultimately collapsed from immobility. Díaz had lost the support of public opinion, that is, of "the aware classes." Public opinion did not support Madero, "but neither did it come to the defense of the government." What ultimately saved the Revolution for Madero was the existence of strong government over thirty-five years.

He was able to take control of it through the cabinet put in place by the interim President Francisco León de La Barra.[73] Here ended Rabasa's narrative, just where he had told Limantour it would end.

Rabasa concluded *Evolución histórica* with a summary of the principal themes of his work and then ended on a rather surprising note.[74] The themes are familiar. The nation at independence lacked experience in self-government, which led to conflict between two tendencies, the "progressive" which invoked liberty, nourished by the theories of Rousseau and Montesquieu, and the "conservative," which sought order through the restoration of the colonial regime. There was in reality no nation until the Reforma, when the progressive tendency triumphed. The post-independence period, said Rabasa, may seem "jumbled and confusing" (especially to foreigners), but actually the movement of the era "in its main outline has a defined direction that obeys the laws of development . . . which can be seen in all peoples."[75] To demonstrate his point Rabasa turned to the recent history of France, which followed a turbulent course from 1789 to 1875 not unlike that of Mexico, even though France had had the advantage of a national government for centuries and an educated populace. Rabasa repeated once again his indictment of universal suffrage adopted in 1857, to which he attributed the sole cause of the subsequent revolutions. Mexico, he added, like all peoples, is "under the influence of natural sociological laws," such that there can be no successful revolts against legitimate elections.[76] Rabasa then returned to "the assessment" of Porfirio Díaz, emphasizing the thirty years of peace and international admiration he bought to the country. But he also emphasized the failure of Díaz to establish institutions, principally strong political parties, "because the transition from a dictatorial to an elective regime depends on the development of parties." Dictatorship can only be replaced by elections, and without them dictatorship will prevail. Finally, Rabasa repeated his contention that the Revolution could not be justified by condemning the regime that preceded it; to do that would be to "deprive the Mexican nation of its means of vindication" and "provide arms to the ignorant or to those who condemn it in bad faith."[77]

Rabasa ended his book unexpectedly with a defense of Latin America against "foreign opinion," particularly in the United States. He dismissed the characterization by Gustave Le Bon that the republics of the south have always lived in perpetual anarchy, and that all twenty-two republics are in the torrid zone and thus inhospitable to the white race; Le Bon is a charlatan, he said.[78] Moreover, by idealizing the United States, Le Bon is merely encouraging its imperialistic tendencies. Turning to the United States itself, Rabasa maintained that "there is general ignorance" about all that is beyond its borders, especially about Latin America.

Rabasa went further and posited a fundamental cultural divergence between "the two races" of the Americas, the utilitarian drive for wealth
as the end in life for the one and the idealism, sense of art, and ties of
family for the other. The dichotomy that Rabasa depicted is reminiscent
of that in José E. Rodó's *Ariel* (1900). Latin America, asserted Rabasa,
must preserve not only its political autonomy, "but also the autonomy of
its civilization and its customs . . . as an integral part of its intimate personality."[79] He obviously sensed the renewed threat of North American
intervention, which he had experienced at close hand in 1914; and although he lived six years in New York and had great admiration for the
United States, particularly its legal tradition, on a deeper level he had
little taste for North American culture. We will see further evidence of
this ambivalence in the final chapters.

We have noted that in the midst of completing *La Evolución histórica*
and trying to arrange for its publication and translation there appeared
in September and October 1917 "El Archivo de la reacción," which obsessed Limantour and which drew him and Rabasa into an extensive
and frank correspondence. The exchange of letters lasted until mid 1919
and revealed not only personal characteristics of the two friends, but
also their private reflections on the critical years prior to the Revolution
of 1910–11. In addition, the publication of the "Archivo" led Limantour
to begin what became his *Apuntes sobre mi vida pública,* a work on
which Emilio Rabasa had considerable influence. However, the reflections actually began a month earlier when Rabasa coincidentally received the news that a second edition of *La Constitución y la dictadura*
was to appear in Spain, with a preface by Rodolfo Reyes.[80]

That news prompted Rabasa's "private thought (*intimidad*)," as noted
in Chapter 3, which dealt first with the circumstances of the original
composition of his masterwork. Rabasa then went on to explain to
Limantour that he had spoken with Porfirio Díaz after completing the
first third of the book in 1909, warning the president that he would not
like its argument, namely that the Díaz dictatorship emanated from the
Constitution of 1857 and that it was essential to amend the document
"to bring about a stable government." In the face of "a certain anxiety"
on the part of the president, continued Rabasa, "I told him in these
very words that my book would in fact be a justification of his regime.
Long after 'those who publish pure praise have been forgotten . . . mine
will be in the library of everyone' who has an interest in his country.
My prediction has been realized," he added proudly to Limantour; and,
concluded Rabasa, "I am very happy to contribute to [Díaz's] vindication with 'a book that is written without fear, without vulgarity, and
with serenity.'" Limantour responded that he could well understand the

President's concern, since Díaz believed that changing the Constitution would expose him to the charge that "he had pocketed it." Limantour said he had had many conversations with Díaz about needed changes, on suffrage, on the composition of the legislature, on the judiciary, and on the press, but that the president had refused to adapt laws to the peculiarities of the people he governed. Instead, "he preferred to let [the people] be occupied with liberty and democracy as playthings," while he proceeded as he wished in a patriarchal and altruistic way. That is why, concluded Limantour, "I want *La Constitución y la dictadura* to have the widest possible circulation."[81]

In his reply of 6 December, Rabasa was of course pleased, but also greatly surprised by Limantour's revelation, since he always thought that his friend supported the president's policies without question, giving in to either silence or conformity. By this time, however, Limantour had received copies of the "Archivo de la reacción," and the two correspondents launched into a more detailed discussion of Díaz, his characteristics, and his policies, especially during the years 1906 to 1911. However, prior to their exchange on matters of substance, Rabasa had to calm Limantour, whom he knew would react strongly to the charges in the "Archivo." Receiving the newspapers before Limantour did, he twice forewarned his friend that though the pirated letters were disagreeable to all concerned, Limantour should not respond publicly. "Neither the letters nor the commentaries really attack you," wrote Rabasa, except for one insignificant article by a "Brígido Caro" in Nemesio García Naranjo's *Revista mexicana*. Rabasa knew well Limantour's obsession with his reputation and his need to defend himself.[82] Limantour finally received the newspapers in question and said he was "deeply upset and disappointed." He claimed not to be sensitive to mere criticism or dissent, but that he could not help being resentful since the letters showed "such indignation and egotism, and were so unjustified in regards to me."[83]

As noted in Chapter 3, Miguel S. Macedo and Rosendo Pineda essentially blamed Limantour privately of treason, bringing about the fall of the Díaz regime through negotiations with senior members of the Madero family in March and April of 1911, when the president was turning more political authority over to him. Pineda had even remarked sarcastically to Pablo Macedo that the "Lord" [Limantour] wonders why the revolutionaries won't leave him in peace: "Well, he's right, since he prepared the banquet and served it to them, but such is the ingratitude of people."[84] On reading the charges of his erstwhile friends and colleagues, Limantour protested that Miguel and Rosendo were quite aware of everything he was doing during the two tragic months of April and May 1911. They both even worked with me, he added, on the final documents prior to Diaz's resignation. Limantour said he didn't have the heart to respond to the charges (a sentiment that would soon change), and he agreed with Rabasa (perhaps reluctantly) that the letters were exaggerations expressed privately in the passion of the moment. Responding to Rabasa that he hoped his own letter would not get into the wrong hands, the ever-cautious Rabasa came forth with another significant "private thought": namely that letters Limantour wrote to him would not suffer the fate of those written to Pablo Macedo, because he routinely destroyed all letters received from friends and family.[85] (Fortunately for this biographer, Limantour not only kept everything that came in but also copies of what went out.) Rabasa was also pleased that Limantour was showing good judgment in his reaction to the "Archivo." These had been difficult times, he added, in which we were all prone to "letting off steam," blaming even our friends. Such reproaches are not even "venial sins" and should be ignored. The problem, added Rabasa, is the publicity they received (always a central concern for him).

Throughout the lengthy correspondence, Limantour constantly expressed gratitude to Rabasa for his wisdom and his candor, including mild criticisms of his friend's actions during the decade preceding 1911. It is clear that Limantour welcomed the opportunity to unburden himself to a discrete friend in whom he had complete confidence. He was surprised, he said, that Rabasa thought of him as passive in his relations with "our great Caudillo." I did try to keep quiet in all that pertained to politics, until "the ill-fated day" in 1911 when I felt it my duty, at the President's insistence, to share the responsibilities of government. Thus "began," he added, "the worst tribulations of my public life." Limantour claimed repugnance for all that smelled of politics and insisted he never interfered in other departments except on issues bearing on finance. He admitted that he should have left the government many years earlier, especially when serious differences with Porfirio Diaz arose, but that when he returned from Europe in March 1911 it was too late. Tell me frankly your opinion of what I have said, he urged Rabasa. I need clarity now more than ever; the revelations of *El Universal* "awakened me from a nightmare after a long and peaceful but deceptive sleep."[86]

Rabasa did not disappoint his correspondent. Taking him at his word, Rabasa announced that the "opinion" he had "of your place and your conduct would be more 'instructive' than his 'reflections.'" Before expressing his opinions, however, Rabasa had to explain to Limantour why he didn't learn from Rosendo Pineda and Miguel Macedo, both longtime friends, about Limantour's relations with "the Chief." Although Rosendo had been his friend "since infancy," said Rabasa, the friendship ultimately cooled because of Pineda's excessive engagement in poli-

tics. "I hated . . . active politics which I got into only when pushed," he
said. "Although Pineda and I had adjacent offices for three years, we
often didn't see each other for six months at a time." As for Macedo,
Rabasa said they did develop an ever-closer relationship beginning in
1902. But, he added rhetorically, who isn't aware of "Miguel's habitual
tendency to withdraw into his shell (*el sistemático enconchamiento de
Miguel*)?" Macedo would never speak of anything not pertaining to
himself unless authorized to do so. The "instructive" part of Rabasa's
long letter dealt with three main topics: Limantour's aspirations or lack
of them; his decision to remain in the government; and the more general
problem experienced by men in high office, namely their isolation from
public opinion.[87]

Rabasa wrote frankly that he never thought Limantour had the aspirations attributed to him by perhaps impatient friends. He was content to dominate in the world of finance. However, in his financial role
Rabasa regarded him as somewhat aggressive; "you oppressed a bit the
other departments." Then, as if to soften his criticism, Rabasa referred
again to his classic positive description of the minister of finance in *La
Evolución histórica*: "No one is less likely to be popular than a minister
of finance" (see above, p. 94) Rabasa went on to add that Limantour's
aggressiveness probably led Díaz to distrust him politically, and that
Limantour was reluctant to express opinions lest the president think
he had ambitions. My only real reproach, continued Rabasa (echoing
Limantour's own admission), is that you and Vice-President Corral did
not resign sooner. Perhaps it was because you feared the government
"would pass to hands of bitter enemies" (i.e., to Bernardo Reyes and
Teodoro Dehesa). From 1906 on Rabasa said he thought the nation
could be saved by such resignations, which might have convinced the
president himself to step down. But of course, added Rabasa, you could
not suggest he resign without him suspecting you of wishing to replace
him. At the same time, I knew how difficult separation from Díaz would
have been, since he was always able to hold others with his "exquisite
courtesy and the care with which he treated them as friends."[88]

Rabasa completed his frank communication to Limantour by saying
that he was not surprised that his friend was unaware of the grave situation of the country, since those in high office seldom get candid opinions
or bad news. He noted this, he added, even in "my little government."
Disinterested friends are afraid of being impertinent, and others only try
to say what they think you want to hear; everyday rumors and gossip
never reach the highest level. Thus a mixture of malaise and respect for
the old leader existed for years, said Rabasa: " 'They all loved him . . . and
wished that he would die,' was a sentiment confirmed for me a thousand

times." In concluding, Rabasa asserted that his long letter simply provided material "for you to judge public opinion" from one who could see
and hear it at various social levels.

Limantour's rebuttal was mild indeed. He accepted most of what
Rabasa had said, thanking him profusely for his frankness. "Your letter," he wrote, "has been an indescribable benefit for me." Although
Díaz had the tendency "to distrust all humanity," continued Limantour,
"I never thought he mistrusted me as much as he did others," such as
Pineda, the two Macedos, and Casasús. Limantour reiterated his general reticence on matters outside finance, except in urgent cases when he
claimed he did speak out openly and directly. As for Rabasa's reproach
that he should have resigned earlier, he wondered if the criticism was
appropriate, considering "that peculiar turf of Mexico in which the political bulls fight." Given the immense prestige of the president and the
danger of handing the country over to Reyes and Dehesa, could Corral
and I have resigned, he asked, without throwing the country into chaos?
I have to be persuaded that Díaz would have also resigned, as you suggest. Limantour ended his rebuttal by asking if Rabasa would read the
first part of some "Apuntes," a copy of which he was enclosing. He said
he had written them the previous December as a defense against the attacks published in *El Universal.* So we see that it took Limantour only
a month to reverse his original impulse to remain silent; however, he
clearly intended to be guided by Rabasa's advice and criticism before
publishing anything.[89]

The correspondence lapsed during the last half of 1918, but resumed
again fuller than ever the following year.[90] Limantour's "Apuntes" and
the events to which they referred was the main topic of discussion, but
for Rabasa, as we will see in more detail later, a crescendo of activities
and personal concerns intervened. He was arranging for publication of
not only *La Evolución histórica,* but also his major juridical study, *El
Juicio constitucional.* Two of his daughters were married in New York in
the spring of 1919; his son, Emilio, Jr., received an architectural degree;
and his long-planned trip to Paris finally became a reality late in the
year. Despite these preoccupations, Rabasa found time to devote himself
to a thorough reading and full commentary on the draft of Limantour's
"Apuntes," responding with his usual incisive criticism and strong personal advice. His basic message to Limantour was to stick to the facts regarding his actions before 1911, avoiding any attempt to respond directly
to the charges made by his erstwhile friends in the "famous 'Archivo.'"
Otherwise, argued Rabasa, your directed (and polemical) response would
justify the publication—which, he claimed (from information he had
heard from Mexico), had not been well received. "How Palavincini would

thank you for reviving the issue with the prestige of your name and in the form of a controversy with your friends!" If you want to respond to individuals, do so privately, avoiding polemics.[91]

Rabasa later elaborated on his advice, telling Limantour that he should only use the pirated letters as a guide for his rendition of facts. What were the accusations against you "that float as questions in public opinion?" he asked rhetorically. They are essentially: that with your arrival in New York and later in Monterrey (in March 1911), you arranged with Ernesto Madero (uncle of Francisco) to "give over the regime (*entregar la situación*)"; that you engineered the resignation of the cabinet and its replacement by one of "automatons" in order to remove obstacles to your plan; that you then pressured Porfirio Díaz to resign and to make the weak Francisco León de la Barra Foreign Minister (and successor to the presidency). Thus, on leaving the country, you would remain on good terms with "the new men" in order to secure your person and your property. In a word, concluded Rabasa, you were accused of "the premeditated betrayal of your friends, General Díaz, and the nation itself." In the face of this accusation, I have insisted "for some time that you need to explain yourself before the nation." Your "Apuntes" can and should do this. Rabasa made it clear that he very much liked the facts presented in the draft.[92]

But Rabasa's critique and freely given advice did not stop here. He even corrected verb tenses, saying that the grammatical errors were understandable since Limantour had been speaking French for eight years. More importantly, he reiterated his opinion that intimate views expressed between Miguel and Pablo Macedo should not be taken seriously; outbursts between brothers are often exaggerated and soon forgotten. Though I was close to Miguel, added Rabasa, he was always discrete and logical, never speaking to me the way he wrote to Pablo. Moreover, his allusions to you that I heard were always "those appropriate about a good friend." Rabasa also reacted against Limantour's intention to circulate the unpublished "Apuntes" to a few selected friends, saying that circulation would be tantamount to publication, without its advantages. In short, he advised his friend: write the "Apuntes" now, but don't publish them immediately; wait for the appropriate moment. Limantour took this advice to heart and accepted Rabasa's criticisms without demur. He also delayed responding to Rabasa's letter of 15 May because of his "ailments," his distress over his wife's periodic illnesses, "and because of my growing intellectual weariness"; at age 64 he said he felt a perhaps incurable physiological decline. Rabasa was quick to send back an encouraging reply: your manuscript and your letters show none of what you complain of; they are always acute and lively. "My dear friend," he concluded, "the sure way to become old is to believe you are are old; this is your true or imagined illness." A week later, as if to buoy up his friend's spirits, Rabasa emphasized that he saw in the part of the "Apuntes" that had just arrived all he had hoped to see, many new details, much that confirmed his convictions, and exposition as he would conceive of it—"strong, serene, and convincing."[93]

On substantive details in the "Apuntes," much of Rabasa's commentary repeated points made in earlier letters. He said he wrote marginal comments in Limantour's text, but that in his letters he would focus on omissions. He urged Limantour to emphasize that he was in accord with the program the Científicos put forth in the National Liberal Union Convention of 1892; it serves as a precedent, he wrote, for your repeated efforts to advise the President "that he develop a broader policy pertaining to public liberties." You have "the right and even the obligation to state it." Such a declaration would point up the fact that you were acting "as an advisor, not as a personal partisan, not as part of a pressure group." In short, Limantour could in Rabasa's eyes legitimately identify himself with "the ideas of the Científicos of '92, which were noble, patriotic, and honorable." I can say all this, added Rabasa parenthetically, because I was not one of them. Rabasa went on to assert that "then and now I deem their effort of '92 to be the most upright and high-minded that has been seen in thirty years." Rabasa's statement is simply one more example of his adherence to the program of 1892–93, a key element in his concept of "democratic oligarchy." Limantour replied that he did support the program in his conversations with the president—particularly pertaining to the vice-presidency and to the irremovabilty of judges—despite the fact that because of Díaz's opposition, the program "remained blocked in the Senate."[94] Limantour's agreement on this historic issue was certainly one reason Rabasa was drawn to him.

Rabasa also repeated his opinion that public support for the regime declined after 1900, a point on which he and Limantour differed. You may disagree, he told his friend as he had earlier, "but you could not hear the talk from the street as I could." He emphasized that for years he heard the same thing from legislators, men of affairs, and students: "all spoke with acrimony, though not out loud and in public"; and the President was the focus, because he was unable to pass blame on to ministers and governors. Rabasa said he followed the revolution with growing concern, because as soon as people believed it would triumph, the defeat of the government was inevitable. By the time you returned, he told Limantour, it was difficult, if not impossible to "contain the storm." You were unable to provide Díaz the force he lacked. There was of course genuine enthusiasm for the president during the Centennial

Celebration of 1910, but as I said earlier, the people were tired of their great man. As for Madero's arrival, added Rabasa, shifting his definition of "the people," it produced no genuine enthusiasm. The *"vivas"* of the people for Madero on 24 May and the *"mueras"* for Díaz came out automatically, mostly by youths eighteen years and younger: "the people in that case were the riffraff."[95] The drafts of the "Apuntes" have not been preserved, but examination of the final published copy makes it clear that Limantour took Rabasa's advice, criticism, and substantive suggestions to heart. The book contains no mention of the "Archivo" nor reference to specific critics such as Miguel Macedo and Rosendo Pineda. It is a straightforward account from Limantour's perspective of his "public life," with emphasis on his relations with President Díaz, particularly in the final days of the regime. As such, the book is strong evidence of Rabasa's influence and his persuasive powers.

Emilio Rabasa's exile years essentially came to an end in 1919. Although he did not return to Mexico until the following year, by the end of 1919 his activities and his mindset had changed dramatically. The two books written in exile, *El Juicio constitucional* and *La Evolución histórica de México* were either published or on the way to publication. With the end of World War I and the marriage of two daughters, his long contemplated trip to Europe could become a reality. Moreover, the postwar environment and the consolidation and subsequent moderation of the revolutionary regime in Mexico engaged Rabasa in ambitious projects for economic reconstruction and development, projects that also involved José Limantour and his friend and former associate William F. Buckley. Rabasa's exile years were obviously trying ones. Although he clearly had the resources to live comfortably on the Upper West Side of New York City and to provide adequately for six children, the failure of the Niagara Falls Conference, the upheaval in Mexico, and the twists and turns of U.S. policy were a continuous source of frustration and distraction for this intellectual and politician of the old regime.

For a few years after 1914, Rabasa was drawn into exile politics and counterrevolutionary projects, but his ever-cautious attitude and his judgment reduced his involvement to a minor role. He kept in close touch with friends, family, and associates who remained in Mexico as well as with the exile community. We know this, not from his own archive (that is nonexistent), but from evidence in the papers of José Yves Limantour, with whom he carried on an extensive correspondence. In fact, it is only this correspondence that allows us more than shadowy information on Rabasa's exile years. For a man who was a compulsive writer, the correspondence with Limantour and undoubtedly with others as well kept him engaged. As he put it, "for me thinking without a pencil in my hand is half thinking." Despite his serious eye disease and the rigors of a northern climate, added to his discouragement about the direction of Mexico, Rabasa appeared not to suffer the malaise that descended on Limantour; writing was his salvation. Besides letters, Rabasa made a brief ill-fated effort to organize a press campaign to turn U.S. opinion away from Venustiano Carranza and Woodrow Wilson. It was followed by a series of articles published anonymously or under pseudonym in the exile journal *Revista mexicana*. By 1916 he had already undertaken his two major works of this period. And then with the news of a second edition of *La Constitución y la dictadura*, followed by the appearance of "El Archivo de la reacción" in late 1917, the correspondence with Limantour increased and turned retrospective, with a focus on the final years of the Díaz regime.

Rabasa's political writing of the exile period perpetuated the themes of his earlier work. In fact, his thought was relatively unaffected by the changes that were taking place in Mexico and the world. He continued to adhere to the ideas of the Científicos of 1892–93, to which he referred repeatedly in his articles in the *Revista mexicana,* in his letters to Limantour, and in *La Evolución histórica.* Guiding the agenda of 1892 was the doctrine of scientific politics—strong government, free of political contention and "anarchy," oriented empirically toward economic development, but tempered by constitutional limitations on excessive executive authority, in short, "democratic oligarchy." Rabasa's target continued to be the theoretical egalitarian democracy enshrined in the Constitution of 1857, which he like the Científicos of 1892 dubbed "jacobin." In a sense, Rabasa regarded Limantour as a statesman who had followed this program, and he urged Limantour to emphasize this connection in his political memoirs, the "Apuntes"—which he did in the final published version.[96] Rabasa greatly admired Limantour's work as minister of finance, a model of scientific politics to which he devoted special attention in his *Evolución histórica.* Rabasa's constitutionalist thought also comes forth repeatedly in his writings of the exile period. He satirized the revolutionary "Constitutionalists" in the *Revista mexicana.* Throughout his defense of the Diaz regime in the *Evolución histórica* runs a strong critique of Don Porfirio's "personal government" of the later years and the need for constitutional change, especially limited suffrage and the irremovability of judges. This theme is also prominent in the extensive correspondence between the two exiles. Drawing from the work of James Bryce, Rabasa looked to the South American republics of the Southern Cone as models of democratic oligarchy under effective constitutional regimes.

Throughout his exile in New York City Rabasa developed a love-hate relationship with the United States. His two sons received their professional education there, a fact he showed no signs of regretting. His daughter Mercedes married a U.S. citizen in New York. As we will see in *El Juicio constitucional,* he had great admiration for the North American constitutional tradition, mixed with ambivalence toward its present juridical system. Much of his view of the United States was conditioned by his antipathy toward Woodrow Wilson, "the saint of the White House," whose mentality he judged as "theological," in terms comparable to those of John Maynard Keynes.[97] This mentality guided what Rabasa regarded as his confused and confusing policy toward Mexico, especially his ultimate recognition of the government of Venustiano Carranza. Rabasa probably would have found exile in France or in Havana more congenial, like others of his circle. It appears that he chose New York for practical reasons. He ended *La Evolución histórica* with an attack on North American imperialism and culture, which could have been a page from José E. Rodó's *Ariel.* And yet, as we will see in the next chaper, he was quite willing to turn to William F. Buckley and a basically North American plan for the economic reconstruction of Mexico. The ambivalence Rabasa showed toward the United States was deeply rooted in the Mexican liberal tradition.

CHAPTER SIX

Europe and the Return to Mexico:
Economic Development and the Social
Agenda of the Revolution (1919–1930)

⌒

Emilio Rabasa finally left for what was his second trip to Europe on 18 September 1919, accompanied by his one unmarried daughter Concepción. The first voyage had been in 1906, with his eldest daughter Manuela, but no details on that venture survive. His daughters Isabel and Mercedes were married in New York in May and June 1919; they and the rest of his family returned to Mexico, probably soon after the weddings.[1] Rabasa's son Oscar had received a law degree from the University of Pennsylvania in 1917, and Emilio Jr. graduated in architecture from Columbia University in mid 1919. Anticipating the dramatic change in his household, Don Emilio wrote to Limantour in April that the large family would soon be reduced to one and a half (himself) "because the two [professional] men are no longer strictly family." "I will feel alone," he added, and "I suppose that my no. 4 [Concepción] feels it even more." He would certainly come to Paris, he said, if it would cheer up his sad daughter. Limantour was delighted by the news, sent lavish congratulations on the two weddings, and added that perhaps their mutual friends could help to animate Concepción. Her disconsolate state was compounded in August on learning from Mexico that her beloved younger sister, Ruth, had died in childbirth. Thus the year 1919 was a momentous one for the Rabasa family, as well as one of major transition in the life and career of Don Emilio himself.[2]

Even though the war was over, Rabasa worried about conditions in Europe for travel, since he hoped to take his daughter to Italy, Switzerland, and Spain, as well as to Paris. He also said the trip depended on the return of properties appropriated by the Carranza government and on the sale of some of them. He was heartened to learn in 1917 that Carranza had ordered the return of Limantour's properties; but his "poor houses" (as he described them) were not returned until February 1919. Limantour wrote that he would be happy to help Rabasa with expenses for the trip to Europe, an offer Rabasa gladly accepted, but only as a loan. He reported in July that a sale of lands was pending, including some to Americans, but that the sale would also have to cover "the expenses involved in returning them (*de desintervención*), pending taxes, etc. which are consuming all my income." Limantour said he would advance his friend 2,000 dollars and find him two rooms in a modest hotel for 100 francs, including meals. As for travel in Europe, Limantour responded that conditions for travel were hard, in part because of postwar bureaucratic obstacles. Everything is scarce, he added, but "don't think that these lands are uninhabitable."[3] Surprisingly enough, this exchange was one of the few over five years pertaining to the war and its effects (except, of course, occasional complaints about disruption of the mail). Writing from Deauville in August 1914, Limantour of course had deplored the outbreak of war, and Rabasa responded soon thereafter with concern for the well-being of his friend, on learning that the Germans were at the gates of Paris. However, he was soon relieved by the news that the enemy was pulling back on 9 September after the Battle of the Marne. In 1915 Limantour had written from Bournemouth and Derby in England, where he had traveled to seek calm for his wife who was terrified by the Zeppelins.[4] But the two friends were too absorbed with their personal concerns and with Mexico's problems to spill much ink over the European catastrophe.

The year 1919 was also significant for Emilio Rabasa because it marked the resumption of his relationship with William F. Buckley after a lapse of four years in their correspondence. Buckley apparently sought out his friend and former associate for two reasons: first to gain information from Rabasa in order to fortify his testimony in a forthcoming committee hearing before the U.S. Senate, and second to engage Rabasa's services in formulating projects for Mexican economic development proposed by the American International Corporation (AIC) of New York.[5] The reconnection with Buckley coincided with Rabasa's plans for his European trip and undoubtedly came to figure heavily in those plans, though he made no mention of Buckley or the AIC project in his letters to Limantour before arriving in Europe. Nonetheless, Rabasa's friendship with Limantour came to be a crucial element in the development schemes of the AIC, a friendship Buckley was clearly aware of. It should be added that Rabasa's engagement by the AIC probably removed any lingering concerns he might have had for financing his trip and his later return to Mexico.

Buckley had been called to testify before the Senate Foreign Relations Subcommittee, designated: "To Investigate the Matter of Outrages on Citizens of the United States in Mexico." The committee was promoted and then chaired by Republican Senator Albert B. Fall of New Mexico, probably the "most militant" antiadministration politician with significant influence on Mexican policy.[6] Fall had strong ties with U.S. businessmen operating in Mexico, including Buckley, and Buckley obviously prepared himself thoroughly for his appearance. In September 1919 he wrote Rabasa in fairly insistent tones, requesting before he left for Europe detailed information on the Niagara Falls Conference and other subjects. Could you analyze the Conference, he asked, "pointing out the inconsistencies and bad faith of the American government." Could you send a copy of your article "Unconditional Surrender" from the *Sun*. Could you hire Lic. Roberto Guzmán (Rabasa's good friend and assistant in New York) at $150 a month to gather information, including articles and clippings on Mexico.[7] The mass of newspaper clippings from 1914–15 in the Buckley collection testifies to the cooperation of Rabasa and Guzmán.

Buckley was questioned by the decidedly friendly counsel to the committee, "Judge" F. J. Kearful, a lawyer in Mexico City representing the Association of Petroleum Producers in Mexico.[8] Buckley's testimony was in large part an interpretation of recent Mexican history, with a focus on the misguided policy of the Wilson administration and the evils of the Carranza regime. Why had Wilson never consulted any of the 5 to 10,000 Americans living in Mexico? he wondered. Instead, he charged, Wilson relied on emissaries like John Lind, who had absolutely no understanding of the country. As for the *carrancistas*, they "devote a great part of their energy to resisting the Americans and robbing them of their property." Buckley condemned the concept of property "as a social function" in Article 27 of the Constitution of 1917, comparing Carranza's Mexico to Trotsky's Russia. Buckley had no faith in the possibilities of popular democracy in Mexico; countries like Mexico can only be "ruled successfully by their educated classes." He had asked Rabasa for a list of the Científicos, individuals he later identified in detail in the hearing.[9] They were the advocates of scientific politics and constitutional reform in 1892–93, the group upon which Rabasa based his concept of "democratic oligarchy." Although the interests of William F. Buckley and Emilio Rabasa were different and although Buckley's bombastic diatribe in the U.S. Senate was hardly in the style of his friend, there were definite points of similarity in their political and social ideas.

As a result of conversations between Buckley and Rabasa in August 1919, the AIC retained Rabasa to consult with Limantour in Paris and to seek his advice on the AIC's financial and development proposals. The AIC was a New York financial group closely tied to National City Bank, which was organized in 1915 to expand aggressively U.S. participation in foreign commerce and direct investment abroad, especially in "new" or underdeveloped countries. Its founders, Frank A. Vanderlip of National City Bank, chairman of the board, and Willard Straight, vice-president, saw great opportunities for U.S. leadership, replacing or cooperating with formerly dominant European Banking interests now weakened by World War I.[10] Though the proposed Mexican projects were not principal ones in the overall AIC vision, they were fueled by the prevailing expansive enthusiasm of the 1919–20 years. From late September through mid-December 1919, Rabasa remained in Europe, combining personal travel with his daughter and consultation with Limantour; he was able to get extensive advice from Limantour, which he conveyed via Buckley to T. M. Streeter of the AIC, in both letters and detailed memoranda.[11] These documents reveal Limantour's continued interest in Mexican finance and economic development and his willingness to impart his knowledge and experience to a trusted friend. They also reveal Rabasa's close familiarity with this world.

The first project proposed by the AIC involved cooperation with French financial interests to reconstitute the Banco Nacional de México (BNM), Mexico's most important bank of the Díaz era, founded in 1881. It was authorized as the bank of emission by the government until 1914, when the Carranza regime intervened and declared its currency "invalid for discharging obligations (*sin fuerza liberatoria*)." Rabasa reported that Limantour was much interested in the AIC project and had arranged meetings with three important European bankers, M. Cretenier, president of the "executive committee" of the BNM; Jacques Kulp, a member of the same committee and of the board of the Banc de Paris y des Pays Bas; and Joseph Simon, on the board of the Societé Génerale and the former manager of the BMN.

According to Limantour and Rabasa, there were two major conditions that the AIC would have to meet in order to secure European collaboration. One was the need to convince the Mexican government that a reorganized BMN could again become the official bank of emission provided for in Article 28 of the Constitution of 1917.[12] Rabasa and Limantour were optimistic on this point because of the Carranza regime's need to raise capital for a *banco único* and to have circulating money that would hold public confidence. The second condition, raised by the three French bankers, was that the firm of J. P. Morgan be invited to take part in the negotiation, a condition seconded by Edouard Noetzlin, a respected and experienced founder of the BNM. The French felt a moral obligation to Morgan, who had been involved in French finances during the war and who also had spoken vaguely with them about reorganizing the BNM. Despite these potential problems, the French bankers emphasized, according to Rabasa and Limantour, that "in general the collaboration has been accepted without restrictions and enthusiastically welcomed."[13]

The second AIC project, on which Rabasa consulted Limantour, was a contract by a Mr. F. Lavis to be proposed to the Mexican government for the construction of a railroad between Tampico and Honey, in the extreme north of the state of Puebla, presumably to be later connected to Mexico City. Limantour, who had successfully established government control of the railroads in 1908, had strong opinions on the AIC proposal, which he conveyed to Rabasa after several meetings. Limantour said that he tended to see these matters from the point of view of the government, rather than from that of the concessionaire, and he hoped that this perspective might be useful to the AIC. Though Limantour agreed that the construction of a direct line between Mexico City and Tampico was highly desirable, the more so now because of the great growth of the oil industry since 1911, he objected in general to the type of contract proposed by the AIC. Drawing on his own experience, he said that due to the uncertainty of revenue, any Mexican government would reject a contract that obligated it to make "indefinite payments." Because of this uncertainty, and because of the unpredictability of construction in difficult terrain, the government would only accept subvention by kilometer, rather than 10 percent of an indefinite cost, as proposed by the AIC. In addition, there was the problem of not transferring 51 percent of the ownership of the railroad to the government until the last bond was paid. Limantour feared this might mean deferring payments indefinitely. In short, according to Rabasa, Limantour made it clear that the project as proposed was not viable, but that if modified the general idea was excellent. It was of major importance, added Limantour, to allow the government some power of intervention, often indispensable for appearances, without being an obstacle for a secure contract.[14]

It is interesting to note that Limantour's ideas, as conveyed by Rabasa, reflected a technocratic mentality, unrelated to current politics. Limantour had no more faith in the financial practices of the Carranza regime than did Rabasa in his articles for the *Revista mexicana* or in his correspondence. Limantour said he was simply presenting the objections he would have to the project as proposed, were he still Secretario de Hacienda. Rabasa returned to New York after a stormy twelve-day journey on 18 December 1919 and reported to Limantour a meeting with Streeter to discuss the memoranda he had previously sent via Buckley.

Rabasa said he responded successfully to questions raised by Streeter, particularly about Mexican political stability. Rabasa believed the situation would be clear in six months, that is, after the election of 1920. The conversation dealt only with the bank matter, about which Streeter remained enthusiastic. Despite his private concern that he knew of no example in which "American capital has gone abroad to fund a strong credit institution," Rabasa continued to be engaged for another year.[15] Apparently the railroad project went no further. Rabasa soon turned his attention to his return to Mexico.

Apart from the primary purpose for the trip to Europe, it was a memorable experience for Don Emilio's daughter, Concepción, as related by her decades later. The trip helped, she said, to replenish their spirits somewhat *(reponerse un poco)*, following the recent death in Mexico City of her younger sister, Ruth. The travelers were welcomed by the then Mexican Consul General in Paris, Lic. José Vega Limón, who showed them around the city, as well as by Limantour, who arranged gatherings of friends at his home. Concepción took note of the unusual interest Porfirio Diaz's widow, Carmen Romero Rubio, took in the as yet unpublished "Evolución histórica de Mexico." Following the business negotiations, according to his daughter, the two left for Spain. Rabasa particularly enjoyed San Sebastián, she said. In Madrid they met by chance Rabasa's good friend Jesús Rivero Quijano, who then apparently traveled with them to Seville, Cordoba, and finally to Barcelona, which was of special interest, "because our name comes from there." They were particularly impressed with the advance of industry, a product of "the vigor of the Catalan character."[16]

Rabasa had begun to consider seriously returning as early as February 1919, when he received news from "a relative" in Mexico that not only was the government giving back his properties, but also that he could return "assured of encountering complete freedom."[17] Limantour surmised that the government was approaching Rabasa because it needed good people in order to improve the opinion of Mexico abroad. He cited the case of Alberto J. Pani, Carranza's delegate who had recently been in Paris but was snubbed, unable to see the French foreign minister. Rabasa was cautious as usual and decided to delay his return, a decision Limantour agreed with, partly because it might assure that Rabasa would come to Paris. But the repatriation of exiles was clearly in the air in early 1919; Rabasa reported that there had even been a false rumor that Limantour himself would be returning.[18] A year later, Rabasa's return to Mexico was imminent, at which point it became the subject of an exchange of letters between him and William F. Buckley from mid February and early March 1920. Buckley tried unsuccessfully to dissuade

Rabasa from returning until after the elections in July. Continuing the diatribe against Carranza he had begun in the Senate hearings, Buckley argued that if Rabasa returned before Carranza left office, it might indicate his acceptance of the regime, or it might expose him to reprisals. Buckley also predicted a "crash" and that Carranza's intention to "place [Ignacio] Bonillas in the presidential chair" would clearly alienate the United States, suggesting to Rabasa the possibility of American intervention.[19]

Rabasa responded with gratitude for Buckley's interest and also with perhaps exaggerated tact, saying that while he agreed with "99%" of what Buckley wrote, in the remaining "1%" he saw "a little very natural anti-revolutionary exaltation." For Rabasa, there was no real point in waiting; a revolt and instability were more probable after the elections than now. As for personal danger, he said that men of the former regime "are not in the second, but in the fifth rank." Although people know I am against Carranza, he continued, "they have to admit that I accept . . . the victory of the revolutionaries, as one accepts accomplished facts." Rabasa concluded his response on a personal note. Staying here, he said, is "prejudicial to my interests." He needed to return to put his affairs in order and to begin to produce, "and not be a simple consumer, because . . . in my family there are many consumers." Moreover, he could "no longer bear the life of solitude and inaction"; better to face "a little danger in Mexico." He did not expect to do any business in Mexico, but at least he could think about it on familiar ground. Rabasa even mentioned the northern climate, which "is intolerable and seems more suitable for punishment than for rational existence. I have endured it from absolute necessity."[20]

Rabasa actually arrived in Mexico sometime prior to 21 May 1920, the date of the assassination of Venustiano Carranza, and in June he could report enthusiastically to Buckley on the positive changes in the country. All of Carranza's "errors" have been reversed, including the "system of robbery" allowed by Finance Minister Luis Cabrera. He said it was difficult to believe what was now happening, "but the fact is that this government [of interim President Adolfo de la Huerta] continues to show signs of moderation and good judgment." He admitted that many problems remained, the major ones being finance and the need to reduce the army. But he noted a general climate of goodwill not seen in any government since 1911. For Rabasa, what brought about the sudden pacification was the "breadth of vision" of the victors to welcome those who appeared to be opponents, to "suspend the exile of the emigrants, and prohibit further persecution." The government is no longer despoiling the rich, he wrote; it is returning confiscated property and giving churches back to the clergy. Rabasa urged Buckley to make a trip that could be "beneficial for your business." If one has money, he added, the field for business is propitious, for I am told the government is eager to promote enterprises. Rabasa's acceptance of the new regime indicated that that he and Buckley were drifting further apart politically; nonetheless, their business and personal relations remained strong.[21]

Throughout the last half of 1920, Emilio Rabasa continued to stay in contact with Buckley over the ongoing and increasingly complicated question of Mexican finances and the reconstruction of the banking system. However, the AIC was giving way to another financial group, the International Bankers Committee (IBC), founded in 1918 to refund the Mexican debt, which had been in default since 1913. The IBC had the support of the U.S. State Department and was led by Thomas W. Lamont of J. P. Morgan and Company, regarded as the leading banker of his generation. Although the IBC included British and French members, it appears that the Europeans were increasingly willing to concede leadership on Mexican financial affairs to the Americans within the IBC.[22] Since the definitive shift in the financial balance of power did not come about until 1921, Rabasa was still engaged throughout 1920 with Buckley and the AIC in negotiations with the French bankers, initiated the year before. In July 1920 Rabasa offered to return soon to Paris (that is, before winter set in), though he first wanted to communicate with Limantour. Apparently, the Mexican government was objecting to the insistence by the Banco Nacional that its concession be officially recognized, including the right to issue currency, and that money extracted by the government from the BNM in 1915 be given back. Rabasa never did go to Paris in 1920, for Limantour's response was not encouraging; he said that the BNM held to its position on issuing currency and balked at the idea of government "control" over a banco único, as specified in Article 28 of the Constitution. Limantour also suggested that some modification of the constitutional article might be necessary to satisfy the bankers. In September, Rabasa reported to Buckley that the government (according to a notice in the press) had accepted "a project modeled on ours," but he still remained optimistic.[23]

Interestingly, Rabasa's final letter to Buckley on financial matters reported a brief conversation with President-elect Álvaro Obregón, who expressed ideas that "were not opposed to our projects." Obregón favored the idea of a single bank if it were funded to the extent of 200 million pesos. He also said he would seek to modify the Constitution, allowing for the establishment of one or more banks independent of the government. Although Rabasa regarded Obregón's proposal as unrealistic (presumably because of the amount needed to capitalize a banco único, he reported that Obregon "has shown much common sense" and that he would probably come to modify his ideas on banks. In light of this information, Rabasa concluded, "tell me your opinion regarding the pending project."[24] The documentary trail ends at this point and we are led to infer that the AIC banking project, including Rabasa and Buckley, also ended, eclipsed by the intensive negotiations between Lamont and the IBC with the Mexican government, which began with the inauguration of Álvaro Obregón on 1 December 1920. Moreover, the AIC was reducing its direct investment abroad in the face of world depression and "became simply a holding company for portfolio investments."[25]

Buckley, for his part, was now deeply involved in opposition to the Mexican government, both as head of his militant lobbying organization, the American Committee on Mexico, and as a collaborator of Senator Albert B. Fall, who was actively promoting open rebellion against the De la Huerta and Obregón regimes. There was even active talk of "intervention" by the United States, particularly with the coming of the administration of Warren G. Harding in 1921, in which Fall became secretary of the Interior. The oil interests, with which Fall was closely connected, looked to replace Obregón with someone more amenable to their interests, whereas the bankers saw the possibility of working with the Obregón regime. Ultimately, the larger oil companies, represented by the National Association for the Protection of American Rights in Mexico, split with Buckley's more militant organization, the American Association of Mexico. The National Association accepted taxation imposed on oil properties and looked to a broader solution, that is, reversal of retroactive application of Article 27 to oil properties. Buckley then joined with Fall to finance a rebellion against Obregón which would bring together Estéban Cantú, governor of Baja California, and Manuel Peláez, the Veracruz caudillo who had been a protector of American oil enterprises during the Carranza era. The rebellion ultimately failed to materialize in 1921.[26] Buckley was probably unimpressed by Rabasa's favorable opinion of Obregón; he certainly did not, like Rabasa, accept the Revolution "as an accomplished fact." Buckley was finally expelled from Mexico as a "pernicious foreigner" under Article 33 of the Constitution in November 1921.[27]

Once back in Mexico City, Don Emilio took up again his professorship at the ELD, the institution he had helped found in 1912. He also served on its Junta Directiva and was elected rector in 1925. He reopened a law office at 84 Calle de Uruguay with his long-time partner, Lic. Nicanor Gurría Urgell.[28] His legal business included, as we shall see, representation of landowners seeking amparos before the Supreme Court, one of whom was none other than William F. Buckley. As a jurist of great renown, Rabasa's speeches were welcomed at juridical conferences as were his articles and studies at the newspaper *Excelsior* and an occasional legal journal. His special concern, to be treated in detail in Chapter 7, was the permanency of judges of the Supreme Court, but his writings dealt with other subjects as well, legal, social, and even political (though clearly avoiding commentary on present regimes or personalities). Although he wrote no books in his final decade, Rabasa recaptured his voice as a notable intellectual in postrevolutionary Mexico.

The widower's household was now sharply reduced. Rabasa's youngest daughter Ruth had died in 1919; his daughter Mercedes died in 1922. His one unmarried daughter, Concepción, married the widower of Mercedes, Leland de Villafranca, two years later.[29] The other children had established separate households on their return to Mexico City. Shortly after their marriage, Leland's business took him, along with Concepción and his young son Edgardo (by Mercedes), briefly to Houston, Texas. Don Emilio stayed in close touch, and his several letters to his daughter (*"Mi querida Concha"*) revealed the special relationship they had developed since their trip to Europe in 1919. He told of his heavy schedule, the possibility that he would have to go to New York on business, and of his successful sale of property, which would allow him to purchase a house for the newly married couple. From the sale he said he could also purchase a new house for himself, within which he anticipated renting out three units. In addition, he added a note for Edgardo (*"Chatito"*), urging him not to resist learning English. Don Emilio complained of migraine headaches and of course his eyes; he said he could now hardly read, but he assured his daughter "that this does not overwhelm me or drive me to despair." I will find a way, he added, "to fend off discouragement, as I have done my entire life, thanks to God."[30]

However, a month later, referring again to his eyes, to his solitude, and his need for family, Rabasa charged his daughter with the task of finding him a wife. It will be difficult, he warned, because I am so demanding:

The bride must have the following qualifications: to be on the threshold of old age, rather homely, and not too short. She must have such an easy-going and undemanding manner that she won't bother me in the least, or interfere with my inclinations, habits, or concerns. I almost forgot one other condition: that she not have a penny to her name. Try to think of a candidate who fulfils these requirements and don't let the notion of a stepmother frighten you, since there is no stepmother who could control me (*no hay madratra* [sic] *que pueda*).[31]

Actually, it was Manuela, the eldest daughter, who ultimately found the candidate, Srta. María Luisa Massieu, a neighbor and family friend; and the marriage took place late in 1924 or early 1925. According to Andrés Serra Rojas, Rabasa, now 68, announced his decision to his children in these terms: "I'm not going to ask your permission to marry, because

Left to Right: Edgardo de Villafranca Rabasa (son of Mercedes), Emilio Rabasa, Marío de la Torre Rabasa (son of Isabel), 1923. Courtesy of RVR.

this is a matter of my own free will; I only want you to know my decision and my reasons for doing it." His daughters Isabel and Concepción were not pleased by the marriage; but his close friend Miguel S. Macedo commented with admiration and surprise simply, "Emilio went and got married on us."[32]

It is evident that Emilio Rabasa's relationship with the United States had a strong effect on his career, his personal and family life, and his intellectual orientation. We will recall that in his legal practice he was an associate of William F. Buckley as early as 1913, a business and personal relationship that flourished for a decade, despite growing political differences between the two men after 1920. His diplomatic mission in Niagara Falls was focused on the futile objective of reaching an official understanding between the two countries. Rabasa's six years of exile in New York brought him into direct contact with American life, cultural values, and individual Americans. His mysterious "friend from Chicago" might have become a collaborator in one of these major works. Rabasa's two sons received professional degrees at leading American universities, and two of his daughters married successively the same American citizen. Rabasa's juridical thought, as we will see in Chapter 7, was much influenced by his experience in the United States. In fact, it could be said that this experience strengthened his comparative approach to the law, making him almost unique among Mexican jurists. However, as much as he admired the United States, Rabasa always revealed, as we have noted, ambivalence toward its legal tradition, its culture, and its customs. This admiration and this ambivalence persisted in his occasional writings of the 1920s.

As an opponent of the Revolution and a former exile, Rabasa shunned political involvement in the 1920s, but he felt free to comment on problems that existed in the electoral system. He could do so as a constitutional expert who could also inject American experience comparatively into his arguments. In 1921 Rabasa called into question the constitutional provision that gave the Senate the power to designate a governor in "a leaderless state" by a two-thirds vote among three candidates proposed by the president of the Republic. Rabasa objected to the measure because he said a minority of the Senate could with persistence impose its will if it mustered more than a third of the votes. He pointed out that the U.S. Constitution (followed by others in the hemisphere) required a two-thirds vote in matters of great importance, but such a requirement in electoral matters was absurd.[33] Another electoral issue caught Rabasa's attention a few months before his death, namely, the intervention of the Chamber of Deputies in the event that there was no majority for either of two presidential candidates. It was a good moment, he said, to present the problem because there had just been an election, but only one candidate, Lic. Pascual Ortiz Rubio.[34] Rabasa pointed out that the U.S. Constitution provided for such a problem by giving the electoral decision over to the House of Representatives; however, he added, in Mexico the Constitution of 1857 overlooked the issue, even though the constitution makers used the U.S. Constitution as a model in many ways. Nor did the Constitution of 1917 deal with the problem. Although the electoral law of 1857 did incorporate the U.S. precept, being a mere law meant that Benito Juárez was able to change it to his advantage in 1871.[35] Rabasa's main point was that Mexico's electoral law should become constitutional. Its absence was "a dangerous omission," which could lead to contention and even rebellion.

In his final articles, published just three weeks before his death, Rabasa returned to the electoral theme, this time with a focus on the perennial problem of the vice-president in Mexico. He said that calling now for the reestablishment of the office would be hopeless, comparable to advocating in 1856 the restoration of the Senate. However, he added, we must find a better procedure for replacing a president who is unable to serve. Rabasa proceeded to review the history of the office: the contention it caused in the 1820s; its elimination in 1857 in favor of making the chief justice of the Supreme Court de facto vice-president; the additional constitutional changes following the open conflict that broke out over presidential succession in 1876; and finally the decision by Porfirio Díaz to reinstate a vice-president in 1904, namely Ramón Corral. The problem in Mexico after 1904 was that, unlike the vice-president in the United States, Corral remained as minister of the Interior and thus continued to be entangled in politics. In the United States, Rabasa argued, the vice-president merely presided over the Senate and remained basically freed of those entanglements. Since the upheaval over the succession to Díaz in 1910 was attributed to Corral (wrongly, he added), the general view arose that the vice-president was always the cause of disasters. "He enjoys the worst reputation in the country." Rabasa had no solution for the problem, but he felt obliged to call attention to it. His long experience and undoubtedly his uneasiness about conflicts that could have arisen recently over succession at the death of Álvaro Obregón led him to assert in conclusion that "the first, most important, and most urgent [necessity] is the necessity for peace."[36]

Rabasa took the opportunity to reveal his ambivalence toward American values in a short interview in 1921 by the newspaper *El Demócrata* on the subject of education.[37] Rabasa sensed that the reporter's questions suggested a critique of Mexico's present system of education, which led naturally to government employment, and that it should be more practical like that of the United States. What the reporter got was a dose of Rabasa's wit and perhaps perverse delight, reminiscent of his novels and his articles in the *Revista mexicana*. Rabasa admitted that the questions were partially true, but they contained unexamined prejudices about the two countries. "The adventurous spirit of individual independence," responded Rabasa, is not the result of the educational system, but of social milieu, family upbringing, and customs in general. An American child grows up from an early age thinking he can work "for himself and on his own behalf" by delivering newspapers or shoveling snow. In Mexico, we produce "sentimental children; the Americans make theirs producers." It is not the schools that can change our children, "but the system of upbringing in the homes"; we would have to change mothers and fathers. Do we want to do that? asked Rabasa. Do we want to renounce our way of being? His answer was clear: "I believe that the characteristic nature of the Latin spirit is not inferior or to be depreciated. It is good that there are Yankees in the world, but it is not desirable that the entire world be Yankee."

Regarding "the mania for public employment," is it really worse here than in the United States? Rabasa proceeded to relate statistics on the civil service, cases of members of Congress who besiege the president seeking jobs for their constituents, and the hordes of public employees in states and municipalities. Taken together, he said, "they could form an auxiliary army for another world war." In Mexico there is a reason people desire public employment, given the insecurity of life and poor business conditions. Moreover, he added, a good office holder is as responsible as any other worker, even a journalist. What is important is "that public employees be good ones, not that they stop being employees." In short, if we have more office holders than elsewhere, the problem cannot be corrected by education. For the disappointed reporter, Rabasa's "conservative opinion" would not be of practical benefit to Mexican youth, but "it does provide relief (*un bálsamo de resignación*) for all those who live from public employment."

Rabasa's skepticism about American values persisted throughout the 1920s, as illustrated by another of his final contributions to *Excelsior*.[38] Echoing the recent "excellent article" by the federal deputy Antonio Díaz Soto y Gama, Rabasa deplored the decline of social mores in Mexico and identified the United States as the main source of the contagion. While admiring the Puritan values of early New England, Rabasa attributed the current Prohibition laws, which had little effect on public drunkenness, to its excessive moral code. He repeated the familiar litany: lack of parental control, adolescent autonomy and license, the prevalence of divorce, the lust for wealth, and gangsterism in Chicago. He said his purpose was not "to condemn (*deturpar*) the people of the United States" but only to "reinforce Lic. Soto y Gama's demonstrations." Rabasa went on to reflect on the "relaxation of family ties" throughout Western civilization since World War I and in Mexico since the Revolution, which he said had an ill effect on customs. With peace, we could have recovered "our good sense," except for the "irresistible tendency to imitate the foreign" in social attitudes, especially those of the United States. Since the holiday season had just passed, he ended with an admittedly "puerile" example, the substitution of the Christmas tree for the "poetic and characteristic 'birth,'" and of "the foreign Santa Claus" for "the wise men"—"almost a first lesson in national treason." One can almost hear from Don Emilio the lament attributed to Porfirio Díaz: "So far from God and so close to the United States."

Emilio Rabasa's ambivalence toward the United States also permeated the only systematic exposition of his social ideas, the final section of *La Evolución histórica de México,* entitled "the national problems." These chapters, probably written in early 1917, constituted his response to the revolutionary agenda and its famous triad—the Indian, land, and education—without reference to specific revolutionary policies. They were also a response to what he regarded as ignorance and "popular prejudices" on the part of foreigners about Mexican society, particularly in the United States. Rabasa frequently characterized these problem areas as "the so-called problems," and the chapters clearly formed part of the principal objective of *La Evolución histórica,* namely to mount a "defense of the nation," which he admitted was essentially a defense of the regime of Porfirio Díaz. We should remember that the book was originally intended as an anonymous publication in English, as well as in Spanish and French, and to that end Rabasa received a subsidy from the Weetman Pearson interests in Great Britain. Rabasa insisted, however, that the subsidy did not affect his treatment, an insistence I would argue we can accept as genuine.[39]

The Indian was the centerpiece of Emilio Rabasa's discussion of Mexico's social problems, directly in two of the four chapters, and indirectly in those on education and land. It is also clear that Rabasa's view of the "Indian problem" was derived principally from his experience in Chiapas, both as a native of the state and as governor in the 1890s. Throughout his discussion ran four principal themes: one, a sharp critique of Indian policy in the United States—particularly the reservation system—drawn from American sources; two, the argument that improvement of the indigenous population could not come directly from education, but rather from the material progress of the country as a whole; three, that association with the "superior castes" was the Indian's sure road to civilization; and four, that through this association Mexico would continue on its course as a mestizo nation. Rabasa acknowledged the exploitation of Indians under the Spanish colonial regime, by colonists, church, and state. The preconquest noble class was nonexistent by the time of independence. Moreover, a kind of segregation existed, which "kept [the Indian] apart from dealings with civilized man," at the same time that the Indian population was basically preserved, constituting by 1910 40 percent of the population, and mestizos another 30 percent.[40]

What did not happen in Mexico was the decimation of the Indian population, as in the United States. Rabasa devoted ten pages to the evils of American nineteenth-century Indian policy, citing U.S. reformist literature of the period 1880 to 1915. Drawing from *A Century of Dishonor* by Helen Hunt Jackson, plus its preface by H. B. Whipple, he noted the rapacious occupation of lands by settlers as they moved West, the removal of Indian tribes after 1830, the killing off of the buffalo (the livelihood of the plains Indians), and finally the establishment of the complex reservation system, which Indians were forced to accept as an alternative to extermination.[41] Rabasa contrasted the stability and even the growth of the Indian population in Mexico with its rapid decrease in the United States. As a jurist Rabasa focused particular attention on the misguided system of reservations in the United States, since it separated Indians from the rest of the population. They were neither foreigners, dependent on another government, he said, nor American citizens. Not being taxed, they had no sense of duty to the population as a whole, and they were under the control of the federal Bureau of Indian Affairs. Rabasa quoted generously from Lyman Abbott, a strong critic of the system. The reservations "are practically prison yards," wrote Abbott: "all the currents of civilization were excluded by federal law. The railroad, the telegraph, the newspaper, the open market, free competition, all halted at its walls . . . No courts existed in these reservations . . . Such law as existed was administered by an Indian agent, a person of ill-defined and . . . illimitable power." From Cato Sells, an Indian commissioner, Rabasa cited the high incidence of tuberculosis and trachoma on the reservations, the lack of sanitary conditions and instruction in personal hygiene. As quoted by Rabasa, Abbott concluded that "the reservation system . . . is wholly bad . . . and should be abolished."[42]

Turning to the second theme in his account, Rabasa was particularly attracted to Abbott's argument because they shared the view that the Indian "must,' as Abbott put it, "take his chance with the rest of us." Though "his rights must be protected by law . . . he must plunge into the current of modern life and learn to live by living," like the immigrants from Europe. In agreeing with Abbott, Rabasa rejected the benign view of the paternalistic reservation system portrayed by his fellow exile, Toribio Esquivel Obregón, whom he said drew his portrayal from official descriptions.[43] The U.S. system, wrote Rabasa, "is . . . neither physically possible for Mexico, nor morally acceptable for Mexicans." He was not accustomed to praise *jacobinismo,* but in the matter of the

Indians he acknowledged that extending them "civil equality" provided the foundation for their future advancement. However, he did not, as we have seen earlier, accept the establishment of universal suffrage in 1857, the product of "an impulse of jacobin generosity." Rabasa emphasized that a specific policy of civilizing the Indian, particularly through education, was misguided. The first priority should be transportation and communication, for example roads and rails, so Indians would no longer be beasts of burden; and he pointed to the work of his government in Chiapas in the 1890s. In attacking the U.S. policy of not taxing Indians, he even suggested, with some ambivalence to be sure, a modern form of per capita tax for Indians, as a way of reminding them that they were part of the nation. "We are not arguing for the head tax," he insisted, "but for the Indian."[44]

Rabasa's third closely related theme was that the advance of the indigenous population must come about naturally from broader association with the rest of society. He noted that the Indian population more than doubled between 1808 and 1910, even though not favored by specific policies. He accepted the view that accomplishment by Indians in various fields of endeavor supported "the conviction that aptitude is unrelated to caste." At the same time, specific cases of social mobility by Indians were inevitably the result of exposure to a higher social group. "In all these cases," he affirmed, "it is life among the superior castes that transforms the Indian's mentality." In the major cities such improvement had come rapidly on a larger scale, as "the Indian disappeared by crossing or by adaptation." But the general process was necessarily slow because most Indians remained in villages apart from "the civilized milieu of a city." Rabasa acknowledged that rural Indians were subject to exploitation, but with some protection by "lower authorities" and "philanthropists," the Indian could learn to defend his rights. "Only in this way can he achieve human dignity (*dignidad del hombre*)." It is significant that Rabasa ended his chapter on "the problem of the Indian" by returning to comparison with the United States. Whereas in the United States each rapid advance by the country "pushes the Indians into a new exile," we have advanced more slowly, but "Mexico has not cast off the burden in order to move speedily."[45]

The theme of Indian improvement by exposure to more "civilized" social groups reappeared in two of Emilio Rabasa's final articles, a rare additional insight into his social thought. A statement by President-elect Pascual Ortiz Rubio, which Rabasa said confirmed ideas he had expressed in 1920, prompted the articles.[46] The articles recounted four visits between 1880 and 1907 to San Bartolo Solistahuacán, a remote village that was a necessary way station between Tuxtla Gutiérrez and San

Juan Bautista, Tabasco (later Villahermosa) en route to Mexico City. On his first visit to this "village of completely uneducated Indians," the villagers housed his mule but provided him only a bare floor and a cup of coffee. Coming again in 1891 as governor-elect of Chiapas, accompanied by twenty people including his family, the party was well treated in "a secluded building (*una hermita*)," but on departing they found the village totally abandoned and its houses closed up. These experiences prompted Rabasa to establish the almost totally indigenous Department of Mexcalapa and to recommend the construction of a dwelling for travelers, attended by a salaried individual. Returning in 1894, he and his family were treated well; the Indians did not hide and even brought them goods. "This transformation," asserted Rabasa, "had been brought about by the simple presence of two civilized individuals of good character," the caretakers. On his final stop in 1907, his party was lodged in the private home of a *ladino,* who was a prosperous coffee cultivator.[47] The town's recent harvest brought 20,000 pesos at the market in Pichucalco, and the previously impoverished Indians were now earning 20 pesos per inhabitant. For Rabasa this was clearly a case of private interest producing public benefit, and he presumed that in the last twenty-three years the "civilizing invasion" had continued, with or without the Revolution.

Emilio Rabasa was always reluctant to speak of the Indian as a "problem"; one reason was that he like Justo Sierra regarded Mexico as "a mestizo nation." Introducing Mexican society to presumably foreign readers, Rabasa not only presented a benign view of colonial society, but also emphasized its basic unity, despite "two races and two civilizations." What the Colony had of unity, he added, "was later the basis of the modern nation." Beginning with the familiar origin of the mestizo in the offspring of Hernán Cortés and la Malinche, he concluded more generally that "in all countries in which there has been a superimposition of races, mixing has produced a distinctive national race." The mestizo nation did not really come into being with Mexico's independence, but only out of the "the unformed human mass" after a half century of struggle. Rabasa asserted that the shades of mixture made racial classification impossible, and that this impossibility sufficed even to produce a spirit of equality "which serves as a basis and a bond for the most numerous part of society, the mestizo population." We have noted that Rabasa saw association with more "civilized" peoples the sure road to Indian betterment, a central feature of which was "crossing (*la cruza*)." However harsh the actual treatment of the indigenous population in Chiapas or in Mexico generally, Emilio Rabasa, like most other Mexican positivists, had abandoned the early nineteenth-century Creole concept of nationality and looked to *mestizaje* (and perhaps racial whitening) as the ultimate solution to the "so-called Indian problem." Moreover, he rejected those "notable writers" [Gustave le Bon?] who concluded that the "mestizo is by blood" incapable "of self government."[48]

In treating "the problem of education," Rabasa first raised the question of statistics. He maintained that the generally cited 80 percent illiteracy rate, which placed Mexico "among the backward peoples," did not do justice to the country. He pointed out that if Indians "who were incapable of schooling," were omitted (for example those who spoke no Spanish), the illiteracy rate would be reduced to about 65 percent, or even to 50 percent if Indians were excluded altogether. How, he asked, would the inclusion of reservation Indians affect the U.S. rate or colonials the British rate? But Rabasa appeared to be hesitant to use this argument, for he quickly added that Mexico "cannot nor has it wanted to disown the primitive race, which is one of trunks forming the future national race." It was as if he did not want to support what is now referred to as "internal colonialism." Rabasa argued that public instruction had advanced greatly during the Díaz regime, but, as we have noted earlier, he also asserted that education could not be the country's first priority, as some "romantics of education" would like. Agriculture, industry, commerce, lines of communication, and highways are indispensable to promote the wealth "that pays for education itself." Thus Rabasa returned to his frequently made general point, namely, that the Indian population must be exposed to "civilization" to make its education effective. He even questioned how significant literacy itself was; Portugal and Italy had large numbers of illiterates (in the conventional sense), but even if they didn't learn arithmetic in school, they applied it in daily life. In short, in the old countries of Europe "the coefficient of national sentiment" is much higher than in Mexico.[49]

In concluding, Rabasa divided the population of Mexico into two main groups, those capable and those incapable of "popular education." Mexico's responsibility is primarily toward the first, which has essentially been taken on by the state, without support, regretfully, by the private sector. It appears, added Rabasa, "that the superior class does not recognize its strengths and has forgotten its obligations." As for the second group, Rabasa quoted an analogous statement by "the renowned" José María Luis Mora: namely that the early missionaries in their zeal tried to make the Indians Christians before making them men, and that they ended up neither one or the other. Applied in our day to public education, said Rabasa , "it is mostly useless for forming men; they must be already formed to receive it."[50]

As a descendant of landowners, a landowner himself, and as a governor who had launched a policy of division of indigenous communal property, Emilio Rabasa was hostile to the agrarian program of the Revolution and sensitive to the rhetoric that supported it. In fact, he began his discussion of "the land problem" with an attack on the charge by President Woodrow Wilson and his emissaries that unequal distribution of land had created agrarian misery. Wilson engaged in "spiritual intervention," said Rabasa, which poisoned opinion in the United States and was worse than the armed interventions of 1914 and 1916. Rabasa then summarized the general history of land tenure in Mexico, focusing on "the system of communal property that is observed in all peoples of rudimentary civilization." He said that the status of nonecclesiastical property did not really change markedly in the nineteenth century. During the Reforma, the effort to make the "communal landholder a proprietor" only had effect among Indians themselves. Rabasa's view of the law of 1863 on idle lands (*terrenos baldíos*) was benign; it only encouraged simple possession, he said. The 1883 and 1894 laws allowing companies to purchase one-third of idle land surveyed had little impact on the holdings of the poor. The companies were aware that in cases of dispute the government "was on the side of the complainants." In short, despite division of communal lands in some places, their status in general changed very little before 1910. The only problem arose when Indian beneficiaries sold off their properties quickly, not having had experience with individual holdings. Perhaps reflecting on his policies in Chiapas, Rabasa suggested that such small individualized plots should be made inalienable. The process of division, he said, "was afterwards called dispossession," and the Indians were deemed "victims" of the purchasers of these properties, the "despoilers."[51]

Communal property, "this residue from the semi-savage era," was of course Rabasa's particular target. Its continued existence, he asserted, though often advocated by the "sentimental partisans of protection, is the best possible way to keep the Indian in a vegetative state," in short, an "intolerable situation." Even the Negro in the United States, despite centuries of "spiritual slavery," is more "individual" than the Mexican Indian. Using the State of Oaxaca as an example, Rabasa described the constant contention between villages over boundaries of communal pasture and woodland and between villages and haciendas. Landowners are intimidated, the spirit of enterprise has declined, and foreign capital refuses to engage in agriculture in Oaxaca. He even labeled this contentious communal spirit a "malevolent instinct," but added that this instinct "is not the Indian's but rather the community's." Although he regarded

division of communal lands as the only answer, he warned that if government did not act cautiously, the result might be "a caste war." Repeating
the classic nineteenth-century liberal arguments against communal holdings, citing Mora and Miguel Lerdo de Tejada, Rabasa concluded that
there is no land problem in Mexico different from what exists among "all
civilized peoples; what exists is a problem of communal lands."[52]

Rabasa acknowledged that the latifundios were a problem when they
posed an obstacle to the development of small private properties, but
failing that they were not detrimental. The general prejudice, he said,
referring again to President Wilson's indictment, is that property in
Mexico remains in few hands, a greatly exaggerated charge designed to
prove that the Díaz regime "had protected an aristocratic bureaucracy
of 'hidalgos.' " Rabasa went on to point out that the large properties of
the Mexican north and the south were quite appropriate, since it was
not economical to raise cattle or extract tropical forest products on
small properties. In fact, he asserted further that the latifundista on the
frontier (like himself?) was a "*pioneer,*" the precursor "of the medium-
sized and even the small property in world history." To prove his point,
he repeated an early statement by the agrarian reformer Pastor Rouaix
of Durango, which he had mentioned in the *Revista mexicana,* on the
folly of limiting frontier properties to fifteen hectares. Rabasa's concept
of property was always governed by the principle of legality, just as had
been that of José María Luis Mora in the 1830s. To proceed illegally
against private property would be "to destroy the foundation on which
all of society rests and to falsify the essential principles of property."
Rabasa ended his discussion where it began, namely with the statement
that a land problem arose when people demanded land to cultivate and
faced great obstacles to acquiring it, conditions that were not present in
Mexico: "In Mexico the land problem does not exist."[53]

As noted above, Emilio Rabasa probably wrote his chapter on "the
national problems" in early 1917, that is, about the same time as the
proclamation of the Constitution in February 1917. In any case, he made
no reference to Article 27 of the Constitution in his discussion. However,
his correspondence with José Y. Limantour reveals that he also wrote
a legal study of the agrarian article soon after it appeared. Though I
have been unable to locate the document, we know that it was published
anonymously, translated into English by his son Oscar, and also sent
to Mexico for publication (omitting the name of the publisher). Rabasa
apparently wrote the study at the request of Herbert Carr, the agent of
Weetman Pearson (Lord Cowdray) in New York, so the firm could better understand the implications of the article for its interests. Limantour
read the work twice and congratulated Rabasa and his son on it; but

unfortunately the correspondence reveals nothing specific about its contents, except Rabasa's general statement that the Constitution entailed "the non-recognition of the most elemental rights and the legal imposition of tyranny."[54] Another clue to the contents of his phantom study comes from a brief discussion in his course at the ELD on Constitutional Law in 1928, in which he asserted that Article 27 "is not an article, it is a treatise on property; It has no legal form."[55]

Although Rabasa did not address agrarian issues publicly after his return to Mexico, he did defend landowners who were affected by the new revolutionary legislation. Of the several amparos he argued before the Supreme Court in the mid 1920s, we have records of one that was a bona fide agrarian case and another that was a significant defense of the urban property of his long-time friend and associate William F. Buckley. Rabasa, like many other lawyers, was able to resort to Article 10 of the Agrarian Decree of 6 January 1915, which allowed landowners to seek redress in the courts against administrative actions by Agrarian Commissions affecting their properties.[56] Yet, juridical confusion was rampant from 1917 until it was partly cleared up by the Agrarian Regulation of 1922, which also inadvertently provided additional openings for lawyers to defend landowners through the amparo process. Moreover, this defense effort was made before a sympathetic court, whose judges after 1923 had life tenure. In fact between 1922 and 1927, 75 percent of the agrarian cases before the Supreme Court were decided in favor of landowners. The result was a legislative reaction in 1927, followed by two constitutional reforms in 1928 and particularly in 1934. By 1934 the Supreme Court was subordinated to the Executive, and life tenure for magistrates instituted in the Constitution of 1917 was eliminated in favor of presidential appointment for a six-year term.[57] Thus two of Emilio Rabasa's major causes, the protection of individual rights through the *juicio de amparo* and the irremovability of judges—as we will see in Chapter 7— were either undermined or eliminated shortly after his death.

Emilio Rabasa's one agrarian case (of which we have records) called for an amparo in favor of the heirs of Pablo Martínez del Río, whose property in Durango of some 75,000 hectares was awarded by restitution to a supposed "community," made up, according to Rabasa, of "covetous men" (mostly peons on the hacienda) who had seized the property by force in 1911.[58] The local Agrarian Commission had initially rejected the community's claim of restitution (a rejection also approved by the governor of the state), but the National Agrarian Commission and the secretary of Agriculture reversed the decision and upheld the claim. Martínez del Río had purchased the property (Hacienda del Pasaje) in 1897, which formed part of Santa Catalina del Alamo, his larger property dating back to the sixteenth century. Martínez del Río also spent 600,000 pesos constructing a dam on Pasaje for the irrigation of land for cotton production. The dam had also been awarded to the petitioning community. Rabasa argued the case on a number of grounds: that the Agrarian Commission and the secretary of Agriculture were acting improperly as a tribunal; that there was a violation of Article 14 of the Constitution, since the titles to the property as a whole preceded the dates (1856 or 1876) set for restitution of properties; that the "community" had no titles to the property claimed and thus lacked "political status" (as defined in the 1922 Regulation); and that there was no provision in the agrarian laws for granting a dam. What kind of law orders "the granting (*dotación*) of dams to villages?" asked Rabasa. In all, he listed ten ways in which the individual rights of the heirs of Martínez del Río had been violated and ended his plea in bold general terms: "The general clamor in the country that arises from the hundreds of thousands of landed proprietors, does not demand the suppression of the agrarian laws, as bad as they are. What they [the property owners] have been demanding for a long time is that the laws be observed as they are and not at the despotic whim of the Agrarian Commissions." The Supreme Court accepted Rabasa's arguments and awarded the amparo by unanimous vote.[59]

The second important amparo case that Emilio Rabasa argued before the Supreme Court dealt with properties of his long-time friend and associate William F. Buckley. This amparo was not an agrarian issue, but rather one that involved, according to Rabasa, the illegal imposition of taxes by the State of Tamaulipas on urban properties developed by Buckley's company, the Cia. Terminal "La Isleta," in Tampico. Buckley's name did not appear in the case; his employee Cecilio Velasco (as representative) officially brought the case to the court. According to Rabasa, Buckley's company had engaged in costly works to expand the City of Tampico by raising the level of land above the Río Panuco, dividing it into lots for commercial and maritime use, and establishing infrastructure for modern utilities and services. The company and the city government of Tampico signed a contract in 1918, approved by the provisional governor, that La Isleta would be treated as a single taxable unit with taxes set at 100,000 pesos; purchasers of the individual properties would pay a proportionate amount of the whole. The company agreed to turn over the public services to the city after eight years. However, in 1921 the legislature of Tamaulipas rescinded the contract, with the approval of the new governor, and began to collect taxes on the separate units of La Isleta. When the company refused to pay, the government embargoed its funds and credits. The company appealed to the district judge, who ruled against it. The government maintained that in accordance with the last paragraph of Article 27 of the Constitution, which authorized the Executive to cancel contracts involving property made after 1876, if such contracts were against the public interest.[60]

Rabasa argued that the contracts could not be legally annulled by an ordinary legislature, only by a constitutional congress conferring such powers on the Executive. Moreover, the legislative decree was applied retroactively, thus contradicting Article 14 of the Constitution. The legislature also violated Articles 15, 17, and 22, which guaranteed protection for individuals against personal harm and illegal seizure of their property. Rabasa went to great lengths to prove his case, citing contract decisions from the U.S. Supreme Court and from French commentators on contract law.[61] Rabasa ended his brief by emphasizing the "traditional submission" of district judges to governmental authorities, whom they seldom challenged. Thus, he said, the plaintiffs place their hopes in this Supreme Court, "on whose vigor and independence they rely and place their trust." The Court voted 8 to 3 in favor of the amparo, ordering that 41,496 pesos in taxes be refunded to the company and that the embargo be lifted. Rabasa announced the result enthusiastically to Buckley in New York.[62]

Our record of William F. Buckley's relationship with Emilio Rabasa ends in 1923, at the moment when Buckley was turning his primary attention to his new Pantepec Oil Company in Venezuela, where he was welcomed by President Juan Vicente Gómez, a latter-day Porfirio Díaz. There were rumors that Buckley might return to Mexico, since President Plutarco Elías Calles was apparently more sympathetic to him than Obregón had been, but that never happened. Buckley made a personal contribution to the ELD in 1923, as well as facilitating another for 10,000 pesos in additional funds from oil companies. Rabasa was cautious about making public any involvement by Buckley, so as not "to stir up ill will or encourage false accusations," though he assured Buckley that he would do so (despite some resistance from ELD colleagues) when the time was right.[63] Prior to his expulsion from Mexico in November 1921, Buckley had planned to build an elegant mansion in Coyoacán, and Rabasa later urged him to carry through his plan to settle in Mexico.[64] Rabasa, who must have been aware of Buckley's conspiracy with Albert B. Fall to support a counterrevolution against Obregón, nevertheless did not resent this activity. He even (surprisingly) accepted without demur Buckley's inflammatory words at the border on his departure, when he told a journalist that Obregón was more of an interventionist than he was, since Obregon benefited from U.S. occupation in 1914 and 1916, whereas he, Buckley, had consistently opposed Wilson.[65] Rabasa only faulted Buckley for "imprudence" but emphasized that he never regarded him as an "interventionist," recalling their general agreement at the time of the Niagara Falls conference and later.

Rabasa and Buckley differed sharply in temperament: Buckley was rash and impetuous, opinionated in the extreme; Rabasa was cautious in the extreme, was always thoughtful, and took great care with all he wrote and did. Yet like Buckley, Rabasa was hostile to the social agenda of the Revolution and was convinced that international capitalism had a positive role to play in Mexico's reconstruction. He welcomed Buckley's financial support toward the survival of the ELD, and he went to great effort to defend Buckley's properties against "illegal" taxation. Rabasa's ambivalence toward North American culture in no way appeared to affect his close and cordial relationship with William F. Buckley, the Yankee imperialist. In short, Emilio Rabasa's continued engagement with Buckley appears to the modern observer as a major contradiction between his interests and his patriotism. Is not this relationship further evidence of the survival of Porfirian liberalism in revolutionary Mexico, a survival exemplified by Emilio Rabasa's career and ideas? Let us now turn to a closer examination of Rabasa the jurist, which not only demonstrates his eminence in the world of the law, but also the clash within his ideas of the two Western legal traditions.

The Constitution of 1917, the Supreme Court, and the Conflict of Legal Traditions (1912–1930)

At the heart of Emilio Rabasa's multifaceted career was the law, and it was upon the law that his reputation was founded and that he continues to be celebrated. His first juridical publication came in 1880, a plea (*alegato*) in a provincial amparo case that caught the attention of the great Chief Justice Ignacio Vallarta. By 1889 he was a cofounder and contributor to the *Revista de legislación y jurisprudencia* in Mexico City, a journal devoted to the new "science of law." However, it was not until 1906 that Rabasa established himself as a leading authority on constitutional law by his exacting study *El Artículo 14. Estudio constitucional*. The year 1912, with the publication of his major political-juridical treatise, *La Constitución y la dictadura* and his leading role in the establishment of the ELD, brought Emilio Rabasa to the forefront of the juridical community, in the midst of political and social upheaval. Despite his antirevolutionary stance and his exile in the United States, Rabasa was a phantom presence at the Constitutional Convention of Querétaro. He could be dismissed, even reviled, as a "reactionary," but his work could not be ignored; by 1917 he had become the master of constitutional law, and traces of his influence abound in the formation of the Magna Charta of the Mexican Revolution. In this chapter we will explore this influence, examine Rabasa's comparative and historical approach to the law—his engagement with the two Western legal traditions—and consider his juridical legacy in the immediate postrevolutionary decade.

The plan for a new Constitution, reforming that of 1857, emerged from the Constitutionalist party of First Chief Venustiano Carranza during the turbulent three-way conflict of 1914 and 1915. In September 1914, the Constitutionalists proposed as a peace measure that a convention of revolutionary governors and generals meet in a neutral city, a proposal that led to the Aguascalientes Convention, ultimately dominated by partisans of Pancho Villa and Emiliano Zapata. The Convention established a type of parliamentary government under three successive weak presidents, a rival regime, pursued by the forces of Carranza from Aguascalientes to Mexico City, Cuernavaca, and Toluca before it finally collapsed in October 1915. Carranza and his civilian followers generally favored a strong centralized government, a conviction fortified by the actions and the rhetoric of the Convention.[1] Radical orators evoked Danton, Marat, and Robespierre of the Convention government of the French Revolution, the classic forerunners of those Mexican "jacobins" who were so often targeted by Emilio Rabasa. Although proposals and publications of the Constitutionalist party did not acknowledge Rabasa (who after all was regarded by many as a "reactionary" and a "huertista"), there was a seemingly natural tendency to look to Rabasa's major critique in 1912 of the Constitution of 1857 and the parliamentary regime it produced.

One of the early expressions of Constitutionalist thinking was *Un Nuevo Congreso constituyente,* a series of articles published as a pamphlet by Félix F. Palavincini in early 1915.[2] Palavincini began by attacking the ineptitude of the Convention and its claim of sovereignty and then turned to the defects of the Constitution of 1857. We cannot create a government with mere theories, he argued; "knowledge of reality and positive conceptions are the base of all contemporary sciences." Though Palavincini claimed to be a good liberal and recognized that the Constitution had served as a triumphant banner, leading to the progressive Reforma, it is, he asserted, in many respects inapplicable. He acknowledged that a new constitution must respond to the revolutionary demands for social justice; and yet "our revolution cannot accept any fanaticism whatsoever. It is the work of a positive generation." He scarcely mentioned democracy and, like Rabasa, called for balance in the Constitution and rejected the infallibility of the popular will as expressed in a legislative assembly. Palavincini even appeared to take on Rabasa's concept of democratic oligarchy, in asserting that "all responsible citizens aspire to a more or less widespread oligarchy." He also emphasized the need for strong executive, even "dictatorial," power. His doubts in 1915 about the benefits of revolutionary upheaval were revealed in references to the social and racial determinism of Vicente Blasco Ibañez, Gustave Le Bon, and Fernando García Calderón. From the latter he quoted a paragraph on the weight of the Hispanic heritage, the futility of revolutions, and the persistence of "the soul of the race," which could only be overcome by national education and the "civilizing contact with other nations."[3] However, Palavincini ended on a more optimistic note, namely that under the firm and disinterested leadership of First Chief Venustiano Carranza, a proper Constitution could be fashioned and common ideals realized.

Assumptions that guided the Constitutionalists' thought can also be found in two proposals for reform that emerged from the circle of lawyers around Carranza. The first proposal was that of José Diego Fernández in October 1914; the second, the *Proyecto de reformas* of August 1916, was based on the Fernández proposal. The Proyecto was the product of a committee of eight, appointed by the first chief from the Secretaría de Justicia, a committee that included Fernández as first numbered member.[4]

The prologue to the Fernández proposal of 1914 emphasized that the objective of the Constitution should not be to seek "social panaceas," but rather to promote harmony between "the state of our society" and our political institutions, to pass laws that conform to our customs. This sentiment was drawn from the antijacobin tradition of historical constitutionalism, from the arguments of Justo Sierra in 1878, the Científicos in 1892–93, and from Emilio Rabasa. It underlay the several proposals that emerged from the Constitutionalist party, including the charge by Venustiano Carranza to the Constitutional Convention of 1916–17. Its most tangible implementation was in reforms that would strengthen the executive power, or as it was generally put by the reformers, to establish the proper "balance" between president and Congress, out of balance in the 1857 document. In the 1914 *ante-proyecto*, José Diego Fernández accorded the president enhanced power to declare a state of siege and in that situation to remove the protection of rights specified in articles 101 and 102 of the Constitution. He was more explicit in the Proyecto of 1916; at the first working session of the committee he called for "dictatorship, in order to strengthen the executive in agonizing situations and in those of urgent necessity." The other committee members, including Fernando Moreno and Fernando Lizardi, who were both soon to be delegates to the Constitutional Convention, agreed with the substance of the Fernández proposal, but balked at the word *dictatorship*. Having secured support for his general point, Fernández acquiesced on the term itself and admitted that there were times when "names become objects."[5]

The points made in the proposals naturally found their way into the address by the first chief to the Constituent Assembly as it began its deliberations on 1 December 1916. Moreover, as many scholars have pointed out, Carranza's directives that pertained to political organization were in the main adopted by the assembly. They were also the ones that clearly revealed the influence of Emilio Rabasa.[6] The famous radical departures in the Constitution from the proposals of Carranza,

Article 27 on property, 123 on labor, and 3 and 130 on education and the church of course bore no relation to the ideas of Rabasa. Carranza began by repeating the assessment of the Constitution of 1857 made in the earlier proposals. "Mexican nationality has been consolidated, and entered the soul of the people with the War of the Reforma"; and yet, he added, its "abstract formulas," though of speculative value, were of little "positive utility." Although the rights of man were declared to be the base of social institutions (Article 1), the Constitution "did not give to those rights the required guarantees."[7] Carranza then proceeded to outline the individual guarantees that should be strengthened. However, the focus of his charge to the delegates was upon the two powers of government, legislative and executive, presented in more detail and made more explicit than in the earlier proposals. Citing Alexis de Tocqueville, he twice evoked the ingrained tendency of Hispanic American nations to oscillate between anarchy and dictatorship, and he argued that the only way to break Tocqueville's "fatal law" was to abandon legislative supremacy, in which "the personal president would disappear, making him a decorative figure."[8] He returned repeatedly to this theme, asserting that a directly elected president could defend individual liberties, gain prestige, and thus command popular support.

There is a certain irony in the first chief's prescription for political organization in postrevolutionary Mexico. He directed his address overtly to the defects of the Constitution of 1857 and not to the political defects of the regime of Porfirio Díaz. He did not, as did Francisco I. Madero, attack the Díaz dictatorship in the name of democracy. In fact, he faulted Madero for not imposing order and thus succumbing to Tocqueville's "fatal law," that is, not finding the effective middle ground between anarchy and dictatorship. His objection to the Constitution of 1857 was the undue power given to a single-chamber legislative assembly, that is, prior to the addition of the Senate in 1874. That reform measure grew out of the Convocatoria of 1867, issued by Sebastián Lerdo de Tejada and Benito Juárez to counteract "convention" government and in effect to perpetuate the strong government imposed by Benito Juárez during the war of the 1860s. It is revealing that Carranza praised Juárez as a strong executive in the same sentence that he pointed out Madero's weakness.[9] Thus Carranza was tacitly accepting the form of governmental organization in place during the Díaz regime; he had no objection to the Senate, nor was a second chamber questioned by the constituyentes. His thesis was essentially that of Emilio Rabasa, namely that because of the inapplicability of the single-chamber legislature as an expression of the rights of man, it became necessary to create the dictatorships of

Juárez and Díaz. Thus, it is ironic that Carranza's prescription for governmental organization, implemented in the Constitution of 1917, kept continuity with the regime that the Revolution overthrew.

Although the basic pre-1910 organizational plan persisted, the first chief did call for a directly elected president, rather than the indirectly elected executive of 1857. The measure had been legalized by the legislature in 1912.[10] Carranza was in effect calling for raising direct election to constitutional status. Interestingly enough, the measure for direct election, though called for by Madero, was actually introduced, as we noted in Chapter 4, by Emilio Rabasa and Miguel Macedo as Senators in 1912. They, however, favored restricted suffrage whereas Carranza called for (rather reluctantly perhaps) universal suffrage. In short, it seems that Carranza, in advocating a strong presidency, was expressing in somewhat different terms the earlier proposals from within his own party. Although he did not mention the Sovereign Convention of Aguascalientes, his attack on parliamentarianism (or what Rabasa called *"congresismo"*) was directed more against Aguascalientes than against the Constitution of 1857, reformed in 1874 to strengthen government. It should be noted that Carranza did not reveal any sympathy for Rabasa's notion of "democratic oligarchy," as did for example Félix Palavincini. In fact, the first chief, as mentioned above, emphasized that the president should become more "personal," that is, acquiring prestige from being more popular. This leaves us with yet another irony: Venustiano Carranza was advocating the kind of "personal" power that Rabasa so clearly rejected during the final decades of the Porfirian regime. Whereas Rabasa suggested in 1912 that dictatorship had run its course and that the constitutional stage must follow, Carranza appeared to construe the presidency as another dictatorship, albeit a dictatorship with its base in popular support.[11]

Despite the evident influence of Emilio Rabasa on the sections of the Constitution pertaining to political organization, he was mentioned specifically in the Congress only during the debates over Articles 94 to 96 on the Supreme Court.[12] The first to speak was José María Truchuelo from Querétaro, who opposed in a long peroration the Constitutional Committee's recommendation that there be nine justices, elected by Congress, with terms initially of four years and life tenure for those elected after 1921. Truchuelo asserted that the proposal contradicted Montesquieu's doctrine of the separation of powers. Clearly, he added, the proposal was inspired by "the reading of a book that is reactionary on many points," *La Constitucion y la dictadura* by Emilio Rabasa, "a man who with great pleasure flew to the White House to represent the usurper Huerta." Truchuelo went on to object to all points in the committee report. For instance, he said Rabasa was totally wrong to call the judiciary a "department" rather than a "power"; moreover, the idea of irremovability "is the greatest mistake that can be imagined." Instead, he proposed that the Supreme Court should be increased in number (to 31, one from each state, territory, and the Federal District) and elected popularly within each jurisdiction. In addition, he asserted that only popular election of judges could ensure the independence of the Supreme Court and that the Court should be divided to distribute its excessive workload. Truchuelo dismissed the argument that in most other countries the legislature or the president selected judges. We mustn't distance ourselves from "true democracy," but rather "position ourselves at the forefront of innovation in legal science."[13] Rafael Martínez Escobar supported his colleague. A vote for the committee's recommendation, he asserted, is a vote for the ideas "of that representative of Victoriano Huerta." Though a man "indisputably intelligent and of the greatest learning," Rabasa's ideas could never be liberal or democratic "because he has lived only under tyranny, because he has breathed in only autocracy."[14]

The committee members and others rose to the occasion with equal vehemence, even though they could not defend Rabasa or the measure as based on Rabasa's ideas. Paulino Machorro Narvaez insisted that Emilio Rabasa had nothing to do with the committee proposal, and that he personally may have read Rabasa's work "many years ago," but did not remember it now. He accused Truchuelo of tilting windmills, of going after Rabasa "like fury," but not attacking the proposal itself.[15] Hilario Medina said he didn't know if the first chief found his inspiration in Rabasa, but he admitted that the committee merely passed on Carranza's proposal. Truchuelo warned us not to depend on one book; but, he added, "it seems that he didn't find any book in his library other than that of Don Emilio Rabasa." Of the several orators who spoke in favor of the proposal, Medina was probably the most eloquent. He emphasized that "scientific ideas . . . have no personality." Just as great histories came from the "traitors" Lorenzo de Zavala and Lucas Alamán, so the principles of "irremovability" can be attributed to Emilio Rabasa—but really "belong to other scholars of other eras long ago." Medina ended his lengthy oration by comparing the Supreme Court to the Roman Senate, which stood rock solid in the face of the barbarian invasions. "Thus I imagine our magistrates . . . through all our tribulations . . . serene and high like the flight of eagles . . . serene, unyielding, immovable."[16] He clearly won over his colleagues, because Article 94 was approved with only Truchuelo and Rafael de los Ríos opposed.[17]

We have noted that Emilio Rabasa's critique of the Constitution of 1857 was guided by the dictates of historical or traditional constitutionalism, a set of ideas infused with positivism or scientific politics, which he carried on after 1906 from his predecessors, notably Justo Sierra and his colleagues, in both *La Libertad* in 1878 and as the Científicos of 1892–93. Historical constitutionalists sought to change precepts of the 1857 document they found abstract and unrealizable in Mexico, arguing that a constitution should reflect social and historical reality. Traces of historical constitutionalism showed up in the proposals for governmental organization that emerged from the Constitutionalist Party and were written into the Constitution of 1917. Carranza and the constituyentes rejected the doctrinaire constitutionalism of 1857, principally the abstract doctrine of rights (Article 1) and the single-chamber legislature as the expression of popular sovereignty. They called for a strong executive to counteract not only the parliamentarianism of 1857 but also that of the Sovereign Convention of Aguascalientes of 1915, and perhaps that of the congresses of the Madero period. With the elements of historical constitutionalism in mind, let us now turn to the comparative aspects of Emilio Rabasa's constitutional thought, which is characterized by a conflict within it between assumptions drawn from the two major Western legal traditions, the common law of the Anglo American world and the European civil law that Latin America inherited. First, however, we must explore in more general terms the relationship between constitutionalism and the civil law tradition.[18]

Legal scholars occasionally treat this relationship, but historians do so more rarely, especially historians of and in Latin America. At the outset we encounter the problem of terminology and translation. Lawyers and scholars of the English-speaking world use the term *civil law tradition* to distinguish their "common law" systems from legal systems that were derived from Rome and later from continental Europe, especially from Germany and, in Latin America, from France. However, since "civil law" (i.e., *el derecho [le droit] civil*) in continental Europe refers only to private law, as opposed to criminal, commercial, and public law, there is no obvious translation of the term into romance languages: I have seen "civil law tradition" rendered as "*la tradición jurídica romano-canónica*," "*la tradición del derecho continental europeo*," "*la famille romano-germanique*," and even (in despair perhaps), "*la tradizione di civil law.*" This problem of translation may reflect the fact that "civilians" (as they are called in English) tend to regard their tradition exclusively as "the law" (el derecho) and are generally less interested in outside comparison than are their common law colleagues. This is certainly the case in Mexico.

Be that as it may, the notion of legal "tradition" goes beyond identifying rules and details of a legal system, and, in the words of John Henry

Merryman, "puts the legal system into cultural perspective"; it is concerned with "deeply rooted, historically conditioned attitudes" about the law, its organization, its teaching, and its implementation.[19] There are four interrelated characteristics of the civil law tradition that set it apart from the common law tradition and that are particularly relevant to our inquiry: one, a depreciation of judges and a resistance to, even a hostility toward, judge-made law; two, the theoretical corollary that law emanates from the legislator, which found its modern expression in the impulse toward legal codification, especially in the French Civil Code of 1804; three, a strict adherence to the separation of powers in government, conceived of differently from the so-called separation of powers in the United States; four, a deeply held distinction between private and public law, a distinction that has been generally unimportant in common law jurisdictions.

The animus toward judges in the modern civil law world arose from the reaction in revolutionary France against the great legal power and privileges acquired by the judiciary during the Old Regime. Judicial authority was one target of the egalitarian fervor that impelled the assemblies of 1789 and 1790 to eliminate "feudalism." By the decree of 16 August 1790, judges were reduced to technicians who would simply apply the laws and refer back to the legislature in case of doubt. By the same decree, "the civil laws shall be reviewed and reformed by the legislatures; and a general code of laws, simple, clear, and in harmony with the Constitution, shall be drafted."[20] Thus came the ideological impulse, not only to eliminate the interpretative role of judges, but also to throw out the accumulation of past legislation in favor of a code that would conform to nature and to the rights of man. It was the ideology driving codification, the utopian idea of replacing the laws of the past that distinguished codification in the civil law tradition from the proliferation of codes that exist, for example, in the United States.[21]

The French Constituent Assembly also decreed on 16 August 1790 that "the courts may not take any part, directly or indirectly, in the exercise of the legislative power"; moreover, it added, "judicial functions are distinct, and shall always remain separate, from administrative functions." The revolutionaries found support for their distrust of judges and their determination to separate the powers of government in the ideas of Montesquieu, who had asserted in *The Spirit of the Laws* (1748) that the judge "is the mouth that pronounces the words of the law." For him, judges were "inanimate beings." The "power to judge," he added, "becomes . . . invisible and nul."[22] In addition, constitution-makers of the revolutionary era could not conceive of a republican government based on the sovereignty of the people becoming oppressive.

As long as a popular legislature applied laws equally to all citizens, no one could claim being deprived of individual rights. Since threats to individual liberty could only come from citizens themselves, judicial action came to be regarded as only complementary, never opposed, to legislative action.[23] Thus, from Montesquieu and from the revolutionary impulse, every French constitution since 1791 has been based on the principle of the strict separation of powers, a principle that for French constitutional scholars has become a dogma.[24]

The first three characteristics of the civil law tradition bear directly on the fourth, the distinction made between private and public law.[25] The basis for the distinction is ancient; the *jus civile* of the Romans applied to relations between individuals, while public law was left to the sovereign. The first was the subject of elaborate scholarly study, commentary, and refinement by medieval jurists; the second was left undeveloped until the rise of the sovereign state. Public law emerged in modern times from theorizing about government in the seventeenth- and eighteenth-century monarchies as it interacted with the liberal and egalitarian ideas of the American and French revolutions. Nonetheless, in European civil law systems, where scholars were the ultimate heroes of the law, the two major branches of public law, constitutional and administrative, aroused far less interest than did the traditional civil or private law. In fact, it is often said that in France constitutional law is still regarded by many jurists as political science. In postrevolutionary France, judges were restricted to decisions based on facts that pertained to articles of the Civil Code.[26] If they misapplied the law, their actions could be appealed to the Tribunal of Cassation, established in 1790 as a nonjudicial body "in the service of the legislature" (*au prés du corps legislatif*) to *casser* (quash or annul) procedurally incorrect judicial decisions. The tribunal gradually took on more interpretative (essentially judicial) functions and was called a "court," but in accord with the doctrine of separation of powers, these functions did not include public law. The High Court of Cassation did not interpret the Constitution, and thus it never became a supreme court in the U.S. sense, nor did any other such court develop in France.[27]

Returning to Emilio Rabasa's historical and comparative approach to the law, it was probably most clearly revealed in the fourth and last of his books, *El Juicio constitucional. Orígenes, teoría, y extensión*, published in 1919. Completion of this major work was yet another event in what we have seen was a crowded and climatic year for Don Emilio and his family. Unlike his experience with *La Evolución histórica de México*, which he began in 1916 and which went through several transformations before being published in 1920, Rabasa apparently wrote

El Juicio constitucional in a short time (while he was also engaged in reading and responding to Limantour's "Apuntes"). He made no mention of the work to Limantour until it was completed and sent off to Bouret, the publisher in Mexico. I have written, he reported "a volume a little shorter than the previous one [*Evolución histórica*] . . . Don't laugh at the timeliness." "I don't know why," he added, "but the fact is that books on free institutions seem to appear (and even to sell) when there is despair of any kind of institution." Rabasa admitted that since there were no higher bidders, he had to accept Bouret's offer of 1,000 dollars for an edition of 2,000 copies, even though he would not make a cent from it; but he did report another thousand dollars for an edition of 1,500 copies "(can you believe it!) of my old novels." [28] Although Rabasa worried that *El Juicio constitucional* would be slow to appear, he could tell his friend on 25 July that he was shipping off a copy of the published volume. Rabasa was definitely displeased with the quality of the publication; it turned out, he wrote, "as bad and cheap as everything that Bouret publishes." Limantour accorded the book high praise. For him, it was the best study he had read on the development of constitutions in the Anglo Saxon and Latin American countries, as well as presenting the true essence of the Mexican juicio de amparo. He noted, however, that Rabasa might have added some treatment of France, which had such influence "especially in Mexico, on the ideas of our learned men." [29]

The purpose of the book, in Rabasa's words, was to give "a synthetic appreciation of the governmental system in which the stability of political institutions is based on the intervention of judges." Only in the United States, he added, has this system (essentially judicial review) become fully developed. Although the North American system was copied throughout Latin America, only the Mexican Constitution of 1857 adapted it to "the conditions of the Latin peoples of America." Thus "the American system is worthy of the greatest interest and deserving of close examination by kindred nations." We must explore its "historical derivation" and not confuse "judicial review (*el juicio constitucional*) with ingenious inventions that substitute artifice for ancestry." But Rabasa made it clear that the Mexican system of judicial review had degenerated and that its principles, doctrines, and laws needed to be restored by "new free and pure minds," that is, by the law students of Mexico, to whom he dedicated the book. In writing the book, Rabasa was obviously contemplating his return to Mexico where he could once again bring his ideas to bear on the juridical life of the country. [30]

In much of the first part of *El Juicio constitucional* Rabasa idealized Anglo American constitutional development compared to that of the Latin American nations. He said that the latter's institutions were "imposed," in contrast to the unwritten and "spontaneous" English constitution and to the North American constitution, which was "proposed," then "ratified" by the sovereign people.[31] The English constitution, from its base in common-law guarantees to persons and property, was able to overcome reactionary tendencies, and by gradual changes in the electoral system become more democratic. The emigrants to North America, being Englishmen, carried the common law in their baggage; it was their birthright "like the language, domestic customs, and the spirit of the race."[32] In drawing up the Constitution of 1787, the delegates were well aware of theory, which they drew from Montesquieu, yet they were sensible and deliberate, keeping invention within limits. Since the baggage of emigrant Spaniards was absolute monarchy and the *recopilación de leyes,* which gave them little to build upon, they turned at independence to "easily propagated abstract theories," drawn from Montesquieu and Rousseau, "condensed into revolutionary slogans."[33] Whereas the North Americans used "science" (i.e., rationalism) "as an aid to empiricism in establishing the principles of the new freedom," the Latin Americans turned exclusively to science and invention, adopting principles presumably proven already in North America. Natural science took precedence over history and sociology.[34]

But Rabasa went further in his indictment of early Latin American constituent congresses, asserting that "more than theories they have employed fictions." Since according to "scientific theory," sovereignty always resides in the people and cannot be delegated, and since "the reliable part of those communities was so reduced," it was pure fiction to establish a junta, to elect a congress, or to write a constitution in the name of the people. Ironically, he added, popular sovereignty, the ultimate democratic concept, in fact constituted an omnipotent power that was incompatible with democracy. The result could only be endless contention between small minorities, each claiming support from "a population incapable of political ideas."[35] No early constitution could be permanent; it could only be the pretext for revolt. For Rabasa, this resort to fictions in forming Latin American governments was yet another example of the jacobin spirit he had identified in the Constituent Congress of 1856–57, ultimately drawn from Hippolyte Taine's critique of the French Revolution.

From his discussion of comparative constitutional development, Rabasa moved on to his principal concern, namely to demonstrate the power of the Supreme Court as the guardian of the Constitution. Although Rabasa showed an interest in the Anglo American judicial process prior to 1914, his extended exile in New York City clearly deepened his appreciation and knowledge. His account shows evidence of considerable study in juridical and historical sources; it is also logical to assume that he had direct contact with American lawyers (besides William F. Buckley), and that his son Oscar's legal studies at the University of Pennsylvania provided something of a stimulus for his discussion of judicial review. In any case, he first sought the "the origins of judicial supremacy" in England, from medieval beginnings to the seventeenth century, emphasizing the role of Sir Edward Coke, who as president of the Court of Common Pleas, arrived "at the concept of a 'higher law' which was above all authorities," including the monarch [James I] and the laws of Parliament. Developing gradually and spontaneously, "what we call in this book 'judicial review (*juicio constitucional*),'" affirmed Rabasa, is from its origin an English institution. Despite the ultimate legislative supremacy of the Parliament, the judiciary became a basic defender of individual rights against "agents invested with governmental power," and English judges acquired great dignity and respect in "the world's most refined society." Nonetheless, he concluded that for judicial review to be elevated to a "juridical system," it demanded a newly organized free people, in which "popular will" is inserted into "the words of an unequivocal, categorical written commandment."[36]

For all Rabasa's admiration for the Constitution of the United States, he was quite cognizant of its vague designation on the role of the judiciary and of the early struggle between the search for autonomy by the new states and the limitations on that autonomy by the federal government. He detailed, for example, among other issues, the threat from the Virginia and Kentucky declarations of 1797, "in favor of the complete sovereignty of the states," which pitted the Republicans Thomas Jefferson and James Madison against the Federalists John Adams and John Marshall. At bottom was a seemingly irreconcilable ideological conflict between popular sovereignty and the "higher law," until the appointment of John Marshall as chief justice by President Adams in 1801. As Rabasa put it, the alternatives that the Supreme Court faced at the beginning of Marshall's term were that either its decisions would become an integral part of the Constitution "or the Court, a useless and insignificant body, would disappear from the mechanism of government." He then devoted two chapters to Marshall's work of the next thirty-five years, citing several key cases, including *Marbury v. Madison* (1803), which established judicial review, *United States v. Peters* (1809), which overruled actions of the state of Pennsylvania, and *McCulloch v. Maryland* (1819), which further enhanced national power. In Rabasa's view, the latter case determined that the states would have been competent to form an association like the Confederation, "but not to constitute a new government with sovereign powers."[37] Rabasa pointed out incidentally, for the benefit of his Mexican readers, the significance of precedents in the American system, that legal treatises "are only the ordered and exceptionally laborious (*laboriosísima*) exposition of precedents"; and (thinking perhaps of his son Oscar's recent experience) that teaching in law schools was based on case books, which often "produce the literal text without any critique."[38]

Rabasa concluded his discussion of the Anglo American constitutional and legal tradition with remarks on "the theory of judicial supremacy" in that tradition. Much of Rabasa's discussion focused once again on the question of sovereignty. He claimed that Americans were always wary of generalizations and "sparing in the application of abstract theories." However, he continued, American federal lawyers generally argued that the people, on constituting the states before 1789, had in effect delegated their sovereignty to local governments and thus had no longer anything to give to the federation. "That is to say, the people as people were devoid of authority." He dismissed the general declaration that sovereignty was inalienable, and added, as he was wont to do, that "philosophical declarations have no practical value."[39] As for the judiciary, he resorted to Montesquieu's dictum that in order to avoid the abuse of power "it is essential that by the arrangement of things power restrains power." But, he added, the solution in the United States did not come from theory; it emerged from addressing practical problems subsequent to the establishment of the Constitution.[40] While emphasizing the need for a strong judicial power, he added that its real strength comes from its moderation and the fact that it cannot use force. "Weakness is the complementary condition of judicial power." As legitimate and definitive interpreter of the Constitution, it is "the shield of individual rights"; it places limitations on the other active powers, and it is "the preserver of the federal system"—all characteristics of the regime of John Marshall, "the great upholder of American judicial power."[41]

The nature and effectiveness of judicial review in Mexico was of course Emilio Rabasa's central concern in *El Juicio constitucional*. He had dealt with this subject before, in both *El Artículo 14* and *La Constitución y la dictadura*, but he now treated it more systematically and comparatively. His comparative perspective, developed in the context of his New York experience, led Rabasa ultimately to temper his seemingly unbounded admiration for the American system, with criticisms of it brought from his own civil law tradition. But these came only at the end of his book, seemingly incidental to his analysis of judicial review in Mexico. He announced with pride at the outset that no Latin American constitution took on and developed American judicial review as successfully as did the Mexican Constitution of 1857. The constitution makers of 1824 knew nothing of the American system, he said, for the simple reason that Alexis de Tocqueville's *De la démocratie en Amérique,* which brought it to world attention, was not published until 1835 (1836 in Spanish). The word *amparar* (to protect) was introduced by Manuel Crescencio Rejón (who had read Tocqueville) into the Constitution of Yucatán in 1840. However, the true founder of Mexican judicial review was Mariano Otero, who in the Acta de Reformas of 1847 "followed the path of the American Constitution, found the formula to make individual guarantees effective, and established in a masterful way the *juicio de amparo.*"[42] Ponciano Arriaga and his colleagues, continued Rabasa, implemented the fundamentals of Otero's formulation in Articles 101 and 102. These fundamentals, we will recall, were that the federal courts (in effect the Supreme Court) would resolve all controversies arising from violation of individual constitutional guarantees and that all suits must be initiated by the "offended" party, that is, by an individual.[43]

Rabasa's examination of judicial review in Mexico was definitely critical, balancing pride in the system with a variety of its defects, and, as in earlier studies, the need for reform. He asserted at one point that it was impossible and undesirable to pursue a theoretical ideal of constitutional government, the removal of all imperfections. He gave the example of justifiable extraordinary executive powers, as assumed by Benito Juárez during the 1860s in order to save the nation.[44] However, protection of individual rights was always Rabasa's principal concern, and he emphasized the importance of Article 14. Despite its defects, as elaborated on in his 1906 study, the article was vital in providing the same protections as the "due process" clause of the Fifth Amendment to the U.S. Constitution.[45] Although Rabasa admired the work of Ignacio Vallarta as chief justice (1878–82), he took issue, as we have noted, with several of his positions on judicial review. For example, Vallarta argued that the Mexican juicio de amparo was derived from the Writ of Habeas Corpus in Anglo American law, an argument Rabasa rejected; they were, Rabasa maintained, simply different procedures.[46] He dismissed criticism of the "*amparo* against laws" (judicial protection of individuals against unconstitutional legislative acts), a provision of Article 101. The critics argued that it would expose the "representation of the people," that is, popular sovereignty, to adjudication. The idea of excluding legislation from judicial review, said Rabasa, "is very jacobin"; the legislature "is not a sovereign power," as it tends to be regarded in continental Europe. "Democratic ideas, sublimated by the fire of revolutions" [presumably in France], idealized popular legislatures as against the executive (construed as an absolute monarch). Rabasa continued by noting that these ideas still permeate "the modern mind" and "produce irresponsible convictions." Here Rabasa revealed once again his attraction to the U.S. model of judicial review and also his orientation toward historical constitutionalism.[47]

The principal defect of the juicio de amparo, what Rabasa called its "corruption," was one he had pointed to in 1906, namely that it swamped the Supreme Court with an overload of cases. The reason was that numerous state and local disputes were brought directly to the Supreme Court as constitutional cases, forcing it to "do in abundance the work of a lower court." In effect, a large part of its activity was devoted to cassation, that is, to examining purportedly incorrect legal procedures by lower courts. He even said that this problem threatened to bring the Supreme Court "to the point of death."[48] Nonetheless, Rabasa remained optimistic in his belief that despite the many defects in the Mexican system of judicial defense of the Constitution, it could be made more effective. In fact, he shifted ground in his final chapter to focus on "the advantages of the system in Mexico."

Rabasa's concluding argument in *El Juicio constitucional* was complex and even contradictory, because of the clash within it between his admiration for the Anglo American system and key assumptions from the civil law tradition. As we might expect, he took strong exception to the plebiscite (referendum and recall) movement in several American states, which threatened to impose "the tyranny of the greatest number." And yet, he wondered, somewhat oddly for an antirevolutionary social conservative (who, as we have seen, argued against agrarian reform), whether the U.S. judiciary could adapt to social change. For example, he pointed out, it had overturned labor legislation regulating wages, hours, and union organization. Is the U.S. Supreme Court, he asked, incompatible with the evolution of ideas, inflexible and old-fashioned, as charged by laboring groups? He even acknowledged the popular complaint in the United States that "the American government is an oligarchy of the robe"; and he repeated the critical phrase used by French theorists, "legislation by judges," which he saw as a serious threat in the United States to "legislation by legislators."[49]

Rabasa stated with pride that legislation by judges could never take hold in Mexico. While Mexico did not enjoy the authority of precedent, one of the great advantages of the common law, at the same time it was spared "jurisprudential petrifaction," the danger that judicial supremacy could be "converted into a dam to hold back the currents of national life."[50] He was confident that the threat of judge-made law would be nullified by Mexico's legal doctrines, its scholarly traditions, and its conception of justice, "which awaken and enliven in the Latin ideal a spiritual liberty that we will never disregard." Rabasa's study of and direct exposure to the U.S. legal system during his years of exile did not make him a convert. He still adhered to the fundamentals of the civil law tradition and revealed, as on this occasion, that he could even idealize them, all of which paradoxically made him appear as a jurist who might be sympathetic to the revolutionary legislation being enacted in his own country.

Rabasa's ambivalence in the face of the two divergent legal traditions was also revealed in his response to the confusing and much-debated theoretical issue: was the juridical branch of government simply a "department" or a true "power?" He initially took the first position in 1912, appearing to follow the French doctrine of the rigid separation of powers; by 1921 he shifted decisively to the second. In 1912 he argued that since the administration of justice was concerned only with the protection of individual rights, it was not dependent on "the will of the nation" and thus not a power as such. It lacked, he added, the three qualities of "the agents of power," initiative, unity, and general authority. He also found support in a passage by Alexander Hamilton on "The Judiciary Department" in *The Federalist,* which in turn referred to Montesquieu's famous phrase on the nullity of the judicial power. Rabasa interpreted the phrase to mean not that the judiciary was insignificant compared with the legislature or executive, but only that its function was different.[51] As we have seen, various constituyentes of 1917 attacked Rabasa for his use of the word *department.* One senses that by 1919 he realized that the term was a red herring and that to be practical he should use the word *power.*[52] Rabasa's basic conviction did not change over these years, namely that Mexico's constitutional system needed a strong supreme court, whether it be called a "department" or a "power." His problem was how to implement this conviction within the dictates of the civil law tradition, in light of the defects he saw in Mexican judicial review.

In September 1921, a year after returning to Mexico, Rabasa again confronted the theoretical issue of "department" versus "power" in the face of the continued backlog of amparo cases in the Supreme Court and a pending measure to divide the Court into multiple chambers (*salas*) in order to expedite cases and meet the problem. In a dramatic speech to an overflow crowd at the Primer Congreso Jurídico Nacional, he reminded his audience that "the Supreme Court is not a tribunal; it is a supreme national power." As such, though it does not command, "it restrains those who do command." He emphasized that its function "is always and exclusively political, as the regulating element of governmental organization."[53] He saw the measure to divide the court as disastrous, leading to anarchy and dissolution.

The dramatic point of the speech came when he proposed, in addition to the Supreme Court, the creation of a court of cassation on the French model, a proposal replete with references to French theorists, French legal history, and lavish praise for French jurisprudence, references and praise that were never explicit in his previous writings. His words bear quoting at length:

Above the monument of the Napoleonic code [was constructed] the monument of French jurisprudence, the wisest and perhaps the most respectable in the world, the rich source turned to by the legislators and jurisconsults of nations that derive their law from the Roman trunk. The product of this work [that is, of the Court of Cassation] is a general system of the highest justice, contributed to by a body of judges equaled by no nation, and by a truly scientific and judicious bar, the pride of the world's most profound and transcendental profession.[54]

The French Court of Cassation, he argued, with its division into civil, penal, and procedural (*la procedencia del recurso*) chambers, can dispatch its business with rigor and clarity and avoid the "perversion of the law" present in the Mexican system. It "shows us the admirable example of a revisionary tribunal within the central government to watch over the exact application of ordinary legislation." The union in Mexico of both judicial functions, cassation and defense of constitutional rights, in a single body, "results in a monstrous institution."[55]

By creating a court of cassation, he concluded, the Supreme Court could be made a true power of government, essentially as it is in the United States; and Mexico's system of judicial review, the juicio de amparo, could be freed to function as it should. The speech was in effect Emilio Rabasa's swan song on this subject, for he wrote only once more on it before his death in 1930. It was his final effort to graft North American judicial review onto the civil law trunk and thus to establish his version of a vigorous constitutionalism in Mexico. The effort was in vain. His proposal aroused some debate at the time; but except for his disciple Manuel Herrera y Lasso, whose influence was limited, it has gone virtually unnoticed since.

There were two other closely related matters of judicial organization that Emilio Rabasa continued to pursue in the final decade of his life: the irremovability or life tenure of Supreme Court justices and the means of designating them—whether by popular election or by executive nomination and legislative confirmation. Although the perennial issue of irremovability seemed to have been solved with the passage of Article 94 by the Constitutional Congress of 1917, we will see shortly that Rabasa expressed justified concern for its future. Therefore, let us turn first to the question of popular election, which he introduced initially in 1912 as part of his critique of the Constitution of 1857. On a note of sarcasm, Rabasa asked rhetorically how the Constitution provided for the all-important independence of Supreme Court justices: by popular election, "the path to universal salvation as proclaimed by revolutionary theories."[56]

He proceeded to attack popular election, building his case by reference to the experience of the United States. Although the wise and irremovable justices of the U.S. Supreme Court remained in place, the "entry of the pure theories of the *Jefferson democrats,* which were nothing but jacobin theories," led to the popular election of judges in two-thirds of the states by the mid-nineteenth century.[57] Rabasa maintained that popularly elected judges were generally less competent and more subject to the influence of bosses than those in other states who were nominated and confirmed. Popular election is incompatible with life tenure, he continued, because the people are obliged "to renew their trust from time to time"; in Mexico this meant a six-year term. In addition, popular election has led to "the invasions by the Supreme Court" in state politics.[58] For Rabasa, the major example of this political invasion came from the application of the "incompetence by origin" doctrine in the 1870s. In contrast to the United States, he wrote, where the Supreme Court was obliged to follow the jurisprudence of the state courts, in Mexico the Supreme Court could declare a state law invalid if proven that its application was by a local official whose election was irregular or illegal.[59] The official and the law could be designated "legally unqualified (*incompetente*) by origin," according to Article 16 of the Constitution. Thus the Supreme Court intervened in cases in several states from 1873 to 1881. These interventions basically brought the Court directly into politics and amounted to encroachment on the independence of the states, at the same time reducing the role of the Supreme Court, in Rabasa's words, to that of "a provincial tribunal."[60]

During his years in the United States Emilio Rabasa encountered the major conflict over the popular recall of judges and even of judicial decisions, an American version of the policy he had opposed so vigorously in Mexico. By 1914 the Supreme Court was faced with mounting criticism from socialists, progressive reformers, labor, and even some jurists for its resistance to social change. Rabasa was clearly sensitive to this mounting opposition, which he appeared to acknowledge positively in his conclusion to *El Juicio constitucional* (see above, p. 147). On returning to Mexico he called attention to the recall issue in a brief summary of a French study of the American Bar Association, a study he said would be useful to his Mexican colleagues. In fact, Rabasa singled out the recall issue from among those that particularly engaged the Bar Association and added his own statement on the subject,[61] a statement that again showed some ambivalence. On the one hand, he said that in the face of the political pressures favoring "the evolution of socialism," the Supreme Court of the United States "has maintained an immobility that borders on being archaic." On the other, he noted, with seeming disapproval, Theodore Roosevelt's proposal that disputed Supreme Court decisions be made subject to popular plebiscite. The adoption of the recall, insisted Rabasa, "would have produced a most sudden change in the governmental system, since judicial supremacy would have turned into legislative supremacy, resulting in the failure of the Union."[62] In his brief critique, he acknowledged that his authorities on the subject were the American Thomas G. Haines and the Frenchman Edouard Lambert, further evidence of Emilio Rabasa's thoroughly comparative approach to the law.[63]

There was no ambivalence whatsoever in Emilio Rabasa's views on the irremovability of judges. He had repeatedly lavished praise on the unsuccessful campaign by the Científicos of 1892 to reform the Constitution of 1857. In fact, as I have argued, irremovability of judges was an important element of Rabasa's broader legal and political thought, that is, the Porfirian historical constitutionalism and scientific politics that he carried into the twentieth century. His position on irremovability clearly influenced the debate on the judiciary in the Constitutional Congress and in part its final decision on judicial organization. Nonetheless, Rabasa once again argued the matter in 1923, presumably responding to at least two strong critiques of the present judicial system and the competence of judges by members (*vocales*) of the Segundo Congreso Jurídico of 1922, Lic. Ignacio Bravo Betancourt and Lic. Luis Sánchez Pontón. Neither opposed irremovablility in theory, but both argued that it should not be instituted at this time. Betancourt called for a "law of responsibility" to hold judges accountable for their actions; Sánchez Pontón emphasized the need for a change in the way judges were selected, namely that nominations should come from judicial organizations.[64]

In a series of four articles directed to the enlightened public, Rabasa reviewed the history of irremovability, once again paying tribute to the constitutional reformers of 1892–93, especially "the most brilliant talent of the Científico group, Don Justo Sierra."[65] Although the Chamber of Deputies passed the 1893 measure by a two-thirds vote, "the project lay buried in the archives of the Senate." Porfirio Díaz was not initially opposed to the measure, but came to be persuaded that an irremovable court was an autonomous power, "and that there is no place for two powers in a dictatorship." In 1911, continued Rabasa, the measure was revived; but despite revolutionary enthusiasm for "civil liberty," the Madero regime rejected judicial independence as inopportune. "So acted the apostolate of the revolution."

Actually, the experience of irremovability in 1911 was more complicated than Rabasa's tart comment suggested. The measure was introduced briefly in early October 1911 by the Chamber of Deputies and sent to the Senate a few days later. The debate in the Senate was unusually long and contentious. Several of the opponents did say that irremovability of judges was inopportune in the midst of a popular revolution, but the arguments in favor were equally forceful, as presented by Esteban Maqueo Castellanos, Victor Manuel Castillo, and Miguel S. Macedo, all friends and associates of Rabasa. Castillo favored separating irremovability (Article 92) from other articles involving the judiciary, and his position was accepted in the revised measure. Rabasa did not participate in the debate, but he did vote for the proposal. It failed in 1911 by 20 to 19 in the Senate.[66] Now, in 1923, in the face of growing opposition to irremovability, Rabasa responded to the view that "we are not at the level of Switzerland to be able to adopt the irremovability of judges," which he took to mean that Mexico did not have "the necessary level of culture." He dismissed this argument, saying that irremovability had nothing to do with "culture"; in fact, an uneducated and weak populace needs all the more the protection of "incorruptible tribunals."[67]

Rabasa then turned to the present renewal of the court, and praised the extensive press coverage of its importance because the eleven justices now selected would have life tenure. He mentioned three in particular noted for their "independence, wisdom, integrity [and] devotion to their work," Victoriano Pimentel, Enrique Colunga, and Manuel E. Cruz, but feared they would be overlooked. He then proceeded to repeat the general arguments for irremovable judges, responding to potential fears that a bad judge could not be removed. In England, he said, an irremovable judge can be removed by Parliament, in France by a plenary session of the Court of Cassation, and in Mexico by Article 108 of the Constitution.[68] Rabasa completed this, his final important statement on the cause that was central to his juridical thought, by calling attention to the continuing problems of administering the juicio de amparo, the heart of Mexico's system of judicial review. He contrasted the effectiveness of the amparo in the days of Ignacio Vallarta, when it was a simple and straightforward defense of individual constitutional rights, with its decline, as a result of "the introduction of *amparo* into civil matters that pertained to inexact application of laws," in other words, cassation. Rabasa was, in effect, repeating his argument of 1906 in *El Artículo 14* and in his proposal of 1921. The Court's agenda was now overwhelmed, with 10,000 cases in arrears. The division of the court into several chambers, then being proposed, would do nothing to alleviate the situation. The only remedy was to "eliminate from the *amparo* all that is spurious, and return it to the dignity it had under Vallarta."

Otherwise, he concluded, the Court will be turned into "a higher court that as a power will be as ridiculous as an emperor of the theatre selling vegetables in the Merced Plaza."[69] Thus ended Rabasa's formal commentary on the Mexican judicial defense of the Constitution.

By 1923 Emilio Rabasa was thoroughly integrated into the postrevolutionary juridical world, even though his argument for irremovability of judges was not widely accepted. In his first article of 1923, Rabasa mentioned that he was currently president of the Orden Mexicana de Abogados, which had initiated and continued to support the Congresos Jurídicos Nacionales, the first of which, as we have seen, took place in 1921. It was there that Rabasa gave his dramatic speech urging the establishment of a court of cassation on the French model. The new lawyers' organization was established in 1917 to restore cohesion to the juridical community, to raise professional standards, and to improve the administration of justice—all of which were in disarray as a result of revolutionary upheaval. The organization was often attacked as "reactionary," but it finally won official approval when President Álvaro Obregón inaugurated the First Juridical Congress in 1921.[70] Rabasa's reentry into the juridical world in 1920 was facilitated by the presence of colleagues like Antonio Ramos Pedrueza (1860–1930), a founder of the Orden Mexicana de Abogados. Ramos Pedrueza was a professor of Penal Law for some forty years at the Escuela Nacional de Jurisprudencia, and later at the university, as well as a long-time federal deputy. He was also a member of the committee of three that introduced the irremovability measure in the Chamber of Deputies in 1911. In 1921 he was a part of the "permanent committee" of the 1921 Juridical Congress, along with Rabasa, Rabasa's law partner Nicanor Gurría Urgell, and Rabasa's close friend Miguel S. Macedo. Ramos Pedrueza is a good example of continuity in the juridical world of the capital through the revolutionary era, a continuity that of course Rabasa himself epitomizes.[71]

We have seen throughout this study that Emilio Rabasa was also a practicing lawyer, in addition to writing on judicial and constitutional issues. Moreover, we examined in Chapter 6 his success in arguing at least two amparo cases against revolutionary laws in defense of the rights of the heirs of Pablo Martínez del Río and of William F. Buckley. There are records of three other Supreme Court cases Rabasa argued unsuccessfully in 1924. Unlike the two above, these do not appear to have involved revolutionary agrarian legislation. The first was a dispute between Eugenio Gorzave and Ulpiano Ruiz Lavín over the cancellation of a complex rental contract involving a third party. Representing Ruiz Lavin, Rabasa argued that the cancellation was legal, but the Court upheld Gorozave's amparo by a 6–4 decision.[72] In the second case Rabasa defended a widow, Anastasia Delgadillo, whose husband had loaned money fifteen years earlier to the firm of Fernández and Parduelas. Although the loan had been made in gold, Parduelas ultimately repaid it in depreciated paper currency. According to Rabasa, Parduelas violated "the spirit and the moral sense" of the 1918 *Ley de Pagos* against taking unfair advantage in such a situation. The Court ruled 6–5 against the amparo.[73] In the third case the Court also voted 6–5 against the Companía Mexicana Holandesa "La Corona," defended by Rabasa, in favor of the heirs of Tomás Valladares (who had leased land to the oil company); the plaintiffs claimed that 6,000,000 pesos had not been paid.[74] There is sketchy evidence of other cases argued by Rabasa, but none after 1924. He appears at this point to have given up the Supreme Court and returned to his teaching and administrative work at the ELD.

The juridical legacy of Emilio Rabasa can be seen both in the experience of the institution which he helped establish and in the ideas of his successors. The survival of the ELD between its founding in 1912 and the official recognition of its degrees in 1930 is one of the intriguing subjects of the revolutionary years. Its survival may also be regarded as an important aspect of the survival of Porfirian liberalism. Although the overt justification for the school, as we have seen in Chapter 4, rested on the guarantee of "freedom of teaching," as stated in Article 3 of the Constitution of 1857, its científico, anti-Madero, and ultimately pro-Huerta orientation was clear. In short, the ELD was a product of the major political conflicts of the Madero presidency. The school rapidly gained prestige, despite the political sympathies of its founders, in part because they were the country's leading lawyers and jurists. The antagonism between the ELD and the official ENJ declined after the fall of Victoriano Huerta in July 1914 and the rise of Venustiano Carranza. Carranza was able to reconcile the political divisions within the university world of the capital, including the juridical establishment. It is significant, for example, that José Natividad Macías, a founding professor of the ELD and a follower of Rabasa, was an author of the draft constitution Carranza presented to the Constituent Congress at Querétaro in December 1916.

After 1920, the Escuela Libre remained vulnerable, both because its leaders Miguel S. Macedo and Emilio Rabasa could be regarded as ex-Científicos, but also because many of its professors and students were strong Catholics. In the harsh political and anticlerical atmosphere of the 1920s, the school's survival strategy was to become apolitical and to preach "tolerance," that is, to avoid entanglement in the church-state conflict. Rabasa set the tone for this strategy. Yet he was also vigorous in his defense of the "free" (that is, nonofficial) character of the school and even argued in 1925 that the ELD might be considered a precursor of the autonomous university.[75] In his courses he did reiterate earlier critical and comparative themes, but in a less vigorous form. He contin-

Rabasa Teaching at ELD, 1928. Courtesy of ELD.

ued to attack the contemporary juicio de amparo as "notoriously defective and corrupting," referring to his 1921 proposal to create a court of cassation on the French model and his articles of 1923. He criticized the failure of the Constituent Congress of 1916–17 to establish full irremovability of judges. And he pointed up differences between the U.S. emphasis on judicial precedent and the French emphasis on scholarly analysis of the law. But Rabasa avoided analyzing in depth the radical articles of the Constitution of 1917, especially Article 27 on property and 123 on labor. He omitted the latter altogether in his course. He said he would only touch on points in Article 27 he considered "as constitutional." Basically, he regarded Article 27 as a treatise on property, not a properly constitutional article. As for Articles 3 and 130, he revealed his nineteenth-century anticlericalism, but said he declined to "touch on religious issues," or "to impose my ideas on such difficult material"; religion and science should be kept apart in education.[76]

As we noted in Chapter 6, Rabasa's relationship with William F. Buckley aided materially in the survival of the ELD, since Buckley not only made a financial contribution to the school, but also facilitated a contribution of 10,000 pesos by Lord Cowdray, the British oil magnate. Although one member of the ELD's Board resisted Buckley's support because of his expulsion from the country as an "interventionist," Rabasa as president of the Board prevailed. But he had to inform Buckley that he was unable for the moment to make either contribution public.[77] The ELD's survival strategy was successful, and the school's future was secured when two of its early students, Emilio Portes Gil and Ezequiel Padilla, became president of the Republic and secretary of Education, respectively in 1929. With the recognition of its degrees, the school was able to withstand continuing pressures during the era of Lázaro Cárdenas. But in so doing, the critical dimension of Rabasa's legacy declined, the study of law and of history diverged, and the juridical establishment made its peace with the revolutionary state.[78]

The divergence of formal law and critical history and the problems of the Rabasian legacy can also be seen in bits of evidence drawn from ideas of his successors. It appears that with the Revolution, interest in comparative legal systems faded in Mexico, though Rabasa's son Oscar attempted vainly to keep it alive. The fact that he received a law degree from the University of Pennsylvania in 1917 made him unique among Mexican lawyers. On his return to Mexico, he sought to perpetuate his father's interests when he vigorously opposed an amparo case that he said involved a strictly political (and nonconstitutional) conflict between the State of Veracruz and the federal government.[79] He maintained that since the juicio de amparo was an adaptation of the Anglo American system of judicial review to the Mexican milieu, it would be quite natural in such a case for jurists to study the decisions of the U.S. Supreme Court. He then berated his colleagues for not doing so. When a juridical problem in civil, commercial, or penal law arises, he said, they "turn to its source or origin, going back if the case demands it to Roman law, or perhaps to French or Spanish law." What a pity, he added, that "we don't see in their libraries, alongside the magnificent French treatises, a single complete work on U.S. constitutional law, or a collection of Supreme Court decisions." While French theorists are extensively consulted in a civil or criminal case, "an American author is never consulted when a constitutional issue arises." Moreover, if Mexican jurists had studied U.S. constitutional law, they could have adapted the juicio de amparo more perfectly to their needs, instead of allowing it to reach "its present state of disintegration."[80] Rabasa then went on to review in detail the U.S. Supreme Court cases that bore upon the amparo suit in question.

Oscar Rabasa's polemic aroused little response, but it is also evident that he himself was determined to fill the void, which he did two decades later with the publication of Mexico's only important treatise on North American law. Once again he took the occasion to lament the ignorance in Mexico of U.S. law, both because few could read Anglo American works in English, but also because there did not exist a single complete translation of such a work into Spanish. His challenge, as he saw it, was "to figure out a system which in its formal aspect, in its juridical forms, in its terms and procedures, differs radically from Mexican law."[81] In addition to Oscar Rabasa's work, there was established in 1940 the Instituto Mexicano de Derecho Comparado and in 1948 its journal devoted to comparative law. However, the journal scarcely acknowledged Oscar Rabasa's study and to date has given little attention to topics from the common law world. Hector Fix Zamudio, long-time director of the Sección de Derecho Comparado of the Instituto de Investigaciones Jurídicas, has clearly pursued comparative topics, but he admitted recently that the teaching of the subject was hindered by the lack of any appropriate texts. It is perhaps too early to tell whether the era of NAFTA will bring a change in the situation.[82]

The fate of the Rabasian legacy is also revealed in the experience of his "most distinguished disciple," Manuel Herrera y Lasso (1890–1967).[83] Herrera y Lasso was one of the student rebels of 1912 whose actions led to the founding of the Escuela Libre de Derecho, and he was closely associated with the school throughout his career. He taught sociology at various times from 1914 to 1927 and became Rabasa's successor to the chair of constitutional law in 1930. A fervent Catholic, Herrera sought exile in Cuba during the Cristero upheaval of 1927–29, and in 1939 he became a founder of the conservative Partido de Acción Nacional (PAN) and a subsequent PAN activist. Despite his uneasy relationship with the revolutionary state, Herrera was tolerated and even recruited to serve as consultant to three presidents from 1947 to 1964. Though he never published a major juridical study, he was celebrated for his teaching at the ELD and respected within the juridical establishment for his eloquence and his numerous occasional commentaries on constitutional issues, collected and published in three separate volumes from 1940 to 1986.[84]

Though Herrera y Lasso took issue with Rabasa's anticlericalism and his narrow construction of individual rights, he remained faithful to the core issues of Rabasa's constitutional thought. He perpetuated Rabasa's attacks on the contemporary amparo procedure, and he was the sole champion of Rabasa's 1921 proposal for the establishment of a court of cassation to separate appeals based on ordinary legislation from amparo suits on bona fide constitutional issues. He continued to pursue the cause of judicial irremovability and criticized severely the half measures taken to restructure the Supreme Court after 1917.[85] He argued eloquently that a statue should be erected to Emilio Rabasa in the Supreme Court building to accompany those honoring the other three great jurists who had guided the evolution of the juicio de amparo. The project has finally been realized in our day.[86] However, Manuel Herrera y Lasso's Catholicism, his PAN militancy, and his failure to

Statue in Supreme Court Building, Mexico City, February 2006. Photo by Rafael Estrada.

publish a notable juridical treatise reduced his influence as a perpetuator of Rabasa's thought within the postrevolutionary establishment.

Not only did the Revolution undercut the Rabasian tendency toward historical and comparative constitutionalism, but it also injected new social assumptions into the juridical process. Rabasa himself was quite aware of this new social thought and actually came to grips with it in one significant publication, an address to the Confederación de Cámaras Industriales in 1922.[87] His subject was Article 5 (the right to work), and his speech was prompted by pressure from radical syndicalist groups essentially to rescind this constitutional guarantee. By this initiative, he maintained, "the dictatorship of the union" would replace the right to work, as well as the right to association (Article 9). Rabasa made it clear that he upheld individual guarantees as "the indispensable balancing element" in political organization. At the same time, he seriously engaged the new social doctrines, particularly those of Léon Duguit (1859–1928), the French legal theorist who claimed to work from positivist premises. Though Rabasa emphasized that Duguit held to "the need for positive methods in research" and referred to his "scientific faith," he criticized Duguit's empirical conception of the state. Duguit had argued the historical decline of two opposing abstract theories, the idea of "the sovereign right of the state" and the "idea of a natural inalienable and imprescriptible right of the individual personality." Both, said Duguit, gave way to a "public service" state, that is, public law guided by realistic social concerns.[88] Rabasa saw Duguit's conception as leading to a new absolutism, an empirically based "dominance of the majority" replacing the old absolutism of Rousseau's metaphysical general will.

But Rabasa's specific concern was radical or violent syndicalism, which he believed threatened the right to work. He quoted a long passage from Duguit, which argued the distinction between revolutionary syndicalism and the more generally peaceful labor movement.[89] The latter was not bolshevist and violent, wrote Duguit, like the general strike it had opposed in 1920, but rather was "a powerful means of pacification and union," which extends to all classes and "tends to bring them together in a harmonic unity." Rabasa appeared to have some sympathy for Duguit's optimistic view, though he ultimately rejected it as utopian, contrary to the basic human instinct to dominate. Rabasa concluded his address by acknowledging that "all of us, even the most stubborn," are imbued with the justice of the "good socialism," not to be confused with "leveling communism." He singled out Jesús Rivero Quijano (1888–1968), the Spanish-born major entrepreneur and president of the Confederation to which he was speaking, a man who had recently made "noble and generous declarations on the rights and the future of the working class."[90] Deploring "violent syndicalism," which seeks suppression of the right to work, Rabasa emphasized that this right did not necessarily imply the "regime of individual egoism" of the old laissez-faire. "All educated nations," he added, have modified their laws in the face of the influence of "pure socialism," and its principles have raised "the moral level of the upper classes." The right to work and the right to association are two compatible individual guarantees that protect the union, he insisted; this is "the destiny of the right to work," which is the "basis of existence." Perhaps the views inherent in this address make Rabasa's critique of the excessively individualistic decisions by the U.S. Supreme Court more credible.[91]

In any case, Mexican legal thought after 1920 moved in new social directions, influenced in part by Duguit, an author much studied at the ELD during the 1920s. The ideas of Felipe Tena Ramírez (1905–94), Rabasa student, eminent constitutionalist, and Supreme Court president were symptomatic of this change. Tena Ramírez studied at the ELD in the mid 1920s, presenting in 1928 a thesis on the shift in the function of law from individualism to socialism. That same year a revision of the Civil Code appeared, specifically construing property "as a social function and not as a subjective right."[92] The constitutional thought of Tena Ramírez revealed clear signs of these new tendencies, as well as certain older Rabasian themes. The interaction of the two was subtle and not always in conflict.

Felipe Tena Ramírez departed from Rabasa when he justified some years later the right of the Mexican people to modify by violent means "the constitutional norms of the Mexican state." Following a detailed discussion of the political and constitutional events of the revolutionary decade, he concluded that revolution can have a moral if not a juridical basis. In short, "the right to revolution," he said, "becomes positive law when it is recognized as such by the people, overtly or implicitly."[93] Tena's construction of the right to revolution seemed to run parallel to his critique, in the manner of Rabasa, of the U.S. Supreme Court's attack on social legislation early in the century, which he termed a defense of the capitalist social order. Citing French theorists Maurice Hauriou and Edouard Lambert, Tena identified the penetration of the "contagion of politics" into the U.S. judicial power; it was paralyzing the work of the legislator. It is necessary, he concluded, that "the Mexican defense of the Constitution (*el juicio constitucional mexicano*), which has taken that system as a model, preserves itself from such risks."[94] Tena Ramírez then went on to discuss at length the juicio de amparo, which continues to be "what it always has been, a defense of the individual within the constitutional order," and not what it perhaps could never have been, "a direct and autonomous defense of the Constitution" (by which he meant a defense against unconstitutional legislation or decrees).[95]

One can definitely sense ambivalence in the treatment of the Supreme Court by Tena Ramírez, an ambivalence pointed to years before by his mentor. Tena outlined a pattern of frequent changes in the organization of the court from the 1920s to the 1950s, a discussion that in effect emphasized its lack of independence in the face of executive authority. He criticized particularly the constitutional reform of 1934, which (as we have noted) abolished irremovability and set judicial terms at six years, that is, to coincide with presidential terms. He asserted that it was the worst of all systems, "because it converts the justices of the Supreme Court into simple agents of the executive."[96] Though his ambivalence was generally subdued, considering his praise of later changes in the organization of the Court, Tena Ramírez probably would have agreed with his colleague Salvador Urbina, the socially liberal president of the Supreme Court in the 1930s and 1940s. In his 1944 prologue to Oscar Rabasa's treatise on Anglo American law, Urbina lamented the limited power of the Mexican judiciary, asserting that the Mexican legal system "places handcuffs on the Mexican judge."[97] Tena Ramírez took great pride in the juicio de amparo as a defense of individual rights, and he resisted any political intervention by the judiciary. Nonetheless, he acknowledged, as had Emilio Rabasa earlier, the weakness of the Mexican Supreme Court in the face of executive authority, now enhanced within the revolutionary state.

Felipe Tena Ramírez may have realized that the year he graduated from the ELD, 1929, had seen the transition in Mexican constitutionalism from limited judicial independence to executive domination, a transition that was complete by 1934 with the amendment to Article 94 of the Constitution. This transition was also marked symbolically by the passing of Emilio Rabasa, who was able, despite his exile and antirevolutionary proclivities, to return to Mexico and still remain a significant presence in the world of the law. Not without its anomalous aspects, Rabasa's juridical thought continued to exert influence, beginning with the Constitutional Congress of 1916–17, where the phantom presence of Don Emilio could be resisted but not ignored. His attack on "jacobin" legislative supremacy in the Constitution of 1857 and his support for strong executive power weighed with those who fashioned the preconstitutional documents of 1914 and 1916 and found their way into Venustiano Carranza's draft constitution and finally into the Constitution of 1917 itself. But Rabasa's main concern was the role of the third branch of government, the judiciary, which in 1912 he had hoped would be the bulwark of the "constitutional stage" following the era of dictatorship. The constituyentes of 1917 responded, making Rabasa, his ideas, and his politics the subject of vigorous debate; and they ultimately approved a measure for partial judicial independence.

Perhaps encouraged by the action of the constituyentes, and perhaps sensing the opportunity to influence the development of "free institutions" on his return to Mexico in 1920, Rabasa published his juridical masterpiece, *El Juicio constitucional,* in which the Supreme Court took center stage. Implementing his historical and comparative approach to constitutionalism and drawing from his experience in the United States, Rabasa presented to Mexican readers the American tradition of judicial supremacy, from its roots in England to its completion under John Marshall. However, for all his admiration for the American system, Rabasa was a product of the continental civil law tradition, which made him resist (rather surprisingly) "legislation by judges" in the United States, particularly when the "Lochner Court" turned hostile to social change. He said hopefully that this "petrification of the law" could not happen in Mexico. Mexico's major judicial problem, a perennial one for Rabasa, was the malfunction of the juicio de amparo, Mexico's unique defense of individual constitutional rights, which produced total overload in the Supreme Court. His solution for the problem, presented in his dramatic speech of 1921, was to create alongside the Supreme Court, a court of cassation on the French model, which would remove from the Supreme Court's agenda the myriad cases that dealt with the misapplication of ordinary legislation. Don Emilio's initiative failed to attract continuing support, except from his successor Manuel Herrera y Lasso; and the problem persisted. However, Rabasa continued to write on the necessity of making life tenure for judges permanent, but again his efforts failed to survive. Moreover, his historical and comparative approach to the law, which guided his campaign for judicial irremovability, went into decline after his death, except for the valiant efforts of his son, Oscar.

Emilio Rabasa can certainly be termed a social conservative, as revealed clearly in his discussion in 1920 of Mexico's "so-called problems"—the Indian, land, and education—and in his refusal to regard Article 27 as properly constitutional. However, he was, surprisingly enough, sensitive to the new social liberalism, which penetrated the younger generation at the ELD, principally through the ideas of the French jurist Léon Duguit. Rabasa could even, as in his address in 1922, announce himself a supporter of "good socialism," while rejecting militant syndicalism and omitting Article 123 from his teaching. Once again, as a jurist, Rabasa straddled the two Western legal traditions, the Anglo American and the French. On the one hand, he argued for judicial supremacy that could control within the Constitution the tendency of the other two branches of government toward revolutionary transformation, and on the other, resist "legislation by judges" which placed obstacles in the way of change. Rabasa never resolved this conflict, nor did his more socially liberal student Felipe Tena Ramirez, and it continues to this day.

CHAPTER EIGHT

Conclusion: The Survival of Porfirian Liberalism

Emilio Rabasa was active until the end. Although he was virtually blind, as described by friends and colleagues, he published several articles in *Excelsior* in the year before his death on 25 April 1930. His final articles, "El Desprestigio de la vicepresidencia," appeared on the third and fourth of that month. Although he probably had given up his work as a lawyer by 1925, he continued to teach constitutional law at the ELD at least through 1928, as well as acting as rector of the institution at the time of his death. Carlos Díaz Dufoo, who had been a fellow editor of *El Universal* in 1889, told of Don Emilio's final project, a proposed collaborative history of the years 1885 to 1910. Rabasa wanted to set the record straight. "The youth of today do not know us, they are mistaken; we are not what they believe we are," he said to his friend. The account must be "impartial, serene, and pure (*limpia*)." Díaz Dufoo left the late March interview, impressed by Rabasa's determination, but knowing that the dream would never be realized. "I had the foreboding," he concluded, "that my friend's idea was the deception by which the angel of death seduces the old."[1] Despite Rabasa's effort during his final month to relieve a severe respiratory ailment at the waters of Tehuacán, he finally succumbed to bronchopneumonia. The burial ceremony took place on 26 April at the Panteón Francés, with several eulogies by colleagues and students, including Felipe Tena Ramírez. The eminent constitutionalist was remembered by numerous articles in the press and at a "solemn gathering" held at the ELD on 2 December 1930. The main speakers were Nicanor Gurría Urgell, Professor at the ELD (and Rabasa's law partner of thirty-five years), and Manuel Herrera y Lasso, successor to the chair of Constitutional Law.[2]

Rabasa Tomb, Panteón Francés, Mexico City. Photo by C. A. Hale.

As a physical personage, Rabasa left strong impressions on those who knew him. Jorge Ferrer remembered him as especially tall and gaunt, "discretely elegant in his dress," and propped up by a stiff cane that "seemed an extention of himself." All commented on his near blindness. Ferrer thought his dark glasses seemed a "sad portent of mourning"; but Jorge Gaxiola, a former student, wrote that teaching for Rabasa appeared to disperse the fog of his vision and light the way for pointing

Memorial Tablet on Rabasa Tomb, Panteón Francés, Mexico City. Photo by C. A. Hale. Top to Bottom: Emilio Rabasa, 25 April 1930; Ruth Rabasa de Escandón, 26 July 1919; Mercedes Llanes de Rabasa (wife of Emilio), 2 May 1910. Photo by C. A. Hale.

out "new horizons." In the interview with Carlos Díaz Dufoo, Rabasa surprised his friend; how could this man, who often seemed externally "disdainful and indifferent," show such zeal for the joint project he was proposing? For him Rabasa displayed at that moment the strength and energy of a "stoic combatant."[3] But such impressions pertained mostly to the outer man. Since Rabasa has been known basically through his books, his speeches, and his presence as a teacher, his personality and personal characteristics have been largely hidden from view. However, thanks to his correspondence with José Yves Limantour, we now have more of an insight into the private man who was exceptionally reserved and even secretive, a man who kept no archive of his own. (He was usually more guarded in writing to William F. Buckley). We also get a glimpse into the inner man through journalistic articles written under cover of supposed anonymity, which express thoughts he would never have uttered in signed writings.

Rabasa's discrete nature did not prevent him from occasionally venting strong feelings privately. We will recall that in 1913 he told Limantour that if someone gave him the cold shoulder, he would respond in kind and then eliminate that person from his thoughts. Though he rarely expressed irritation at the actions of friends and colleagues, he freely wrote Limantour of his displeasure at the self-important manner of Francisco León de la Barra when he came though New York in 1916. Don Emilio later regretted his comments after Limantour chided him for his lack of solidarity with "the good Mexicans." León de la Barra never again entered their correspondence. The appearance of the "Archivo de la reacción" in 1917 troubled Rabasa less than it did Limantour, but the revelations led him to express freely his reflections on the final tumultuous days of the Díaz regime and on Limantour's actions, reflections he purposely eliminated from his books. The appearance of the "Archivo" also prompted him to reveal the "private thought" to his friend concerning his delay in completing *La Constitución y la dictadura*. He also felt free to comment frankly and critically on the draft of Limantour's political memoirs (the "Apuntes") and on many occasions to give him strong advice. In his anonymous articles for the *Revista mexicana,* Rabasa was quick to ridicule the oratorical style of Francisco Bulnes, to satirize the inconstancy of Jesús Urueta, or to expound upon Luis Cabrera's mediocrity. In doing so he seemed to revert to the barbs against fictional characters that infused his novels. He admitted that he was a man of passion, though he usually tried to suppress it.

"Serenity" was Rabasa's watchword. He used the word again and again in his correspondence with Limantour. He justified caution and even disinterestedness toward counterrevolutionary exile schemes because he was thus able to remain serene. He said repeatedly to Limantour that he wanted his *Evolución histórica* to be serene, since only a serene and dispassionate book would acquire certainty, be convincing, and survive. To achieve his goal, he even eliminated the section he had written on the Revolution. His dispassionate stance also allowed him to keep his equanimity in dealing with others. Rabasa was temperamentally able to take William F. Buckley's rashness in stride, even to the point of not turning away from him when he was expelled from the country as an "interventionist." Rabasa's equanimity showed up even more clearly in his numerous efforts to calm Limantour's obsession with defending his honor. He persuaded Limantour not to pursue the legal case against José Barros, not to defend himself against attacks by Manuel Calero or against accusations by Francisco Bulnes, and particularly not to engage in recriminations against his erstwhile friends Rosendo Pineda and the Macedos after the appearance of the "Archivo de la reacción." Rabasa's calm and levelheaded demeanor obviously enhanced his persuasive powers, for example to keep Limantour from circulating or publishing immediately his political memoirs and to rid them of polemics. In fact,

Limantour's "Apuntes" did not appear until thirty years after his death and made no mention of the "famous *archivo*."

One of Emilio Rabasa's principal characteristics was his determination to maintain a low public profile, which contrasted with his actual eminence—as governor, senator, diplomat, jurist, and major intellectual. If it was true, as he told Limantour, that he hated active politics and that he only entered when pushed, it must be said that he rarely passed up a political opportunity, at least until after the Niagara Falls Conference. That experience certainly must have disillusioned him, but it did not keep him from engaging in exile politics, albeit cautiously behind the scenes. He acknowledged once that he was identified as a "sphinx," an enigmatic and perhaps mysterious person. Rabasa's friend and relative, Victoriano Salado Álvarez, writing after Rabasa's death, expressed great admiration for him and referred to "our spiritual bond (*espiritual parentesco*"; but he said he frequently reproached Rabasa for "his zeal for minimizing and hiding himself," for not bringing his wisdom and his thought "to the general public."[4] The example Salado Álvarez used was his failure to write an account of the 1914 Conference (an account that he did actually contemplate writing). Another example of Rabasa's sphinxlike quality was his refusal to identify his "friend from Chicago," a man with whom he was obviously in close touch over several years and whom he even considered as the surrogate author of his "Evolución histórica de México." We will also recall Rabasa's comment to Limantour in 1917, proud of the fact that he destroyed all mail he received (after answering it), so there would be no chance of his correspondence being made public, as happened to that of Pablo Macedo. Above all, it was publicity that he most feared, which led him to even secretive tendencies.

Don Emilio was a reserved and private man who was devoted to his family, a devotion perhaps enhanced by several tragedies and much hardship. He began married life in Oaxaca with the news of the death of both parents from cholera in Chiapas. The tragedy prompted the romantic poem to his wife, Mercedes, that together, "let us fearlessly cross/through this painful vale of tears." However, in 1910, after bearing seven children, Mercedes died. Devastated by the death, Emilio put aside *La Constitución y la dictadura* for a year and a half, completing it only at the urging of his brother Ramón. He took his children to Niagara Falls in 1914 and chose to settle in New York City afterwards, in part because he could stay in closer touch with his one married daughter, Manuela, who had remained in Mexico. When she came to New York in 1915 with her children, there were eleven in the Rabasa household. Though two daughters married in New York in the spring of 1919, tragedy struck once again: the youngest, Ruth, having married two years earlier, died in childbirth in July 1919. Rabasa's response was to take his doubly saddened unmarried daughter, Concepción ("la Magdalena"), with him on his business trip to Europe later that year. Although his letters to Limantour reveal virtually no details of family life in New York, we know from Concepción's reminiscences that he encouraged gatherings of friends and associates, which probably led to the daughters' marriages. The presence of his family in New York certainly buoyed him against depression and gave impetus to his writing, which in a sense was his personal salvation as the years of exile wore on. Their presence also must have helped him face the growing affliction of macular degeneration. On returning to Mexico, his need for intimate companionship and care propelled him into his second marriage in 1925 to María Luisa Massieu. Although much about Don Emilio's family life must be left to our imagination, its important role in his survival is clear.

Emilio Rabasa's survival, however, was far more than a personal matter. He was basically an intellectual who enunciated political and social ideas that continued from the old regime to the new regime, from the era of Porfirio Díaz to the Revolution, and beyond. To study Emilio Rabasa as an intellectual is to study a set of ideas that endured in a period of upheaval and change. Since Rabasa has been celebrated principally as a jurist, as an iconic figure in the world of the law, there has been a strong tendency to separate his strictly juridical thought from his ideas on political and social questions. It has been my premise that this separation is misguided, that to understand Rabasa, the political and the juridical must be examined together. The jurists tend to view Rabasa as the severe analyst and defender of individual rights under the Constitution, as the "consummator" of the juicio de amparo, the crown jewel of Mexico's constitutional system. The historians and sociopolitical analysts, notably Daniel Cosío Villegas, view him as the critic of the democratic Constitution of 1857 who had little faith in the popular (particularly the indigenous) masses, the apologist for Porfirio Díaz, and more generally for the authoritarian presidency. This study has attempted to bring together his juridical and sociopolitical ideas as put forth throughout a multifaceted career, a fascinating and enigmatic career that was replete with ambiguities and even contradictions.

Rabasa's political ideas were based on the transformed liberalism of the late nineteenth century, consisting of scientific politics, derived from positivism, and historical constitutionalism, also of European origin but thoroughly rooted in earlier Mexican history. Both strands of transformed liberalism emerged with the first term of Porfirio Díaz in 1878 (as espoused by the newspaper *La Libertad*) and came together in the program of the National Liberal Union in 1892, followed by the great debate of 1893 over reforms to the Constitution. Those advocating constitutional reform in 1892–93, led by Justo Sierra, were dubbed "científicos," their opponents "jacobinos." Emilio Rabasa and the 1893 Científicos were intellectual soul mates, although Rabasa at the time was serving as governor of Chiapas, where he was attempting to implement scientific politics, in order to modernize his remote state. Scientific politics emphasized strong administration based on science, that is, on empirical study, history and social reality, and directed toward practical economic objectives. Governor Rabasa was also concerned with constitutionalism in 1893 (in fact, he put in place a new constitution for his state), but his dedication to historical constitutionalism really came later, in his two works *El Artículo 14* of 1906 and *La Constitución y la dictadura* of 1912, supplemented by his actions in the Senate of the Republic during these years. Historical constitutionalism, as pursued by Emilio Rabasa, entailed a critique of popular sovereignty (as enunciated in the Constitution of 1857), the adaptation of the Constitution to the political and social realities of the nation, and protection of individual rights through precise juridical procedures, and not by following abstract declarations of equal or natural rights.

Rabasa's juridical thought drew from two legal traditions: the civil law of continental Europe and Latin America and the common law of the United States and England. This was particularly true because Rabasa was a constitutionalist, dedicated to public as opposed to private (civil) law, and because his approach was historical and comparative. This approach to the law was a major strength of Rabasa's thought but it also led to significant ambiguities, especially because his principal concern was the characteristics and problems of the Supreme Court. These ambiguities were apparent in his earlier works, but they came into full view in his juridical masterpiece of 1919, *El Juicio constitucional*. The ambiguities also appeared in occasional speeches and writings of the 1920s. Much of *El Juicio constitucional* was devoted to examination and praise of the North American system of judicial review, its origins in England, and its consolidation under Chief Justice John Marshall. The establishment of an independent supreme court in Mexico, including the North American practice of making judges permanent or irremovable, became Emilio Rabasa's lifelong cause. And yet, as an exile in New York during the years of the U.S. "Lochner Court," when conservative judges routinely struck down Progressive social legislation favoring better wages and hours for working people, Rabasa seemed to return to his civil law roots. He ended *El Juicio constitucional* with "the advantages of the system in Mexico," criticizing in the French mode "legislation by judges" as opposed to "legislation by legislators." On another judicial issue, Rabasa called in 1921 for a court of cassation, also on the French model, to deal with improper application of the law by lower courts in amparo cases involving protection of individual rights. Such a court, he argued, would free up a now overburdened Supreme Court and allow it to become a true third power of government.

The specific influences on Emilio Rabasa's juridical and political works naturally enough came from both Anglo American and French sources. Though his citations were few in number and often poorly identified, definite patterns and authors do emerge. On the Anglo American side, he clearly drew from prepresidential Woodrow Wilson for his discussion of *congresisimo*, or exaggerated parliamentary power in the Constitution of 1857. Through Wilson, Rabasa also turned to the British analyst Walter Bagehot. Of greater significance for Rabasa was James Bryce, the British student of American political institutions, a latter-day Tocqueville. In the judicial and constitutional realm Rabasa drew from leading U.S. scholars, for example Thomas H. Cooley on the pre–Civil War relation between the states and the federal government, and on Thomas G. Haines for later issues and problems involving judicial supremacy. In all probability Rabasa was in touch personally with U.S. legal scholars while in New York (and through his son Oscar who was studying law at the University of Pennsylvania), but unfortunately his correspondence is mute on the subject. Of equal importance for Rabasa were French authors, such as Émile Boutmy on the U.S. courts and Joseph Barthélemy on executive power and the veto, scholars who built upon the foundations laid by the earlier advocates of historical constitutionalism— Montesquieu, Constant, Tocqueville, and Laboulaye. Rabasa's frequent reference to "jacobin" tendencies in Mexico clearly revealed the continuing influence of Hippolyte Taine, so important for the Científicos of 1893. On his return to Mexico, Rabasa emphasized the importance of Edouard Lambert's recently published critique of legislation by judges in the United States. On a given topic, Rabasa occasionally cited both an Anglo American and a French source, yet another indication of his thoroughly comparative approach to law and history.

Emilio Rabasa did not write at length on social questions, though his early novels revealed that he was a keen observer of the society around him. His views were basically elitist and were evident throughout his career, both in his actions as a politician and as an intellectual in several of his works. He occasionally made the distinction between different levels of "the people," between those who were educated and aware of their rights and the unthinking horde that made up many revolutionary armies. His view of the indigenous population of the country was conditioned by his experience in Chiapas. Unlike Justo Sierra, he did not believe that education was the best means for uplifting the Indian; better to institute modern transport, thus freeing the Indian from his role as beast of burden. Most of all he regarded contact with "civilization," in the form of both material improvements and "the superior classes," as the Indian's sure road to progress, a point he illustrated graphically in one of his final articles, "San Bartolo Solistahuacán." He was sharply critical in his *Evolución histórica de México* (1920) of the American reservation system, which kept Indians apart from more civilized inhabitants, and he cited prominent U.S. reformers in support of his critique. Like other Porfirian liberals, he abandoned the earlier Creole concept of nationality and looked to mestisaje (and perhaps to whitening) as central to the positive evolution of society and the future basis of the nation. Moreover, like Justo Sierra, Emilio Rabasa rejected the argument of the influential publicist Gustave Le Bon that racial mixture led to social degeneration.

As governor, Rabasa's agenda for Chiapas was modernization, which meant placing control of the state in the hands of the commercial and agricultural entrepreneurs of the central valley, the social group from which he had come, as opposed to the traditional landholders of the highlands. To do this he moved the capital of the state in 1892 from San Cristóbal to Tuxtla Gutiérrez. Rabasa had a classic liberal attachment to individual property and was hostile to indigenous communal holdings. As governor he launched a policy of division of communal lands. He (and especially his successors) also attempted to "free" indigenous labor from traditional highland peonage, making it more available for coffee production in the lowlands, where labor was scarce, as well as for the plantation economies of the north. Unfortunately, in many cases "freedom" merely led to a new form of social exploitation under a system of contract labor. Rabasa also personally acquired landed property for commercial use in Chiapas, but there is no evidence that he developed it. He later showed little sympathy for Article 27 of the Constitution of 1917 and the revolutionary agrarianism that followed. During the 1920s he defended through the amparo process in the Supreme Court the individual rights of several property holders affected by agrarian legislation. In short, Rabasa was not a democrat in his political or social ideas, even though he did envision in 1912 the coming of a "democratic oligarchy" as the constitutional stage to follow the era of dictatorship; and he even optimistically repeated the idea in 1920.

Emilio Rabasa was not only an enigmatic personality, who shunned public attention (albeit selectively) and feared notoriety, but also a figure whose ideas revealed contradictions. One interesting example can be seen in the difference between his relationship with José Yves

Limantour and with William F. Buckley, Sr., as shown in their private correspondence. Rabasa's close association with Limantour seems consistent throughout. Limantour was one of the Científicos of 1893, even though he was part of the Díaz administration; Rabasa was a fervent admirer of the group and was at least spiritually one of them. Both Rabasa and Limantour were at one in their critique of the last phase of Don Porfirio's "personal government." Limantour expressed great enthusiasm for Rabasa's works, particularly *La Constitución y la dictadura* and *El Juicio constitucional*; Rabasa obviously admired his friend's role as minister of Finance. They could be quite frank with one another, and Rabasa could give firm advice regarding "El Archivo de la reacción" or the "Apuntes," without triggering defensiveness on Limantour's part. Limantour secured a subsidy for *La Evolucion histórica de México,* and Rabasa could turn to Limantour for advice on potential banking and railroad projects in 1919. The two were clearly intimates on an ideological and political level.

Rabasa's close association with Buckley is more difficult to understand. Despite his opposition to the Revolution, Rabasa was a Mexican patriot who had an ambivalent relationship with the United States and its culture. Buckley was a Yankee imperialist, one ultimately expelled from Mexico as a foreign interventionist. Rabasa could develop a professional relationship with Buckley in the early days of the oil boom and recruit him as counsel to the Mexican committee in Niagara Falls, even though Buckley had urged U.S. intervention in 1913. It is difficult to believe that Buckley's interventionist views were totally unknown to Rabasa, despite the fact that his letter to Colonel House urging intervention was private. In 1921, Rabasa, after returning to Mexico and accepting the Revolution as a fait accompli, was able to tolerate Buckley's now open engagement in interventionist activities. Moreover, he could accept financial support from Buckley for the ELD and in return defend before the Supreme Court Buckley's Tampico properties against "illegal" taxation. Are we to understand Rabasa's tolerance of Buckley as a personal matter, as loyalty to a long time associate and friend, despite growing political differences between them? Or does it represent a contradiction within the Porfirian liberalism that Rabasa espoused, a liberalism that could accommodate North American capitalism (and even intervention) within a national political program based on scientific politics and constitutional reform? Or perhaps this association merely reflects the limits of patriotic nationalism in the early twentieth century, especially in the relationship between Mexico and the United States.

Emilio Rabasa's close association with José Yves Limantour and William F. Buckley raises the question of "conservatism." Should Rabasa be identified as a "conservative," rather than as a "liberal" (as we have done in this study)? Rabasa, like Limantour and Buckley, was of course an opponent of the Revolution and in the revolutionary rhetoric of the day labeled a "reactionary," or like many other Mexican antirevolutionaries also a "cientifico" and a "porfirista," an adherent of the old regime of Porfirio Díaz. But more than a porfirista, Rabasa was remembered as a huertista, a supporter and diplomatic representative of Victoriano Huerta, the general responsible in February 1913 for the overthrow of the government of Francisco I. Madero, the "apostle" of the Revolution, and his assassination. Rabasa could thus be identified as an accomplice of "the usurper" and of the crime of "lesé majesté *(lesa patria)*."[5] Moreover, Rabasa was strangely silent regarding the assassination of Madero, as well as that of Senator Belisario Domínguez, a fellow Chiapan. If we also consider the social record of Rabasa's governorship and his subsequent social ideas pertaining to the indigenous population and to property, the label "conservative" might seem quite appropriate. And we could add Rabasa's adherence to the ELD, which was established by professors sympathetic to the old regime, and which during the 1920s included many strong Catholics in its ranks. The problem with the designation "conservative" is that it has been rarely used in Mexican politics, from 1867 to the present.

Following the victory of the Liberal Party under Benito Juarez over the Conservative supporters of the church, the French Intervention, and the Empire of Maximilian, liberalism became thoroughly identified with the restoration of the Republic and the nation itself, conservatism with treason. All those with political ambitions had to be "Liberals." Outside the Church, it was difficult to find self-designated Conservatives. Conservatism in the pre-1867 sense was marginalized, and the Liberal establishment, whether led by Benito Juárez or Porfirio Díaz, reigned supreme. The anticlerical measures of the Reforma were incorporated into the Constitution and foreign monarchy permanently rejected. And yet, as we have seen, the dominant political doctrine of the era after 1878 was scientific politics, to which Rabasa adhered. Its advocates also called scientific politics a "new" or "conservative" liberalism, as opposed to the "old" liberalism, epitomized by the egalitarian features of the Constitution of 1857.[6] Former Conservatives were brought back into the government, and the anticlericalism of the Reforma was muted. Still, the proponents of scientific politics thought of themselves very much as "liberals." In 1903 Francisco Bulnes called for the revitalization of Mexican politics through parties and did suggest that the Científicos might become the new Conservatives. However, *El Imparcial,* the newspaper identified with the Científicos, rejected the suggestion, saying "conservative" implied a return to midcentury, to the reign of the church and foreign empire.[7] Of course, the emphasis on development within scientific politics brought forth a new economic elite, often closely tied to foreign interests and to the advance of private property at the expense of indigenous communal holdings. After 1910 this elite acquired the labels "científico" or "reactionary," but rarely if ever "conservative." Such was the case with Emilio Rabasa.

Finally, we encounter the question of Emilio Rabasa's survival, both as a personal journey during tumultuous times and as the survival of the set of ideas he espoused, Porfirian liberalism. Rabasa's survival as an exile in New York is impressive in itself. As a widower with a large household and plagued by a debilitating eye disease, he managed to return to his writing after dabbling in exile politics and counterrevolutionary schemes. In addition to his contributions to the *Revista mexicana,* he produced two books, a notable history, and a formidable juridical study that drew from his American experience. He also continued his private work as a lawyer, though we know little about it, except for his final effort, in concert with Buckley and Limantour, to advise the AIC in its (ultimately unsuccessful) banking and rail projects. Next was Rabasa's return to Mexico, which he was determined to do for personal and family reasons, and, one senses, out of a desire to solidify his reputation as Mexico's leading constitutional scholar. In doing so, he accepted the Revolution as an accomplished fact; he expressed praise for the flexibility of the interim government of Adolfo de la Huerta, and he had a successful interview with President-elect Álvaro Obregón. Once again in Mexico, he resumed his role as a leader of the ELD, spoke and wrote on judicial subjects, and took up his private legal work. He of course scrupulously avoided politics, maintaining his customary low public profile. Rabasa's survival was due in part to his nature, his ability to accept inevitable change, and to find a way to adapt to it. He had done this with the death of Madero, the rise and fall of Huerta, and his own exile in 1913 and 1914. He did it again in 1920 on his return to Mexico. Adaptation may not be a heroic quality; to be sure, it brought him personal gain. But accepting the inevitable also allowed Emilio Rabasa to continue his major work as a master of the law.

Emilio Rabasa's survival also depended on the flexible and even tolerant nature of the Revolution itself. The Revolution in Mexico City began moderately and remained so until the death of Madero and the coup d'état by Huerta in February 1913. The most severe period for exiles and for others of the Old Regime who remained in Mexico was the era of Venustiano Carranza, particularly from August 1914 to 1916. Several of Rabasa's friends, including Nicanor Gurría Urgell, Miguel Macedo,

and Emilio Pimentel were detained (though only briefly); many properties were taken; and the rhetoric against "reactionaries" and "científicos" reached its highest level. However, as early as November 1916
Rabasa noted that the government had returned the properties of Pedro
Lascurain; and those of Limantour were returned the following year.
Rabasa's holdings (more meager by his account) were given back in early
1920. President-elect Álvaro Obregón was apparently willing to have an
interview with Rabasa on his return, and Rabasa could write Buckley
that the government was no longer despoiling the rich and that the climate was "beneficial for your business." Another indication of the new
tolerance was the sumptuous reburial ceremony in September 1920 for
Joaquín Casasús, a former Científico who had died in New York in 1916.
President Adolfo de la Huerta even personally supplied the coffin.[8] The
new era was clearly one of reconciliation—though there was no tolerance for a foreigner like Buckley who was actively involved with remaining counterrevolutionaries. By the end of the decade, the Party of the
Revolution had been formed and the ground laid for full reconciliation
after 1940. The Revolution became an all-embracing myth, not unlike
the liberal myth of the late nineteenth century.[9] In short, the nature of the
Revolution itself not only facilitated Emilio Rabasa's personal reintegra-
tion after 1920, but it also brought his descendants to high government
posts.[10] In addition, it can be said that the flexibility of the Revolution
also allowed for the survival of his ideas.

On one level, it is evident that the social ideas of Emilio Rabasa did
not survive the Revolution; on another level the matter is not so clear.
Rabasa was hostile to Article 27 of the Constitution of 1917, which developed a social conception of property, gave new legitimacy to communal
holdings (*ejidos*), and limited the subsoil rights of foreign property owners. In fact, he regarded Article 27 as a treatise on property, not worthy
of a constitutional article. Nor did he accept Article 123, an elaborate
code establishing the rights of labor. He declined to discuss these articles in his course on constitutional law at the ELD. However, Rabasa
did make a surprising statement in 1922 in favor of "good socialism,"
as opposed to violent syndicalism. This acknowledgment of the new social liberalism was similar to his seemingly incongruous critique of the
conservative U.S. Supreme Court that stood firm against congressional
labor legislation. Rabasa was aware of the pressure of social change, but
this awareness hardly indicated a conversion. He continued to uphold
private property and individual interests as demonstrated by his legal defense of the doctrine through the juicio de amparo during the 1920s. His
Porfirian attitudes toward the indigenous population, derived from his
Chiapas experience, also stayed firm. Contact with civilization and the

more civilized classes, assimilation, and mestizaje remained for him the Indian's road to progress, a view that had some durability in twentieth-century Mexico. Mestizaje even took on by the 1960s the character of a national social myth, not challenged until the Chiapas rebellion in 1994. Emilio Rabasa was mostly silent in the face of the strong anticlerical current in the Revolution. He seemed to cling to his Porfirian views, as revealed in his novelette "La Guerra de tres años," namely celebration of the Reforma, yet muted anticlericalism in practice, and respect for and adherence to Catholicism. These views are still alive today.

The survival of Emilio Rabasa's political and juridical ideas is less ambiguous. The establishment of strong executive power in the Constitution of 1917 clearly reveals traces of Rabasa's critique of the parliamentary regime of 1857, reinforced by a reaction against the popular revolutionary Convention of 1914–15. These traces informed the constitutional proposals of Felix Palavincini and José Diego Fernández, and found their way into Venustiano Carranza's address to the constitutional congress and ultimately into the Constitution itself. The result was a Porfirian-style presidency that held sway until at least 2000. Moreover, it was a presidency that followed the dictates of scientific politics, or "developmental liberalism," as termed by Alan Knight.[11] Its premises were administration as opposed to political contention, policy based on empirical experience and history instead of on abstractions, and orientation toward practical capitalist economic policies. Rabasa himself was a direct participant in the effort to reinstate scientific politics through his work in 1919 with the AIC. As noted above, Daniel Cosío Villegas has attributed the authoritarian presidency to Rabasa's influence, a presidency that guided what he characterized in the 1940s as the "Neo-Porfiriato."[12] But the Porfirian liberalism that Rabasa espoused also included constitutionalism that would—following the program of the Científicos of 1893—place limits on personal executive authority. This constitutionalism, which Rabasa termed "democratic oligarchy" in 1912 and again in 1920, was based on an independent Supreme Court, to be achieved through irremovable magistrates. Rabasa carried the Científicos' cause into the revolutionary era, and irremovability was partially implemented in Article 94 of the Constitution. In the deliberations of the constituyente, Rabasa and his ideas now became the center of debate, which included polemics from all sides. Judicial independence did not survive the decade of the 1920s; it succumbed to presidential supremacy in 1934 and has only been reinstituted in the reforms of 1994. The future of judicial independence, however, remains in doubt in the present political climate.[13]

Also problematic has been the legacy of Emilio Rabasa's distinctive historical and comparative approach to the law. The impact of the Revolution brought a divergence between critical history and law as scholarly enterprises, in contrast, for example, to the their remarkable convergence in postrevolutionary France a century earlier.[14] In Mexico, the jurists tended toward formalism, became less interested in comparative legal systems, and abandoned critical constitutional history. There were exceptions, for example Felipe Tena Ramirez and particularly Rabasa's son Oscar (who brought his U.S. legal education to Mexico), and later practitioners of comparative law such as Hector Fix Zamudio and Lucio Cabrera. Critical historiography of the national political experience remained weak during the postrevolutionary years, until its revival by Cosío Villegas in the 1940s. Although Cosío admired Rabasa's knowledge of both history and law, he had little sympathy for the juridical scholarship of his day. Curiously enough, the critical history of Mexican constitutionalism in the style of Rabasa, was in a sense perpetuated by Edmundo O'Gorman, even though he departed sharply from Rabasa by rejecting positivism and "scientific" historiography. It is not without significance that O'Gorman was a graduate of the ELD in 1928 and was exposed to Rabasa's interpretation before he abandoned law a decade later.[15] More recently, there are signs of Rabasa's method in the "revisionist" study of the Mexican political system by Luis Medina Peña.[16]

One measure of Rabasa's survival is that his books continue to be reprinted, including his novels. For example, his literary work has drawn the attention of Carlos Monsivais, one of Mexico's leading cultural critics of recent decades. In fact, Monsivais argues that Rabasa missed his true calling by abandoning fiction for renown in law and politics. He was, concludes Monsivais, "a bad interpreter of his own true talent."[17] Nonetheless, Rabasa has continued to be greatly celebrated throughout the Mexican juridical world—despite the ambiguities and contradictions in his thought—especially but not exclusively at the ever-prosperous Escuela Libre de Derecho. In 1945, one ELD graduate, Manuel González Ramírez, called forth Rabasa's liberalism as inspiration, at a time when the doctrine seemed under threat.[18] The generation-long effort by some jurists to have a statue of Emilio Rabasa placed in the Supreme Court building was finally realized in February 2006. One might be tempted to attribute this remarkable event to the decline of the revolutionary establishment and to what a foreign observer might term the "conservative" turn in Mexican politics. Whatever the reason, Emilio Rabasa has perhaps now received his just reward.

Reference Matter

A Castelar

Source: *El Espíritu del siglo. Órgano oficial del Gobierno del Estado Libre y Soberano de Chiapas. Segúnda Época,* 17 Abril 1873, p. 3

A Castelar

Y te habre de cantar! . . . Con torpe acento
Mi labio invocará, genio fecundo,
Tu nombre que ha llenado,
De uno al otro confín, el ancho mundo?
Cantaré de tu voz el poderío,
Tu corazón, tu noble inteligencia,
Que absorto admira el universo entero?
Digno de hacerlo es solo
El que pulse la cítara de Homero. . . .
Mas yo tambien lo haré; porque si falta
Robusta entonación ¡ay! a mi acento,
Entre mi pecho siento
Entusiasmo ardoroso que me exalta,
Entusiasmo ardoroso
Que agita con violencia
Mi corazón que admira
Tu sin igual, gigante inteligencia.

Pasó el siglo fatal que en la ignorancia
Sumido se encontró; pasaron
Los tiempos de la guerra en que tan solo
Ella daba la gloria.
Los nombres de los heroes de la espada
Los guarda entre sus páginas la historia. . . .
El siglo ilustrador, el del talento,

Le sucedió por fin; la inteligencia
Venció y el hombre de la fuerza bruta
Se doblegó ante el hombre de la ciencia

Siempre, siempre en la lucha
La que la fuerza y la raza pelean,
No se puede dudar quien es vencido.
Y los que duden, incesantemente
Dudarán del Señor Omnipotente
Que siempre tiende justo
Su mano bondadosa,
No al que peleando con feroz encono
Mas fortaleza tenga, si al que airado
La justicia, al pelear, lleve en su abono.

Mirad, sino, en la España
Que bajo yugo de opresór extraña
Algún tiempo llevó su cuello atado,
Como al impulso de una voz potente
Su cuello irguió como en pasados tiempos.
Mirad que la palabra
Bastó de un hombre á contrastar la fuerza
Del que rey se llamó a un pueblo bravo
Que ama la libertad y no es esclavo

Mirad á Castelar! Ved al gigante
Que dió la libertad al pueblo Ibero
Y levantó altanero
Su frente ante el monarca que arrogante
Quizo domar á un pueblo todo entero.
Mirad a Castelar; su nombre augusto
Grabado está en los pechos
Que amen la libertad; y su memoria
Jamas borrará del pecho mío
Con acento robusto
Solamente cantara
La inmensa Gloria de tu nombre augusto
Pero ¡mísero yo! ¿Qué con mi acento
Te pudiera ofrecer? Solo profunda,
Inmensa admiración que tu talento
Inspira al corazón que bien comprende
Esa infinita gloria
Que alcanzaste dichoso
Al alcanzar tu espléndida victoria.

Marzo 29 de 1873—J. Emilio Rabasa

To Castelar

How shall I, with uncouth accent, sing your praise
How can my lips invoke, oh prolific genius,

Your name that has filled
The wide world, from one end to the other?
How can I praise the power of your voice,
Your heart, your noble intelligence,
The whole universe so intently admires?
Only he who plucks Homer's lyre. . .
Is worthy of the task
But I will do it too; because
If my voice lacks a robust note,
Woe to my accent!
In my breast I feel a fervent enthusiasm
That exalts me,
A fervent enthusiasm that violently stirs
My heart that admires
Your vast and peerless intelligence.

The terrible century immersed in ignorance
Passed; Passed the times of war when only
War provided glory.
The names of the heroes of the sword
Are preserved in the pages of history. . .
The century of enlightenment, of talent,
Finally followed; intelligence
Triumphed and the man of brute force
Knelt before the man of science.

Always, always in the struggle
Between force and the human race
There can be no doubt which is vanquished.
And those who persist in doubting,
Will doubt the all-powerful Lord,
Who always extends his just and benevolent hand
Not to the one who, battling with fierce rancor,
May be the stronger,
 But to the one fighting with justice on his side

But look upon Spain
Which yoked by alien oppression
Long had its neck in shackles,
Yet prompted by a powerful voice
Lifted its head as in times past.
Consider the word
Of a man whose work was enough
To match the strength
Of one who called himself monarch,
Of a valiant people
That loves liberty and will not be enslaved

Look upon Castelar! Regard the giant

Who freed the Iberian people
And raised his head in pride
Before the arrogant monarch
Who sought to subjugate them.
Look upon Castelar; his illustrious name
Is engraved on the breast of those that love liberty
And his memory will never be erased
From my breast
The immense glory of your illustrious name
Should only be sung in a strong voice
But poor me! What could I hope to offer you
With my uncouth accent? Only the deep,
Immense admiration that your talent inspires
In my heart that knows too well
That infinite glory
Which you happily achieved
With your splendid triumph.

Emilio Rabasa's Immediate Family

Emilio Rabasa Estebanell (22 May 1856–25 April 1930)
  m. Mercedes Llanes Santaella (11 September, 1882–2 May 1910)
  m. María Luisa Massieu, 1924

CHILDREN

Manuela Rabasa de Barranco (1885–1976)
  m. Dr. Antonio Barranco
Mercedes Rabasa de Villafranca (1888?–May 22, 1922)
  m. Leland de Villafranca 1919
Isabel Rabasa de la Torre (b.1891?– ?)
  m. Agustín de la Torre 1919
Concepción Rabasa Villafranca (1893–1977)
  m. Leland de Villafranca, 1924 (after death of Mercedes)
Emilio Rabasa Llanes (1894?–1969)
Oscar Rabasa Llanes (1896–1978)
  m. Lilian Mishkin 1919
Ruth Rabasa de Escandón (1898–July 26, 1919)
  m. Antonio Escandón 1917

Notes

CHAPTER ONE

1. On the original Científicos, see above, p. 10. Defined variously, the group will figure prominently in this study.

2. Cosío Villegas, *Constitución de 1857*.

3. See Díaz y Díaz, "Rabasa y Molina Enríquez."

4. Cosío Villegas, *Constitución de 1857*, p. 64.

5. *La Libertad*, 4 January 1879.

6. It should be noted that I use *ideological* to connote political ideas that are directed in defense of or in opposition to an institutional or social order, suggesting a situation of conflict. "Ideological consensus" indicates the absence of a basic conflict of political ideas (e.g., of liberalism versus conservatism), which was the case in Mexico from 1867 to at least 1900. Anyone with political aspirations during that era necessarily had to be a "liberal." See further, my *Transformation of liberalism*, pp. 18–19; also my "Reconstruction of Nineteenth-Century Politics," pp. 62–63.

7. For further discussion of these three episodes, see my "The Revival of Political History"; also my *Mexican Liberalism* and *Transformation of Liberalism*.

8. Constant, "Principes de politique," p. 146.

9. Tocqueville, *Démocratie en Amérique*, Vol. 1, pt. 1, 97. (English ed. [1954]), 1: 100.

10. Mora, "Discurso. La Suprema Autoridad civil no es ilimitada" (1822), *Obras sueltas*, p. 473.

11. The "Convocatoria para la elección de los supremos poderes" and Lerdo's "Circular de la ley de convocatoria" (both dated 14 August 1867) can be found in Dublán and Lozano, *Legislación*, 10: 44–56.

12. Laboulaye, *Historia de los Estados Unidos*, 2 vols. (1870); "Dictamen de la comisión de puntos constitucionales" (1869), in Tamayo, ed., *Benito Juárez*, 14: 403–39.

13. Laboulaye, preface (dated 15 July 1855) to vol. 1 of *Histoire des États-Unis*, pp. ii–xiii. Vol. 1 was first published in 1855, vols. 2 and 3 in 1866.

14. Tamayo, *Benito Juárez*, 14: 419–20 (quoted from Laboulaye, *Histoire*, 3: 375–76; also 426).

15. Laboulaye, "avertissement" to Montesquieu, *Oeuvres complètes,* 7 vols. (1875).

16. Idem, *L'état et ses limites* (1863), p. 96. See also Ruggiero, *European Liberalism,* pp. 197–99. On Savigny, see Kantorowicz, "Savigny." Laboulaye's essay on Savigny (1842) can be found in *Études contemporaines,* pp. 239–310. In English (1831): reprint ed. (1975). The first recognition of Savigny in France may have been by Jean Louis Eugéne Lerminier, who in his *Introduction générale à l'histoire du droit* (1829), vi, testified to the impact Savigny's manifesto of 1814 (*On the Vocation of Our Age for Legislation and Jurisprudence*) made on him as a law student forced to "learn the meager and dry formulas without animation or life" of the French Civil Code. Savigny, he said, made him realize the difference between *loi* and *droit*. On this general topic, see the illuminating study by Kelley, *Historians and the Law.*

17. Laboulaye, preface to Constant, *Cours.*

18. *El Universal,* 22 November 1893.

19. Constant, "Principes de politique," pp. 154–55; Laboulaye, introd. (1861) to ibid.; Laboulaye, *Histoire,* 3: 490–98, passages from which Sierra probably drew his historical argument in the debate of 1893.

20. Bulnes, speech of 12 December 1893, *DDCD,* 16th legis., 3: 495.

CHAPTER 2

1. Serra Rojas, 1: 34. Serra Rojas is the best general source for Rabasa's family background and and early life. See also Glass, *México en las obras de Emilio Rabasa.* Emilio's father was born in the coastal town of Rabasada, near Barcelona.

2. "A Ynés" (date unknown) in Rabasa, *La Guerra de tres años* (1955 ed.), pp. 87–103. Cited passage, stanza xvi, p. 95.

3. "A Castelar" (65 lines) was published in *El Espíritu del Siglo* (San Cristóbal, Chiapas), 17 April 1873, but has never been reprinted in a modern publication. For the entire poem, see Appendix A. Castelar was a major figure in the establishment of the First Spanish Republic in February 1873. He served as president from September 1873 until its demise in January 1874. On Castelar's influence, see my "Castelar and Mexico." The poem was signed "J. Emilio Rabasa." The name "José" appeared on his baptismal certificate, a copy of which is in Ruiz Abreu, *Emilio Rabasa Estebanell,* p. 23. There is no evidence that he used "José" beyond his youth.

4. On Rosendo Pineda and his ties with Rabasa and Pimentel, see Salmerón Castro, "Política y redes sociales." On positivism in Oaxaca see Lempérière, "Formación de las élites liberales," p. 78. On positivism in the Escuela Nacional Preparatoria, see my *Transformation of Liberalism,* chaps. 5–6.

5. Rabasa, *Amparo* (1880). The amparo can also be found in Vallarta, *Obras completas,* 1a. ser. (*Cuestiones Constitucionales. Votos*), 2: 282–99.

6. Serra Rojas, 1: 47.

7. O. Rabasa, "Breves apuntes," quoted in Serra Rojas, 1: 50.

8. The poem can be found in ibid., pp. 55–66.

9. The "Discurso" can be found in ibid., pp. 77–82.

10. Castillo was married to Rabasa's half-sister, Manuela Acebo Estebanell.

11. Rabasa, "La Prisión preventiva" (1889).

12. Rabasa, *Luis Huller* (1889). On Huller, a German-American land specu-lator, apart from his employment by the English company, see García de León, *Resistencia y utopía*, 1: 173–74.

13. Rabasa, "El Arbitrio judicial" (1889); "El Caso Estrella" (1890), pp. 36–40. It should be noted that Rabasa also wrote an "Opinion" dated 12 November 1894 in support of "La Difamación y las personas morales," a judicial case published by Victor M. Castillo.

14. Bernardo Reyes to Emilio Rabasa, 24 February 1891, Archivo Bernardo Reyes (BR).

15. Rabasa, "La Enseñanza de la historia" (1889).

16. Rabasa, *Musa oaxaqueña* (1886), p. ii.

17. Pio Gil, pseud., "La Inundación" (1888) *El Universal*, 22 July 1888, in Serra Rojas, 1: 131–35.

18. Pio Gil, pseud., "Los Tercetos del Señor Sierra" (1888).

19. Pio Gil, pseud., "Otra Vez ' *Miau* '" (1888).

20. Pio Gil, pseud., "Copias simples de documentos vivos. Juan B. Pérez" (1888?).

21. Pio Gil, pseud., "La Cosa juzgada" (1888).

22. González Peña, "Rabasa" (1930), p. 131.

23. Pola, "En Casa de la Celebridades" (1888).

24. Rabasa, *La Bola y la Gran Ciencia; El Cuarto Poder y Moneda falsa* (1948). 1st ed. 1887–88.

25. Salado Álvarez, introd. to Rabasa, *La Guerra de tres años* (1931), p. 11 (the 1st ed. in book form of the novelette).

26. Rabasa, *Guerra* (1955 ed.), p. 83.

27. See Ramos, "Emilio Rabasa."

28. Federico Gamboa, author of the famous *Santa* (1903), wrote that Ra-basa's novels gave him "the solution that I needed to hazard my attempts": *Im-presiones y recuerdos*, new ed. (1922), p. 163. 1st ed. 1893. See also Idem, *Mi Diario*, 1st series., 2 (1910): 238 (entry for 1899). It should be noted that Rabasa won membership in the Academia Mexicana de la Lengua, in recognition for his literary works.

29. Carballo, "prologo," Rabasa, *Guerra* (1995 ed.), pp. 9–10.

30. Rabasa, *Gran ciencia*, p. 308.

31. *El Universal*, 18 July 1888. For Castillo see above, n. 10; Rabasa's brother Ramón was married to an Esponda.

32. Carlos Díaz Dufoo maintained that it was the general view at the time that Rabasa was destined to become Minister of Justice, replacing Joaquín Baranda (which of course never happened). Baranda remained in the post till 1901. See Díaz Dufoo, "Último Pensamiento de Emilio Rabasa" (1930), in Serra Rojas, 2: 319.

33. Benjamin, *Rich Land* (1989, 1996), p. 37. The 1996 edition added a foreword by Lorenzo Meyer and a revised and expanded epilogue by the author. Otherwise the text and pagination of the two editions are the same.

34. Quoted in ibid., p. 24.

35. For a clear discussion of the ties between Chiapas and Guatemala in the nineteenth century, see Lewis, *Ambivalent Revolution,* chap. 1.

36. Rabasa, *Constitución y la dictadura,* p. 243.

37. Wasserstrom, *Class and Society in Central Chiapas,* p. 156; Rus, "Coffee and Recolonization," p. 273; García de León, *Resistencia y utopía,* 2: 16.

38. Benjamin, *Rich Land,* pp. 1–34.

39. Rabasa to Díaz, 28 March, 4 April, 23 August 1892 (transcriptions and notes by T. Benjamin from Archivo Porfirio Díaz [PD]).

40. Benjamin refers to the 1911 conflict over the site of the capital as the "last [regional] conflict of the nineteenth century": *Rich Land,* p. 118. The continuing deep antagonism toward Rabasa is exemplified in a retrospective statement by Rosauro de J. Trejo, dated 8 August 1937, entitled "Causas del odio." This *cristobalense* resentment of Rabasa and the *rabasato* persisted at least into the 1970s, according to Jan Rus from interviews he carried out (personal communication).

41. *Discurso* (1892), Serra Rojas, 1: 194.

42. Rabasa to Díaz, 14 October 1893. PD. On the situation in Soconusco, see Spenser, "Soconusco," pp. 131–32.

43. Benjamin, *Rich Land,* p. 283, n. 37.

44. Espinosa, ed., *Chiapas* (1925), quoted in Benjamin, *Rich Land,* p. 45.

45. The 1858 Constitution can be found in *Colección que comprende la constitución general de la república* (1884), 1: 136–93, that of 1893 (which went into effect 1 January 1894) in Serra Rojas, 1: 165–78. See also Clagett, *Guide,* pp. 20–26.

46. The phrase is from Niceto Alcalá Zamora, *Impresión general de las Leyes de Indias* (Buenos Aires, 1942), p. 21, quoted in Haring, *Spanish Empire,* p. 111.

47. Benjamin, *Rich Land,* pp. 36–38.

48. Rabasa, "San Bartolo Solistahuacán" (1929). See further details in Chapter 6.

49. Ramon Rabasa, *Estado de Chiapas* (1895).

50. Rabasa to Reyes, 17 November 1892; Reyes to Rabasa, 12 December 1892. BR.

51. Benjamin, *Rich Land,* p. 50; Rabasa, *Discurso* (1893), in Serra Rojas, 1: 183–84. *El Universal* was a consistent supporter of Rabasa's governorship. See 19 November 1893: "El Gobierno de Chiapas cumple."

52. Rabasa, *Discurso* (1892), Serra Rojas , 1: 198.

53. Rus, "Whose Caste War?" pp. 43–77; also Vos, *Vivir en frontera,* pp. 157–90. On indigenous *baldíos,* see Rus, "Caste War," p. 47.

54. Rabasa, *Discurso* (1893), Serra Rojas, 1: 181. *El Universal* (28 December 1893) responded sharply to the Catholic *El Tiempo*'s critique of Rabasa's speech, defending Rabasa's dismissal of the continuing existence of a "caste war."

55. On the land survey process and results, see Holden, *Mexico and the Survey of Public Lands.*

56. Rabasa, *Discurso* (1893), Serra Rojas, 1: 186. The decrees can be found in ibid., pp. 200–01, 202, 211–15, 216–18. The key decree was "Reglamento para la división y reparto de ejidos" (11 August 1893), pp. 211–15.

57. On the national initiatives of 1893 and the decree of 1894, see my *Transformation of Liberalism*, p. 237.

58. Rabasa, *Evolución histórica*, p. 237.

59. Benjamin, *Rich Land*, p. 49.

60. See Washbrook, "Exports, Ethnicity, and Labour Markets"; also García de León, *Resistencia y utopía*, 1: 184.

61. Rus, "Coffee and Recolonization." Rus even argues that Governor Rabasa's modernization program, guided closely from Mexico City, was designed in large part to promote the interests of coffee.

62. Benjamin, *Rich Land*, p. 60.

63. Rus, "Coffee and Recolonization," pp. 279–82.

64. See Washbrook, "Indígenas, exportación y enganche," and for greater detail, idem., "Exports, Ethnicity, and Labour Markets."

65. Rabasa to Díaz, 2 March 1892. PD.

66. Byam, *A Sketch of the State of Chiapas,* (1897). Byam dedicated his book to the "Honorable Emilio Rabasa, illustrious as citizen, governor, senator and statesman." He also credited Rabasa with selecting many of the views for the profuse illustrations throughout the book. Though the book covered all the districts of Chiapas, the emphasis was on Palenque. Byam advertised himself and his partner F. E. Parsons as "Mexican mine and land brokers and managers of the Palenke Coffee Land Company."

67. On Rabasa's involvement in speculation in the "rubber belt," see Vos, *Oro verde*, pp. 141–43 and "Los Linderos sudorientales" pp. 113–15.

68. Reported in *El Democrata,* 10 March 1895. José Mora was mentioned as representing the State of Chiapas.

69. Rabasa's first request to leave was in a letter to Díaz, 4 April 1892. PD.

70. Rabasa had also suggested Moguel as a replacement in 1892. Díaz's positive response to Rabasa came on 25 January 1894. Moguel announced his accession to office to Díaz on 28 February 1894. PD. Rabasa's brother Manuel was married to a sister of Fausto Moguel.

71. Rabasa, *Discurso* (1892), in Serra Rojas, 1: 189.

72. Benjamin, *Rich Land*, pp. 33–34.

CHAPTER 3

1. Leonardo Pasquel, "Biografía."

2. Macías, *Alegato* (1899). José N. Macías was a future founding professor of the Escuela Libre de Derecho in 1912 and author of Venustiano Carranza's draft constitution in 1916. See Chapter 7.

3. Rabasa, *Fallo* (1903).

4. Rabasa, *Laudo arbitral* (1906).

5. For further discussion of the extensive debates prior to reestablishment of the Senate, see Luna Argudín, *El Congreso y la política mexicana,* chap. 2.

For the important influence of the French theorist Edouard de Laboulaye on the Senate project, see current Chapter 1, also my *Transformation of Liberalism,* pp. 80–83. The "disappearance" clause can be found in the "Adiciones y reformas" of 13 November 1874, Article 72, III, B, clause V: Tena Ramírez, *Leyes fundamentales,* p. 703.

6. See Luna Argudín, *Congreso y la política,* chaps 3–4.

7. Ibid., pp. 495–98.

8. Luna Argudín, personal communication.

9. *DDCS,* 20th legis. 3rd periodo, p. 16 (16 September 1901). Another typical response came in the 21st legis., 2nd periodo, p. 17 (16 September 1903): "It is not fresh news, as it was previously, to know that peace and order continue to guarantee the security that society has the right to expect from governments, but that information will always be a pleasure to receive." The full response was ten pages.

10. The Pineda and the Casasús contracts can be found in ibid., 19th legis., 4th periodo, pp. 401–06 (24 May 1899) and p. 355 (16 May 1899), respectively; the Pearson contracts in ibid., 3rd periodo, p. 201 (11 December 1899) and in ibid., 21st legislatura, 4th periodo, p. 373 (May 1904). For further information on Pearson's contracts, see Paul Garner, "Politics of National Development"; also Connolly's highly detailed *Contratista de Don Porfirio.* On Pearson and Rabasa, see current Chapter 5.

11. Rabasa was also chair of the Colonization Committee, which authorized the executive to make a grant of "unoccupied land" (*terrenos baldíos*) to Benito Gómez Farías, justified by his father Valentín's great patriotic services. The grant had been originally authorized in 1861, but never actually made. See *DDCS,* 18th legis., 2d periodo (25 May 1897).

12. Rabasa, *Artículo 14,* p. 2.

13. Oscar Rabasa, "Breves apuntes," p. 4, quoted in Serra Rojas, 1: 249–50.

14. The text of the three articles from the Proyecto de Constitución is as follows: Art. 4. "No retroactive or ex post facto law can be issued nor one that changes the nature of contracts."

> Art. 21. "No one can be deprived of his properties or rights, nor be banished, exiled or imprisoned, except by judicial sentence, delivered according to form and under conditions established by the laws of the country."
> Art. 26. "No one can be deprived of life, liberty, or property, except by a sentence delivered by the appropriate authority and according to the forms expressly fixed by law and exactly applied to the case."

15. Rabasa, *Artículo 14,* pp. 3–18. The 1843 article reads as follows: "No one can be judged or sentenced in a civil or criminal suit except by judges of his own order (*fuero*), and by laws issued and tribunals established prior to the relevant fact or the crime."

16. Rabasa, *Bola,* pp. 167–68.

17. Rabasa, *Artículo 14,* pp. 69–70, 86–87.

18. Ibid., p. 20

19. Ibid., p. 70.

20. Lozano's major work was *Tratado de los derechos del hombre* (1876). Rabasa said that Vallarta followed Lozano's interpretation of Article 1 as Chief Justice of the Supreme Court: *Artículo 14*, p. 33.

21. Ibid., p. 25.

22. Rabasa's reference to the U.S. Constitution is in ibid., p. 56.

23. Ibid., p. 71. On Vallarta's interpretation, see *Cuestiones constitucionales, Votos*, which Rabasa cites (*Artículo 14*, p. 74). On the "the metaphysics of law," Rabasa (ibid., p. 73) said Vallarta referred to "Ahrens." Heinrich Ahrens was a German popularizer of the abstruse philosophy of K.C.F. Krause (see my *Transformation of Liberalism*, p. 174). For Rabasa's critique of Lozano's interpretation of Article 14 (and at the same time his general admiration for Lozano's treatise), see *Artículo 14*, pp. 32–33.

24. Ibid., pp. 45–50.

25. On Vallarta's juridical thought, which emphasizes his positivist orientation and his later influence, see Lira González, "Derechos del hombre y garantías individuales." See also James, "Law and Revolution," chap. 2.

26. Rabasa, *Artículo 14*, pp. 85–87. Rabasa's italics. The text of the two articles are:

> Artículo 101. The tribunals of the federaion will resolve all controversies that are caused:
>
> I. By laws or acts from any authority that violate individual guarantees.
> II. By laws or acts of federal authorities that violate or restrict the sovereignty of the states.
> III. By laws of the authorities of the states, which encroach on the sphere of federal authority.
>
> Artículo 102. All trials referred to in the previous article shall be carried out, by petition of the injured party, according to proper judicial procedures and forms, as determined by law. The sentence shall always be such that it only pertains to particular individuals, being limited to guarding and protecting them (a protejerlos y ampararlos) in the particular case dealt with by the trial, without making any general declaration with respect to the law or the act on which the complaint is based.

27. Rabasa, *Artículo 14*, p. 12.

28. For further discussion of cassation, and Rabasa's attempt to incorporate it formally into the Mexican system, see current Chapter 7, pp. 24 ff.

29. Ibid., pp. 103–10. The chapter in question is entitled "La Imposible Tarea de la corte."

30. Ibid., p. 113.

31. Ibid., p. 120.

32. Rabasa footnoted (p. 121) the first sentence from Bryce, American Commonwealth, probably the 3d ed. (1893), 2: 538. He did not footnote the second long paragraph (Artículo 14, pp. 121–22), which came from American Commonwealth, 1: 340–41.

33. Rabasa, *Artículo 14*, p. 123.

34. Ibid., p. 126, statement put in italics by Rabasa for emphasis. He was referring to the phrase from the 5th amendment to the U.S. Constitution: "nor shall any person . . . be deprived of liberty, or property, without due process of law."

35. The proposed amendment, to be added to Article 102 (see note, n. 26), was as follows: "When the controversy is caused by a violation of individual guarantees in judicial civil cases, it can only be brought before the Federal Tribunals after the sentence that ends the litigation has been delivered and against which no appeal whose effect could lead to revocation is provided by law."

36. Rabasa's speech (24th legis., 13 June 1908) can be found in Serra Rojas 1: 309–23. The amendment to Article 102 was made official on 12 November 1908. For further discussion of the juridical context of the 1908 amendment, see James, "Law and Revolution," chap. 2.

37. Cosío Villegas, *Constitución de 1857*, p. 67.

38. Rabasa to Limantour, 4 August 1917. Archivo Jose Yves Limantour (JYL). Rabasa waited a month before deciding to send the letter (from New York to Paris) for fear it would get lost or fall into the wrong hands. He also said he had first intended to reserve the "private fact," which included a discussion of his encounter with Díaz in 1911, until he met personally with Limantour (see Chapter 6). Limantour sent a note of condolence to Rabasa (4 May 1910) on the death of Mercedes Llanes de Rabasa. JYL.

39. See Rabasa to Limantour, 3, 6 April 1911; Limantour to Rabasa, 5, 7 April 1911. JYL.

40. Cosío Villegas, *Constitución de 1857*, p. 67. The interview with Porfirio Díaz was published as "President Díaz: Hero of the Americas" (1908). A Spanish version appeared in *El Imparcial,* beginning on 3 March 1908. An English facsimile, plus a new Spanish translation, appeared as Entrevista Díaz-Creelman (1963). On the Creelman interview and its aftermath see Stanley R. Ross, *Francisco I. Madero,* pp. 46 ff.

41. Moheno, *¿Hacia Donde Vamos?* (1908). On Moheno see Pablo Piccato, *Congreso y revolución,* pp. 57–67. It should be noted that Rabasa did, however, devote a chapter to "La Conferencia Creelman y sus consecuencias" in his *Evolución histórica* (1920), pp. 151–68.

42. Rabasa to Limantour, 3 April 1911. From the subsequent exchange of notes (5, 6, 7 April), it is evident that they did meet (in Limantour's office in the Palacio Nacional), but we have no record of their conversations. JYL.

43. Rabasa, *Constitución y la dictadura,* p. 8.

44. Ibid., p. 145.

45. Ibid., p. 66.

46. Le Bon, *Les Lois psychologiques* (1894). Examples of Le Bonian intellectuals were Carlos Bunge of Argentina, Francisco García Calderón of Peru, and Alcides Arguedas of Bolivia. See my "Political and Social Ideas in Latin America," pp. 399–402. Rabasa did not actually quote Le Bon in *Constitución y la dictadura* here, but he did on p. 96 and in later works.

47. Ibid., pp. 29, 78–80.

48. Ibid., pp 34–35, 68–69.

49. Ibid., p. 242. Though positivist theories were of course present in Europe before 1857, their appearance in Mexico probably dates from the 1860s. See my *Transformation of liberalism,* pp. 140–41.

50. Rabasa, *Constitución y la dictadura,* pp. 4–5. It seems clear that Rabasa favored the last definition, which also coincided with the second, those capable of exercising political rights.

51. Ibid., p. 242.

52. Ibid., pp. 62, 65, 171–72.

53. Taine, "Psychologie du Jacobin," (1881).

54. Rabasa was less influenced by Tainean psychology than was Francisco Bulnes, who according to Federico Gamboa, imagined himself the Mexican Taine. See Gamboa, "prologo" (1920) to Bulnes, *Grandes Problemas* (1926).

55. This second section of *Constitución y la dictadura* is entitled "La Dictadura en las instituciones," the first, "La Dictadura en la historia." The entire epigraph Rabasa quotes is: "Political philosophy must analyze political history; it must distinguish what is due to the excellence of the people, and what to the excellence of the laws; it must carefully calculate the exact effect of each part of the constitution, though thus it may destroy many an idol of the multitude." Rabasa probably took Bagehot's epigraph from Woodrow Wilson, *Congressional Government* (1885). Wilson inserted it at the beginning of his "Conclusion" (p. 294). On Bagehot, see the introductory essay by Alonso Lujambio and Jaime Martínez Bowness to Bagehot's *Constitución inglesa.* 1st English ed. 1867.

56. Rabasa, *Constitución y la dictadura,* chap. x (pp. 117–37). Rabasa refers to and quotes Bryce, on pp. 122–24 (*American Commonwealth,* 2: 177), and Joseph Barthélemy on pp. 134–35: *Role du pouvoir exécutif* (1906), p. 204.

57. On Wilson's work and his influence on Rabasa, see Lujambio, introd. to Wilson, *Gobierno congresional.*

58. Rabasa, *Constitución y la dictadura,* pp. 156–61. The Tenure of Office Act was finally rescinded in 1886. Rabasa cites Bryce, *American Commonwealth,* 2: 140 on p. 159, and quotes him on p. 160.

59. Rabasa, *Constitución y la dictadura,* p. 177, quoting from Barthélemy, *Role du pouvoir exécutif,* p. 107; also on p. 175 (Barthélemy, *Role,* p. 118 [sic], actually p. 113). Barthélemy was a major constitutional theorist and later deputy, who became disillusioned with parliamentarianism; with the fall of France he joined the Vichy government of Marshall Petain in January 1941 as Minister of Justice. Though an adherent of Vichy's authoritarian "National Revolution," he returned to liberal constitutionalism in 1944. On Barthélemy, see Saulnier, *Joseph Barthélemy.*

60. Rabasa, *Constitución y la dictadura,* p. 67.

61. Ibid., p. 90.

62. Ibid., p. 95.

63. Ibid., pp. 91–92, 96. Rabasa does not identify the quoted phrase from Le Bon, which comes from *Lois psychologiques,* p. 146. On Le Bon, see above, p. 16.

64. Rabasa, *Constitución y la dictadura,* pp. 28, 97–99, 102, 242.

65. Ibid., pp. 109–12.

66. Ibid., p. 243.

67. Ibid., 243–44. For the French analogy, Rabasa cited Madelin, *La Revolutión* (1911), chap. 1, but Madelin makes no reference to Taine.

68. For the presidential veto, see above p. 20; for restricted suffrage, Rabasa, *Constitución y la dictadura*, p. 191; for judicial independence, see chaps xiv–xv, on the Supreme Court, its relationship to the executive, the legislature, and the states. We will treat this subject at length in Chapter 7.

69. Ibid., pp. 245–46, also p. 114.

70. Limantour to Rabasa, 5 July, 31 August, 1 November 1912; Rabasa to Limantour, 22 November 1912. JYL.

CHAPTER 4

1. The remarkably brief treaty, besides calling for an end to hostilities, also provided for Francisco León de la Barra (minister of Foreign Relations) to act as interim president and to call general elections. For the confusing events leading to the fall of Ciudad Juárez and the subsequent treaty, see Ross, *Francisco I. Madero*, pp. 150–73 and Knight, *Mexican Revolution*, 1: 201–04. For the text of the treaty, see Isidro Fabela, ed., *Documentos históricos* , 1: 400–01.

2. In a letter to Limantour (9 March 1918), to be discussed in Chapter 5 in more detail, Rabasa wrote: "between Rosendo [Pineda] and me there has been a true and very cordial friendship since childhood"; and of Miguel Macedo he said, "my friendship with him became close by 1902 and has continued closer each day." JYL. On the Convention of 1903, see my *Transformation of Liberalism*, pp. 130–38.

3. See [Cabrera], *Obras políticas*, p. 7 ("Prefacio" 1921 to reprinted articles of 1909.)

4. All letters are part of the "Archivo de la reacción" (AR), published in *El Universal*, September and October 1917: Miguel to Pablo Macedo, 5 July, 2 August, 9 October 1911 (*El Universal*, 29 September 1917, 9 October 1917); Rosendo Pineda to Pablo Macedo, 24 August 1911 (28 September 1917); Roberto Nuñez to Pablo Macedo, 3 September 1911 (6 October 1917). I am indebted to Alicia Salmerón, who passed on to me her transcriptions of the "Archivo" letters.

5. Ramón Corral mentioned in passing "Rabasa's precious book [i.e., *Constitución y la dictadura*] de Rabasa" to Pablo Macedo, 22 June 1912, ibid., 16 October 1917. The letters contained some omitted sections, marked by ellipses in the *El Universal* publication. It is possible that Rabasa was mentioned in those sections. Salmerón is of this opinion. However, if he was mentioned further, it was probably only incidentally. The letters referred to and commented on many people—friends, associates, and prorevolutionary enemies.

6. In relation to the states, the Treaty of Ciudad Juárez stated merely that as of today (21 April 1911) hostilities between the forces of Díaz and the Revolution shall cease, and "they must be discharged so that each state may take the necessary steps to reestablish and guarantee tranquility and political order."

7. For the confusing set of events in Chiapas between May and November 1911, see Benjamin, *Rich Land,* pp. 99–112.

8. *DDCS,* 25th legis., 3 (5 October 1911): 104–06. The committee characterized the Chamulas as "a small ethnic island, till now impenetrable by civilization," like sun worshippers, who were indifferent to all politics except the autonomy of their *municipio.*

9. Ibid., 6 October 1911 (Serra Rojas, 1: 339–61).

10. Benjamin, *Rich Land,* p. 118. The "sons of Tuxtla" cut off the ears of the Chamula prisoners as a warning against further indigenous rebellion.

11. See Rabasa, "Las Cuestiones de límites entre los estados" (2 February 1911), in Serra Rojas 1: 226–46 (only the portion dealing with Chiapas and Tabasco was reprinted). On the personal interests of Rabasa and Valenzuela, see Washbrook, "Exports, Ethnicity, and Labour Markets," p. 232 and García de León, *Resistencia y utopia,* 2: 15–16.

12. Garciadiego, *Rudos contra científicos,* p. 173.

13. For the Senate session on Puebla, see Serra Rojas, 1: 373–79, on Tlaxcala, pp. 373–95, including a technical discourse by Rabasa on the powers of the Diputación (or Comisión) Permanente, and an interpretation of Article 116 of the Constitution (intervention by the federal government in the states in the case of internal conflict.)

14. *DDCS,* 25th legis, 1: 423–426.

15. Excerpts from Díaz's address can be found in *Papers Relating to Foreign Relations of the United States, 1911* (1918), pp. 445–47.

16. *DDCS,* 25th legis., 1 (8 May 1911): 430–32.

17. Ibid., pp. 441–42.

18. *DDCS,* 3: 133–38. The initiative appeared again on pp. 203–08 (26 October 1911); also in Serra Rojas, 1: 361–67. The authors said they purposely omitted Article 92, election of Supreme Court officials, from the initiative because it was the subject of a separate *dictamen* in the Chamber of Deputies. However, that dictamen did not prosper. We will deal further with the Supreme Court in Chapter 7.

19. Rabasa, *Constitución y la dictadura,* p. 137. In this chapter, Rabasa made his only direct reference in the book to the revolutionary overthrow of Díaz (p. 133).

20. *DDCS,* 25th legis., 3, 200–02. The discussion came on 10 November 1911 (pp. 248–63).

21. Ibid., p. 259.

22. Ibid., p. 262.

23. *DDCS,* 25th legis., 4, 780–82, 788 (15, 16 April 1912).

24. Ibid., 3: 261

25. Mac Gregor, *XXVI Legislatura,* pp. 31–32.

26. On parliamentarianism, see Piccato, *Congreso y revolución*; also Mac Gregor, "XXVI Legislatura frente a Victoriano Huerta," pp. 10–23.

27. Mac Gregor, *XXVI Legislatura,* pp. 11–15; Piccato, *Congreso y revolución,* pp. 79–89.

28. On *zapatismo,* see Miguel to Pablo Macedo, 8, 22 September, 1911 (*El Universal,* 6, 10 September 1917), 28 January, 4, 12 February 1912 (8, 11, 12 October 1917); on Reyes, see Rosendo Pineda to Pablo Macedo, 5 October, 27 November, 24 December (6,7, 8 October 1917), M. to P. Macedo, 31 August 1911 (29 September 1917); on Orozco, see R. Nuñez to P. Macedo, 12 March, 2 April 1912 (12, 13 October 1917). AR.

29. R. Pineda to P. Macedo, 27 March 1912 (12 October 1917). AR.

30. M. to P. Macedo, 28 January 1912 (8 September 1917). AR. President Madero appointed Sierra in January 1912, but he did not arrive in Europe until July and finally presented his credentials to King Alfonso XII on 16 August. See Sierra, *Obras,* 15: 235–50.

31. Serra Rojas, 1: 402.

32. Limantour to Rabasa, 6 March 1913. JYL. Rabasa's letters to Limantour during this period were almost entirely devoted to details on the José Barros case.

33. Senate session of 14 May 1913: Serra Rojas, 1: 418.

34. Ibid., session of 30 September, pp. 419–21.

35. There is much commemorative literature on Belisario Domínguez, the democratic martyr. The best serious and documented biography is Mac Gregor, *Belisario Domínguez.*

36. Arenal, "Pablo Macedo."

37. Garciadiego, "Movimientos estudiantiles," pp. 132–33.

38. See Arenal, "Luis Cabrera;" idem, "La Fundación de la Escuela Libre de Derecho;" Garcíadiego, "Orígenes de la Escuela Libre de Derecho."

39. Rabasa's statement is in Article 1 of *Escuela Libre de Derecho. Estatuto* (1912), pp. 6–7. The *Estatuto* lists all founding members, professors for the rest of 1912, and officials of the new institution. Rabasa, like several others, was in effect a part-time professor, in his case because he was also a senator. Garciadiego, in "Orígenes," emphasizes convincingly the political aspects of the school's founding: see especially pp. 217–18. Arenal tends to emphasize the basic ideas guiding the ELD: see especially "Luis Cabrera," p. 25.

40. Arenal, "Fundación," p. 664. Arenal's publication includes the transcript of the Senate proposal and debate on it: pp. 654–77 (5 November 1912).

41. Ibid., pp. 681–705 (6, 29 November, 4 December 1912). See also Mac Gregor, *XXVI Legislatura,* pp. 116–19.

42. On Novelo and Pino Suárez, see Garciadiego, *Rudos contra científicos,* pp. 161–63.

43. On the recognition of studies in the ELD by Zacatecas, Aguascalientes, Jalisco, and México, see Arenal, "Fundación," pp. 709–10. On the ELD under Huerta and its later reconciliation with the ENJ, see Garciadiego, *Rudos contra científicos.*

44. Joaquín Casasús to Limantour, 10 July 1912; Limantour to Diputados que forman la sección de Gran Jurado, 11 July 1912; Limantour (from Deauville) to Rabasa, 13 July 1912. JYL. Apparently, Carlos Olaguíbel also played a small but significant role in the defense. Barros was the son-in-law of Justo Sierra, but there is no evidence that Sierra supported the accusation.

45. Rabasa, *Acusación de Don José Barros* (1912). The ministry reports were signed by the Sub-Secretario Jaime Gurza, in the absence of the Secretario Ernesto Madero. It should be noted that Ernesto Madero, uncle of the president, was a long-time friend of Limantour. Luis Cabrera listed him as a Científico: *Obras politicas*, p. 7. On the Barros case, see also Salmerón, "Porfiristas expatriados," MS, pp. 11–14.

46. Rabasa to Limantour, 7 September, 5 October 1912. JYL. The Chamber of Deputies was authorized to set itself up as a Gran Jurado to hear accusations against public officials under Article 74, Section V of the Constitution.

47. Rabasa to Limantour, 22 November 1912. JYL.

48. Rabasa to Limantour, 12, 28 December 1912; Limantour to Rabasa, 1 November 1912, 14 April 1913; Rabasa to Limantour, 6 March, 8 May 1913. JYL. Surprisingly enough, Rabasa reported in this last letter that Rendón had said to him that he would continue to work actively in "our" favor. Rendón openly denounced the assassination of Madero and Pino Suárez in the Congress and was later murdered by order of President Huerta on 22 August 1913. In his correspondence with Limantour, Rabasa unexplainably made no specific reference to the events of February 1913, nor did he mention the murder of Serapio Rendón.

49. Rabasa to Limantour, 2 June 1913. JYL.

50. Limantour to Rabasa, 4 July, 14 August 1913; Rabasa to Limantour, 21 July 1913. JYL.

51. For a summary of the conflict between powers of government, see Mac Gregor, "XXVI Legislatura," pp. 18–20. For Rabasa's account of the judicial issue, see Rabasa to Limantour, 8 October 1912. For the news to Limantour, see cables, Rabasa to Limantour, 28, 30 September 1912. JYL.

52. Limantour to Rabasa, 14 August, 30 October 1913; Rabasa to Limantour, 8 October 1913. JYL. Rabasa said Carlos Olaguíbel made an important speech in Limantour's favor prior to the vote, one of his few references to his fellow defense attorney in the correspondence with Limantour.

53. Rabasa to Limantour, 4 February, 6, 16 March, 16 April 1914. JYL. On the complexion of the Supreme Court during this period, which undoubtedly made it sympathetic to Limantour, see James, "Law and Revolution," chap. 3. The Court disbanded in August 1914 until June 1917.

54. Rabasa to Limantour, 16 July 1914. JYL.

55. Limantour to Rabasa, 2 December 1913, including a note to Guillermo Brockmann in Mexico instructing him to deliver a check to Rabasa: Rabasa to Limantour, 10 February, 16 July 1914; Limantour to Nicanor Gurría Urgell, 4 July 1914. Nicanor's brother José María also aided in the legal work. JYL.

56. Limantour to Rabasa, 1 October, 17 November 1913, 3 August 1914; Rabasa to Limantour, 24 October 1913, undated (late September 1914). JYL. Miguel Macedo was more sympathetic to Limantour's concern for self-vindication. In any case Limantour in late 1913 began to accumulate material to refute the accusation against him. Though Rabasa did not want to bring the press into the case, it did attract some polemics: Salmeron, "Porfiristas expatriados," p. 14.

57. Limantour to Rabasa, 4 June 1913; Limantour to Calero, 2 June 1913; Rabasa to Limantour, 21 July 1913. JYL. Calero was a prominent Porfirian

deputy and sub-secretary of Development (Fomento) before 1911. He was later minister of Justice in the in the De la Barra administration and (as we have noted) foreign minister under Madero.

58. See Anders, *Boss Rule in South Texas*, chapter 9. On Buckley's background and early life see Buckley and Buckley, eds. *W.F.B. An Appreciation*. Buckley died in 1958.

59. Letter from Buckley to L. M. Garrison, U.S. Secretary of War, 29 August 1914. SMU.

60. Brown, *Oil and Revolution* p. 107.

61. Ibid., pp. 95, 176.

62. Buckley (from New Willard Hotel, Washington, D.C.) to Walter Pope, 27 May 1914, in Buckley and Buckley, *W.F.B.*, pp. 20–21. Unfortunately, this is the only letter contained in the volume. Buckley also told Pope he had come to Washington at the request of Rabasa to deliver a message to "the President," which the ABC commissioners could not "with dignity deliver themselves." Buckley would have been an assistant to Robert J. Kerr, the civil governor in Veracruz who was ultimately replaced by a military officer: Quirk, *Affair of Honor*. pp. 105–06.

63. Huerta put Rabasa's name before Ambassador Wilson as early as 27 February 1913 (i.e., five days after the assassination of Madero and Pino Suárez): Grieb, *United States and Huerta*, p. 37.

64. Rabasa to Limantour, 4, 6 March, 8 May, 2 June 1913. The emphasis is by Rabasa. Limantour to Rabasa, 6 March, 14 April, 4 June 1913. JYL. On 21 July Rabasa wrote that he was sure to still be in Mexico in September; but, he added, nothing was certain for twenty-four hours. On the extreme turnover of ministers, due to Huerta's unwillingness to delegate authority, see Meyer, *Huerta*, pp. 140–41.

65. Limantour to Rabasa, 30 October 1913. JYL. In the same letter Limantour also mentioned an appointment to the Junta Directiva of the National Railroads, but I have found no other evidence of that possibility. On 20 September Rabasa requested a leave from the Senate to accept the university rectorship (Serra Rojas, 1: 418), but declined it on 29 September because the Senate would not permit him to hold two paid positions. See Garciadiego, *Rudos contra científicos*, p. 262. The official reason he gave was health: UNAM Archivo Histórico. Expedientes de la Dirección General de Personal.

66. Buckley (Tampico) to E. M. House (Austin), 3 November 1913. House papers. Yale University Library. The 17-page letter is cited in Hart, *Revolutionary Mexico*, p. 289; also in idem., *Empire and Revolution*, p. 306. The letterhead "Buckley and Buckley, Attorneys at Law" (Tampico) lists Lic. Nicanor Gurría Urgell (Rabasa's partner) as "consulting attorney" (San Francisco 10, Mexico, D. F.—Rabasa and Gurría Urgell's office). The absence of Rabasa's name may be simply another of his efforts to maintain a low profile. Hart argues that this letter was the beginning of the campaign for intervention, promoted by those concerned with protecting U.S. economic interests in Mexico.

67. On the House interests and E. M. House's political role in Texas, see Hart, *Revolutionary Mexico*, pp. 151–5, 285–86, and passim; Neu, "In Search

of Colonel Edward M. House;" Richardson, *Colonel Edward M. House.* The House mansion was at 1704 West Avenue, the Buckley home at 1801 Lavaca. Both houses have been demolished. Period photographs are in the Austin Historical Society.

68. On the Tampico incident and U.S. occupation of Veracruz, see Quirk, *Affair of Honor*; Grieb, *United States and Huerta*, pp. 142–58.

69. Emilio Rabasa's son Oscar described the meeting in a conversation with Lorum H. Stratton in June 1969: Stratton, *Emilio Rabasa*, p. 30.

70. Grieb, *United States and Huerta*, p. 161. Grieb provides an excellent account of the ABC Conference, drawn especially from U.S. diplomatic sources.

71. Rabasa to Limantour (from Clifton Hotel, Niagara Falls), 22 May 1914. JYL.

72. Grieb, *United States and Huerta*, p. 163. The official American representatives were Associate Justice of the Supreme Court Joseph E. Lamar and Frederick W. Lehman, former solicitor of the Department of Justice.

73. Rabasa to Buckley at the New Willard Hotel, 21 June 1914. WFB. Rabasa added that "your judgments and instructions are very beneficial for us," and that he should continue to send them.

74. Rabasa to De la Lama (minister of Hacienda), 15 May 1914. ER. (This archive deals only with the Niagara Falls Conference). Rabasa communicated initially with De la Lama because the post of minister of Foreign Affairs was vacant and Sub-Secretary Roberto A. Esteva Ruiz was conducting its business. For Mexican acceptance of the mediators' proposal, see Rabasa to Secretario de Relaciones, 30 May 1914; Esteva Ruiz to Rabasa, et al., 1 June 1914. ER.

75. Confidential Memorandum (undated). ER. Rabasa made the point that the United States would definitely not accept Carvajal, Huerta's choice of successor and a man identified with the Científicos.

76. U.S. Department of State. *Foreign Relations of the United States* (1914), pp. 508–10. Quirk described the ABC Conference as "an elaborate quadrille from *Alice in Wonderland*, in which nothing anyone did or said made sense to anyone else": *Affair of Honor*, p. 118.

77. Rabasa to Buckley (at 1809 Lavaca Street, Austin, Texas), 29 June 1914. WFB. Rabasa added his usual thanks to Buckley for "the interest that you took in aiding truth and justice, which was, as you say, aiding the legitimate interests of your own country."

78. Rabasa to Buckley, 14 October 1914. WFB.

CHAPTER 5

1. Limantour's mansion was at 8 Rue de Presbourg. For a listing of Limantour's real estate and other holdings, see María y Campos, *José Yves Limantour,* pp. 185–88.

2. On Manuela's arrival, information from Arq. Ricardo de Villafranca Rabasa, Emilio's grandson. Personal communication. Three of the four apartments Rabasa rented were on Riverside Drive, numbers 440 (at 116 Street), 230 (at 96th Street), 400 (at 112th Street); the fourth was 542 West 112 Street at

Broadway (the Devonshire Apartments). The original buildings, except number 230, are still standing.

3. Rabasa to Limantour, undated (probably late September 1914); 30 November 1916; 2 April 1917. It appears that after 1914, he turned exclusively to the typewriter. His first reference to an eye problem was 29 January 1913. JYL.

4. Rabasa to Limantour, 12 April 1917; 31 May 1917. He described the condition as "a new tissue or scarring on the macula, exactly at the point where direct images are formed . . . The rest of the visual field is good, such that I have peripheral vision, which means I see little. The left eye is still useful using strong glasses for direct vision." JYL. Villafranca said the disorder was macular degeneration, which also afflicted his mother (Concepción Rabasa de Villafranca), and now afflicts his cousin (Emilio O. Rabasa) and himself. Personal communication, March 2005.

5. Limantour to Rabasa, 8 March 1917 (from Biarritz); 18 July 1917; Rabasa to Limantour, 16 April 1914; 31 May 1917. JYL.

6. According to Antimaco Sax, *Mexicanos en el destierro*, pp. 64–65, Rabasa was depressed in New York. However, his correspondence with Limantour reveals little indication of depression (apart from complaints about his eyes and the weather). Ramírez Rancaño, in *Reacción mexicana*, p. 441, says "Sax" was undoubtedly José Elguero, journalist and editor of the Catholic newspaper *El País*, brother of Luis, Rabasa's colleague at Niagara Falls and close companion in New York.

7. Concepción Rabasa de Villafranca, "Apuntes para la biografía de Don Emilio Rabasa" (1968). RVR.

8. Rabasa to Limantour, undated (probably 16 July 1914), from Hotel Netherland, New York; undated (probably late September); Limantour to Rabasa, 8 August 1914 (from Deauville). JYL. On Fuller's mission to Villa and its aftermath, see Katz, *Life and Times of Pancho Villa*, pp. 358 ff.

9. Buckley to Garrison, 21 November 1914. The ten letters to Garrison run from 21 July to 29 December 1914. SMU.

10. Limantour to Rabasa, 15 October 1914. JYL.

11. Ricardo Villafranca, personal communication (March 2005). He added that the family jewels were hidden under the mattress of one of Manuela's children and thus preserved.

12. On the Convention era, see Quirk, *Mexican Revolution*.

13. Rabasa to Limantour, 4 April 1915. On Villa's manifesto, which broke with Carranza, see Katz, *Pancho Villa*, pp. 370–71; on Duval West, Gutiérrez, and Angeles see Katz, *Secret War in Mexico*, pp. 276–79 and Quirk, *Mexican Revolution*, pp. 156–57, 210–11. On Iturbide (subject of a plan promoted by León Canova, head of the State Department's Mexican desk), see Katz, *Secret War*, pp. 303–05. Secretary of State Bryan and ultimately Wilson later rejected Canova's plan.

14. On Esquivel Obregón, see *Desde el Exilio*, Estudio introd. by Mónica Blanco, pp. 15–40, plus letters from Esquivel to Ismael Zuñiga (28 February, 8 March, 19 April, 1915), pp. 237–42, 251–55, 267–70. Equivel was the subject of occasional exchanges between Limantour and Rabasa. Limantour wanted

to know whether Equivel was still critical of him as minister of Hacienda (now that he had filled the same post in 1913.). Rabasa didn't know, but both agreed that Esquivel was often carried away by passion. Rabasa added that though he had "friendly relations" with Esquivel in Mexico, "we are now very far apart" since he lives in Brooklyn and I "uptown": Rabasa to Limantour, 31 August, 25 October 1916; Limantour to Rabasa, 5 October 1916. JYL.

15. Federico Gamboa reported in 1916 that Iturbide and Rabasa were making good money in their law office in New York: *Mi Diario* (1995 ed.), 6: 344 (entry dated 22 April 1916). See also Ramírez Rancaño, *Reacción mexicana*, p. 416. Iturbide's legal association with Rabasa apparently continued after Rabasa's return to Mexico. See Chapter 6, n. 62.

16. Rabasa to Limantour, 4 April, 3 May 1915. JYL. Actually, he finished the letter of 4 April on the 8th, saying he delayed because he had to move his residence to 230 Riverside Drive.

17. Limantour to Rabasa, 3 May 1915; undated (June 1915). JYL.

18.˙ Limantour to Rabasa, undated (early June 1915?); Rabasa to Limantour, 18 June 1915. JYL. Limantour's letter was handwritten from Derby, because of "the fact that I find myself on the road fleeing the zepplins, a source of great fright for my wife."

19. Rabasa to Limantour, 4 June 1915. JYL. Wilson's statement on 9 January was: "Haven't the European nations taken as long as they wanted and spilt as much blood as they pleased in settling their affairs, and shall we deny that to Mexico because she is weak? No, I say!" The key phrase on June 2 was: "if they cannot accommodate their differences and unite . . . within a very short time, this Government will be constrained to decide what means should be employed . . . in order to help Mexico save herself and serve her people." See Link, ed., *Papers of Woodrow Wilson*, 32: 39; 33, 304.

20. Rabasa to Limantour, 18 June 1915. JYL. It should be noted that Weetman Pearson (Lord Cowdray), the public works contractor and oil magnate, was also disposed to finance the campaign: John B. Body to Limantour, 16 June 1915. JYL. See also Pearson correspondence, June 1915 with Limantour (document from S. Pearson and Son Archive supplied to me by Paul Garner). As late as 1916, Limantour said he and Guillermo Landa y Escandón were still willing to contribute small amounts to the press campaign, but he was pessimistic about getting money from other sources. Limantour to Rabasa, 16 November 1916. JYL. For more on Pearson, see p. 89, above.

21. A draft of the article (in both Spanish and English) is in WFB. Buckley asked Rabasa in a letter of 2 September 1919 to send him a copy of the article "which you called 'Unconditional Surrender', and which I had published in the *Sun*," to support his testimony to the Senate Foreign Relations Committee (see Chapter 6). Internal evidence suggests that the article was written in June 1915. However, I was unable to find the published article in the New York *Sun* between June and December 1915.

22. Rabasa to Limantour, 3, 14 April, 5 July 1916; Limantour to Rabasa, 25 April 1916. JYL.

23. Jefe del Servicio de Seguridad to Secretaría de Relaciones Exteriores, 29 June 1916. Archivo Carranza. For details on "the last gasp of *felicismo,*" see Henderson, *Félix Díaz,* chapter 8.

24. Rabasa to Limantour, 30 November 1916; 18 July 1917. JYL. For the period 1916–18 in Chiapas, see Benjamin, *Rich Land,* pp. 128–38.

25. Information sent to Secretaría de Relaciones Exteriores from the Consulado General de Mexico en El Paso, Tex., September 1918. Archivo Histórico "Genaro Estrada," SRE, Fondo Revolución. Salmerón supplied notes from this archive and from the Carranza archive.

26. Rabasa to Limantour, 22 July 1916. JYL. Beginning in April he addressed his letters from 400 Riverside Drive.

27. Limantour (from Biarritz) to Rabasa, 14 August 1916; Rabasa to Limantour, 31 August 1916. JYL. Rabasa announced in this letter that he would be moving once again as of 1 October, to 542 W 112th street. All of his moves were within the same general neighborhood, near Columbia University.

28. Rabasa to Limantour, 31 August, 14 September, 22 July 1916. JYL.

29. Rabasa to Limantour, 19 November 1916. JYL.

30. Speech by León de la Barra, June (?) 1913. Archivo León de la Barra; Commentary on León de la Barra's proposal by governors of various states, 1 July 1913. Archivo General de la Nación, Fondo Manuel González. Documents supplied by Salmerón. For León de la Barra's political activities, including a brief period as vice-president in the presidential campaign of Félix Díaz, as Huerta's foreign minister, and later as a diplomant, see Henderson, *In the Absence of Don Porfirio,* pp. 202–14.

31. Rabasa to Limantour, 14 April 1916. JYL.

32. Rabasa to Limantour, 23 May 1916; Limantour to Rabasa, 12 June 1916; Rabasa to Limantour, 5 July 1916. JYL. Limantour's original reaction to Rabasa's attack on León de la Barra was included in a letter to Luis Elguero, which Rabasa apparently saw.

33. Buckley to Rabasa, 27 September 1915. WFB. Victoriano Salado Álvarez said that Rabasa did a disservice to the country by not writing an account of the Niagara Falls Conference: *Memorias,* 1: 344.

34. García Naranjo, *Memorias,* 8: 229–41. Stratton (*Emilio Rabasa,* p. 32) was the first to take note of García Naranjo's claim.

35. García Naranjo, *Memorias,* 8: 240. He added: "In one paragraph, he [Rabasa] came off as a *pensador,* and in the next as a child playing a prank."

36. [Rabasa], "Un Libro de Francisco Bulnes." The pseudonym Rabasa used was "Pablo Martínez." Bulnes noted that he completed writing the book on 16 July 1916 (p. 394). García Naranjo said that Francisco Elguero delivered Rabasa's articles on Bulnes to him.

37. Rabasa to Limantour, 6 October 1916; also 23 October. JYL.

38. [Rabasa], "Francisco Bulnes," *Revista mexicana,* 22 October 1916.

39. Ibid., 12 November 1916.

40. Rabasa to Limantour, 2 October 1916; Limantour to Rabasa, 16 March 1917; Rabasa to Limantour, 12 April 1917. JYL.

41. Limantour to Rabasa, 16 November 1916; Rabasa to Limantour, 10 December 1916. JYL.

42. Rabasa to Limantour, 30 November 1916; 9 March 1918. JYL.

43. "Galería constitucionalista": on Rouaix, (21 October, 1917); on Ureta (4, 11 November 1917); on Cabrera (18 November 1917); on Manero (25 November 1917); on Iglesias Calderón (3, 17, 24 February; 3, 10 March 1918). These articles were all anonymous. García Naranjo said Rabasa sent these to him directly, but asked him not to attach his name: *Memorias*, 8: 239.

44. The articles on Iglesias Calderón ("Como se escribe la historia: Fernando Iglesias Calderón"), were reprinted, plus the "sketch," as *Dos Últimos Marqueses de Prado Alegre* (1918).

45. Rabasa to Limantour, 5 July 1916. JYL. On Pearson, see Garner, " Politics of National development"; Connolly, *Contratista de Don Porfirio*; Brown, *Oil and Revolution*, pp. 48–55. Garner is preparing a full study of Pearson. On Pearson's intention to subsidize Rabasa's work, see John B. Body to Limantour, 4 August 1916; 31 August 1917. JYL. Body was Pearson's longtime manager in Mexico.

46. Rabasa to Limantour, 31 August 1916. JYL.

47. Rabasa to Limantour, 14 September 1916. JYL. Rabasa also said he was sending Limantour a series of articles by his unnamed friend in Chicago, "the best that have appeared on Mexico." Despite considerable investigation (and much frustration), I have been unable to identify with any certainty who Rabasa's friend might be, or to track down the referred to articles.

48. Limantour to Rabasa, 5 October 1916. JYL. Limantour said he was responding to three of Rabasa's letters (31 August; 14 and 18 September 1916), which all arrived together in Biarritz. He attributed the difficulties of the mail to the war. JYL.

49. Rabasa to Limantour, 30 November 1916. JYL.

50. Rabasa to Limantour, 12 March, 9 July, 4 August 1917. JYL.

51. Limantour to Rabasa, 6 September 1917; Rabasa to Limantour, 13 October 1917. JYL. The opinions came from J. B. Body and Luis Riba y Cervantes, a lawyer close to the Científicos who handled some of Limantour's affairs in Mexico and advised him on political developments. Body urged immediate publication; Riba was opposed and apparently persuaded Body of his view. (Information on Riba from JYL, provided by Salmerón).

52. Limantour to Rabasa, 17 November 1916; Rabasa to Limantour, 9 March 1918; 15 May 1919; Limantour to Rabasa, 20 June 1919. JYL.

53. Rabasa, *Evolución histórica de México* (1920); *Évolution historique du Mexique*. Trans. Carlos Docteur (1924).

54. Rabasa, *Evolución histórica* (2d. ed.), p. 275.

55. Ibid., p. 37. Bolívar's phrase: "America was denied not only its freedom, but even an active tyranny," Jamaica Letter of 6 September 1815, in *Selected Writings*, 1: 110.

56. Rabasa, *Evolución histórica*, pp. 274, 34, 49, 44.

57. Ibid., pp. 274, 56–57.

58. Ibid., pp. 44, 58, 61–62.

59. Ibid., pp. 90–91.
60. Ibid., p. 104. My italics.
61. Ibid., p. 77.
62. Ibid., pp. 116–20.
63. Ibid., p. 113.
64. Ibid., p. 115.
65. *Ibid.* Rabasa was perhaps influenced in this view by James Bryce, whom he cites (n. 66 below), though not here.
66. Rabasa, *Evolución histórica,* pp. 142–44. Rabasa quoted but did not identify passages from Bryce, *South America* (1912), pp. 546–47, in support of the need for order and security at a certain stage in the development of nations, even though, quoting Bryce, "the love of liberty is a nobler thing than the love of security."
67. Rabasa, *Evolución histórica,* p. 122.
68. See above, Chapter 3.
69. Rabasa, *Evolución histórica,* pp. 152–53.
70. Ibid., p. 156.
71. Ibid., p. 161
72. Ibid., p. 172. The reference to Le Bon probably came from *Révolution francaise* (1912).
73. *Rabasa, Evolución histórica,* pp. 180–81.
74. I should remind the reader that this conclusion (*resumen*) appeared as the final chapter of part 3, entitled "Los Problemas nacionales" (to be discussed in Chapter 6).
75. Ibid., p. 264.
76. Ibid., p. 268.
77. Ibid., pp. 274–75
78. Ibid., p. 275. Rabasa probably based his comments here on Gustave Le Bon, *Lois psychologiques,* 12 ed. (1916), Livre III, chap. ii. Interestingly, he condemned Le Bon here while citing him approvingly above. See note 72, above.
79. Rabasa, *Evolución histórica,* p. 277.
80. Rabasa, *La Organización política de México. La Constitución y la dictadura* (2d ed.; Madrid, [1917], "prólogo" by Rodolfo Reyes. Limantour dated his *Apuntes* as 1921, but the work was not actually published until 1965.
81. Rabasa to Limantour 4 August, 7 September 1917; Limantour to Rabasa, 12 October 1917. JYL. Although Rabasa hesitated to reveal his "private thought" to Limantour and finally sent both letters together, Limantour said that good friends, particularly those no longer in public life, should not hesitate to share such thoughts.
82. Rabasa to Limantour, 13, 26 October 1917. JYL. "Caro" had said that the letters in *El Universal* proved that Limantour was "the unaware instigator of the revolutionary movement of 1910." (*Revista mexicana,* 18 November 1917). Limantour did write to García Naranjo protesting the publication, a letter he sent by way of Rabasa, and got an unsatisfactory response. Rabasa said he had no idea who "Caro" was.

83. Limantour to Rabasa, 17 November 1917. JYL.

84. Pineda to P. Macedo, 24 August 1911, published in *El Universal,* 28 September 1917. AR.

85. Rabasa to Limantour, 16 December 1917. JYL. The text of Rabasa's statement is as follows: "What happened to D. Pablo's archive cannot happen to mine, for the decisive reason that I don't have one. For many years, I have had the habit of not keeping letters from family or friends longer than the time needed to answer them: I read them several times and then tear them up. I didn't leave in Mexico a single letter from you or anyone else, except those relating to business and my file as governor."

86. Limantour to Rabasa, 3 February 1918. JYL.

87. Rabasa to Limantour, 9 March 1918. JYL. For Rabasa's early friendship with Pineda, see Chapter 2. For his ties to Macedo, see Chapter 3.

88. Rabasa to Limantour, 9 March 1918. JYL.

89. Limantour to Rabasa, 11 May 1918 (from Biarritz). JYL.

90. There were at least two letters lost during 1918, probably because of the uncertainty of the mail during the climactic final months of World War I (see Rabasa to Limantour, 26 September 1918. JYL). This disruption was the cause of anxiety on the part of both correspondents. Limantour was especially concerned lest the drafts of his "Apuntes" go astray, which apparently did not happen.

91. Rabasa to Limantour, 15 May 1919. JYL. Félix Palavincini was the Director of *El Universal.* On Emilio Rabasa, Jr., see his note to Limantour, thanking him for sending congratulations, 18 August 1919. JYL. I will treat the daughters' marriages and the trip to Paris in Chapter 6, *El Juicio constitucional* in Chapter 7.

92. Rabasa to Limantour, 15 May 1919. JYL.

93. Rabasa to Limantour, 4 February, 15 May, 11, 18 July 1919; Limantour to Rabasa, 20 June 1919. JYL. Limantour said that his wife's health was the reason he spent so much time in Biarritz.

94. Rabasa to Limantour, 4 February 1919; Limantour to Rabasa, 7 March 1919. JYL.

95. Rabasa to Limantour 12 May, 11 July 1919; Limantour to Rabasa, 20 June 1919. JYL.

96. Limantour, *Apuntes,* pp. 14–22, and passim.

97. See Keynes, "Council of Four," pp. 16–17.

CHAPTER 6

1. Isabel married Agustín de la Torre. Mercedes married Leland de Villafranca, an American citizen, descended from a wealthy Costa Rican landowner, on his return from France after serving in the war. Following the death of Mercedes in 1922, Leland remarried Concepción in 1924. Family information from Ricardo de Villafranca Rabasa (son of Concepción and Leland). Personal communications 2005 and 2006. For a list of Emilo Rabasa's immediate family see Appendix B.

2. See Rabasa to Limantour, 1 April 1919; Limantour to Rabasa, 6 May 1919. JYL. The exchange pertaining to Concepción and the prospect of a trip to Paris used a traditional saying. Rabasa remarked: "¡Ya lo creo, si la Magdalena estuviera para tafetanes!" Limantour responded: "En cuanto a los tafetanes de la Magdalena, los amigos, tal vez, podrían servirle en algo." "La Magdalena" refers to the sad biblical Mary Magdalen (whose image has been greatly transformed in our day). "Tafetanes," literally *taffeta*, suggests pleasing distractions. See Rabasa to Limantour, 16 December 1917. JYL. Ruth married Antonio Escandón in New York in late 1917. She died 26 July 1919. According to Villafranca, Rabasa was beside himself on receiving a telegram from Mexico stating simply that a daughter had died. Which one? When he finally learned, he chose not to mention the death in letters to Limantour.

3. On the return and sale of properties, see Rabasa to Limantour, 9 July 1917; Limantour to Rabasa, 18 July 1917; Rabasa to Limantour, 25 February, 11 July 1919. JYL. Rabasa did not identify the properties or to whom he was selling them. For Limantour's offer of help and comment on travel conditions, see letter to Rabasa 3 August 1919. JYL.

4. See Limantour to Rabasa, 8 August 1914; Rabasa to Limantour, undated (September or early October 1914?); Limantour to Rabasa, 26 June 1915 (from Bournemouth), undated (June 1915?) from Derby. JYL.

5. Buckley to Rabasa, 1 August 1919, a short note enclosing a memorandum "which I prepared a couple of weeks ago for some business acquaintances [presumably of the AIC] in New York." Buckley said he wanted to seek Rabasa's advice in person. WFB. The memo is missing from the archive.

6. Hall, *Oil, Banks and Politics*, p. 36.

7. Buckley to Rabasa, 2, 13 September 1919. WFB.

8. Hall, *Oil, Banks and Politics*, p. 40.

9. U.S. Senate, *Investigation of Mexican Affairs*. (1919), pp. 796, 777, 772–73. For the Buckley-Rabasa list of Científicos of 1892–93, see my *Transformation of Liberalism*, pp. 124–27.

10. On the AIC, see Schieber, "World War I as Entrepreneurial Opportunity"; Wilkins, *Maturing of Multinational Enterprise*, pp. 19–23. Straight was a former Foreign Service officer in China who joined J. P. Morgan and Company in 1909 but later left the firm for the AIC post. According to Schieber, he strongly supported "dollar diplomacy."

11. Rabasa to Buckley, 22 October 1919; Rabasa to Streeter, 22 October 1919, 11 January 1920. The extensive memoranda are undated. Rabasa asked Buckley to send mail to Limantour's residence (8 rue Presbourg). WFB. See also an undated and unidentified memorandum (early November?), probably Rabasa to Buckley. JYL.

12. Article 28 prohibited monopolies, one exception being "the emission of bills through a single bank controlled by the Federal Government."

13. "Memorandum" (undated). WFB. M. Cretenier was also very interested in securing an exclusive government concession for a dynamite enterprise.

14. "Memorandum sobre el proyecto de contrato presentado al gobierno de México por el Sr. F. Lavis en nombre de la American International Corporation para la construcción de un ferrocarril entre Honey y Tampico" (undated). WFB.

15. Rabasa to Limantour, 24 December 1919. This letter is the final Rabasa document in JYL. Rabasa and Streeter also discussed the possible participation of "M" (the firm of J. P. Morgan), to which there had been some opposition within the AIC, now apparently resolved. See also "Memorandum sobre el movimiento bancario en México," dated 11 January 1920, a detailed financial statement on the Banco Nacional de México and other banks up to 1910. WFB.

16. Concepción Villafranca de Rabasa, "Apuntes." On Rivero Quijano, see Chapter 7. Concepción's relation of events conflicts slightly with evidence from Rabasa's correspondence with Limantour. According to the latter, the trip to Spain apparently caused confusion (and anxiety on the part of Limantour) in the progress of the negotiations with the French bankers and with the AIC. Rabasa (and presumably Concepción as well) were forced to return to Paris on 5 November, and again soon after 19 November, on receiving cables from Buckley, reported to Rabasa by Limantour. Rabasa received the reports at the home of Alfonso Reyes in Madrid, where they were staying. See Rabasa to Limantour, 4 November 1919; Limantour to Rabasa, 19 November 1919, plus undated telegrams, Limantour to Rabasa. JYL.

17. Rabasa to Limantour, 25 February 1919. JYL.

18. Limantour to Rabasa, 18 March 1919; Rabasa to Limantour, 1 April 1919. JYL.

19. Buckley to Rabasa, 23 February 1920. WFB.

20. Rabasa to Buckley, 2 March 1920. WFB. This letter was translated into English, the only one from Rabasa in the Buckley Archive not in Spanish.

21. Rabasa to Buckley, 22 June 1920. WFB. Rabasa referred to "the fall and death of Carranza" after his arrival in Mexico. Rabasa appeared before the Junta of the Escuela Libre de Derecho on 25 May: Arenal, "Un Rector y una escuela liberales," p. 363.

22. Hall, *Banks, Oil, and Politics*, p. 85. Hall makes no mention of the AIC. On the IBC, see also Smith, "Formation and Development of the International Bankers Committee."

23. Rabasa to Buckley, 23 July 1920; Limantour to Rabasa, 7 August 1920; Rabasa to Buckley, 2 September 1920. WFB.

24. Rabasa to Buckley, 16 November 1920. WFB.

25. Wilkins, *Maturing of Multinational Enterprise*, pp. 51–52.

26. Hall, *Banks, Oil, and Politics,* pp. 56–58. For Buckley's version of his support for the would-be rebellion, see Buckley and Buckley, *WFB*, pp. 142–48; for his close tie to Pelaez, pp. 33–35 (account by Cecilio Velasco, a Buckley employee in Tampico).

27. On Buckley's expulsion, see ibid. pp. 142–48. On the split between the National Association for the Protection of American Rights in Mexico (founded by Edward L. Doheny, a major oil magnate) and Buckley's organization, The American Association of Mexico, see Thomas F. Lee (Executive Secretary, NAPARM) to Buckley, 26 August 1921. WFB.

28. Serra Rojas, 2: 179.

29. Rabasa through Buckley arranged for Leland to interview officials of Amsinc Inc., an import-export firm in New York. See Rabasa to Buckley, 2 March 1920 WFB. Leland took a position with this firm upon his return to Mexico.

30. Rabasa to Concepción Rabasa de Villafranca, 10 April 1924. RVR.

31. Ibid., 14 May 1924. RVR. It is possible that part of this charge to his daughter was tongue-in-cheek, given Rabasa's sense of humor. I leave that possibility to the reader's decision.

32. See Serra Rojas, 2: 181. Ricardo de Villafranca conveyed to me in conversation Manuela's role in the marriage and her sisters' reaction. María Luisa Massieu was probably about age 50 at the time of the wedding. One younger brother, Wilfrido Massieu Pérez (1878–1944), was a prominent military engineer who served both Madero and Huerta, and later in 1940 became the first director of the Instituto Politécnico Nacional. Wilfrido's son (María Luisa's nephew), Guillermo Massieu Helguera (1920–85), was also director of the institution from 1965 to 1970. María Luisa's grandnephew was José Francisco Ruiz Massieu, governor of Guerrero and secretary general of the PRI, assassinated in September 1994.

33. Rabasa, "Una Invención electoral" (1921), in Serra Rojas, 2: 228–29. The two-thirds provision appeared in Article 76, section IV of the Constitution of 1917. It has not been amended.

34. Rabasa, "Un Vacío peligroso" (1929). Ortiz Rubio was elected the third Sunday of November 1929 and took office 5 February 1930.

35. In the second article (25 November), Rabasa related in detail the confusing U.S. electoral conflict between Rutherford B. Hayes and Samuel J. Tilden in 1876 and concluded, interestingly, that the case would have been more easily solved in Mexico.

36. Rabasa, "El Desprestigio de la vice presidencia" (1930). In yet another two of his final articles, Rabasa called for a clarification of Article 84, which would require a two-thirds quorum of the entire Congress for it to meet as a Colegio Electoral (which Rabasa termed an "Asamblea Nacional") to select a substitute president. There had been a conflict between the Deputies and the Senate on the quorum issue in 1923, in which a minority of the Senate refused to provide a quorum. See Rabasa, "La Asamblea nacional" (1930). For further discussion of the quorum issue, see Chapter 7, n. 68.

37. "Nuestra encuesta sobre la educación nacional" (1921). The reporter interviewed Rabasa at his home at Nápoles 40. He also interviewed Federico Gamboa for the same article.

38. Rabasa, "El Desquiciamiento moral" (1930). It is interesting that Rabasa chose to praise an article written by Díaz Soto y Gama, a former collaborator of Emiliano Zapata.

39. On the original plan for *Evolución histórica*, its transformation, and the subsidy, see Chapter 5, pp. 89–91. As noted above, Rabasa wrote to Limantour on 9 July 1917 that he had completed the work.

40. Rabasa, *Evolución histórica*, pp. 191–93.

41. Helen Hunt Jackson (H. H.), *Century of Dishonor* (1881). Jackson was an eastern writer who became a crusader for Indian justice after hearing a lecture by Standing Bear, the chief of the Ponca tribe that had been removed from the Dakotas to Oklahoma. Whipple was Episcopal Bishop of Minnesota, who appealed to Congress after the "Minnesota massacre" of 1862. Rabasa quoted from Whipple in *Evolución histórica*, p. 201.

42. Abbott, "The Indian Problem," (1905). For Rabasa's quoted (and translated) passages, see *Evolución histórica*, pp. 208–09. Rabasa also cited Cato Sells, "Report to the Secretary of the Interior, 1913," as summarized in Eastman (OHIYESA), *Indian Today* (1915), p. 145. See *Evolución histórica*, p. 207. Abbott (1835–1922) was a Congregational clergyman, editor, and author who advocated a rational and evolutionary view of Christianity. He wrote *Theology of an Evolutionist* (1897). Eastman (b. 1838) was the offspring of a Sioux father and a mother descended from a Sioux and a U.S. army officer. He grew up as an Indian, attended Dartmouth College, became a physician serving Indian reservations, and ultimately an international advocate for Indian causes.

43. Abbott, "Indian problem," p. 24 (quoted by Rabasa in *Evolución histórica*, p. 218); Rabasa refers (Ibid., p. 204) to Esquivel Obregón, *Influencia de España y los Estados Unidos* (1918). The pertinent section can be found on pp. 227–89.

44. Rabasa, *Evolución histórica*, pp. 195–98, 218–24.

45. Ibid., pp. 216–17, 225.

46. Rabasa, "San Bartolo Solistahuacán" (1929). Rabasa also referred to an unnamed speech by Manuel Puig Casauranc, Secretario de Educación Pública, probably *Organización técnica* (1924).

47. *Ladino* is capitalized in the text. Rabasa went on to explain (presumably for the benefit of Mexico City and foreign readers) that in Chiapas inhabitants are classified as Indians or *ladinos*. The classification *ladino* "applies, not to color or race, but to level of education, whether acquired by schooling, by commerce, or by other means, and thus put in contact with the life of the educated class." I am not aware that Rabasa used the term in other writings.

48. Rabasa, *Evolución histórica*, pp. 15, 27–28, 51–53, 64, 210. His passage rejecting biological racism (p. 260) is admittedly subtle, because he did acknowledge the continual turmoil of "the Indoamerican peoples" (mestizos and Indians), which he said stemmed from an uncivilized environment. For Sierra's views on mestisaje, see my *Transformation of liberalism*, pp. 234, 243.

49. Rabasa, *Evolución histórica*, 251, 258–260. I have used "instruction" and "education" interchangeably, as I believe it was more common to use their Spanish cognates in 1920 than it was in the late nineteenth century. For a discussion of this question see my *Transformation of liberalism*," pp. 162–63.

50. Rabasa, *Evolución histórica*, p. 261. For Mora's statement, see *Mexico y sus revoluciones*, 1: 196–97.

51. Rabasa, *Evolución histórica*, pp. 226–33.

52. Ibid., pp. 233–37.

53. Ibid., pp. 248–49. For Rabasa's earlier reference to Pastor Rouaix, see Chapter 5, p. 88. For a strong critique of Rabasa's interpretation of the issue of land acquisition, see García de León, *Resistencia y utopía*, 1: 186–87.

54. See Rabasa to Limantour, 12 March 1917. The study of Article 27 was a subject in letters from Rabasa to Limantour, dated 12 April, 31 May, 9 July, 7 September, and 13 October 1917, and those from Limantour to Rabasa, 6 September and 12 October 1917. JYL.

55. "Derecho constitucional mexicano, 2 May 1928 (Serra Rojas, 2): 607.

56. The Decree of 1915 was made "a constitutional law" in section VII of Article 27.

57. For a treatment of the complex changes in agrarian legislation from 1917 to 1934 and their effect on the judicial process, see James, "Law and Revolution," chapter 5. See also Mendieta y Nuñez, *Problema agrario*. Narciso Bassols, a law professor at UNAM, wrote a clear rationale for the 1927 law: "La Nueva Ley agraria."

58. Rabasa, *Amparo promovido por la testamentaria Martínez del Río*. The document is dated 8 December 1923.

59. See *Semanario judicial de la federación (SJF)*, 5th época, 16 (1925): 1275–82. Some of Rabasa's arguments in the Martínez del Río case were presented by Lic. Ramón Sánchez Albarrán (director of the Sindicato Nacional de Agricultores) in "Autorizada Opinión del Señor Lic. Rabasa" (1925).

60. Rabasa, *Cia. Terminal "La Isleta,"* (1923). The plea was dated 20 September. For Cecilio Velasco's relationship to Buckley, see Velasco's eulogy in Buckley and Buckley, *W.F.B.* pp. 25–35; on "La Isleta" see also ibid, pp. 135–36.

61. Rabasa published a separate 36-page pamphlet, *Cia Terminal "la Isleta"* . . . *anexos a los alegatos,* which included the texts (in translation) of Fletcher vs. Peck (1810) and Dartmouth vs. Woodward (1819), cases that featured opinions by Chief Justice John Marshall.

62. The Court's decision is spelled out in *SJF*, 5th epoca, 12 (1923): 884–92. Rabasa's letter to Buckley is dated 10 November 1923. WFB. He said "we" were in effect winning three amparos, since the case also involved two other "colonies" that were part of "La Isleta." For the Court's decision on those subsidiary cases, see Ibid., 12: 1302–03. In his letter to Buckley, Rabasa acknowledged that Eduardo Iturbide and his partner Nicanor Gurría Urgell had also worked on the case.

63. See Rabasa to Buckley, 22 July, 10 November 1923. WFB. For further comment on Buckley's contribution to the ELD, see Chapter 7, pp. 155–56.

64. Walter H. Kilham, Buckley's architect, wrote to Governor Calvin Coolidge of Massachusetts (11 February 1921), gratuitously urging Coolidge to confer with Buckley, whom he described as a "disinterested" expert on Mexican affairs. Kilham mentioned Buckley's association with Rabasa. WFB. For an illustration of the planned mansion, see Buckley and Buckley, *W.F.B.,* p. 49.

65. The interview was reported by Nemesio García Naranjo, "A Friend of Mexico," in ibid., pp 36–50. García Naranjo said that he and Buckley became good friends following García's "second exile" in 1926. He also remarked that when they meet in the hereafter, "we will both solemnly promise never to speak of Mr. Woodrow Wilson again."

CHAPTER 7

1. On the Convention see Quirk, *Mexican Revolution*.

2. Palavincini was a former supporter of Madero who served as minister of Education under Carranza from August 1914 to September 1916. He then founded and edited *El Universal*. The pamphlet was published in Veracruz in August 1915, when Carranza's government was occupying the city after the withdrawal of the Americans the previous November. It appeared as an addi-

tion to Palavincini, *Historia de la Constitución de 1917*, Appendix, 2: 1–81. Facsimile of 1st ed., 1938.

3. Ibid, pp. 67–68. On social pessimism, Le Bon, and García Calderón, see my "Political and Social Ideas in Latin America," pp. 399–402. Arnaldo Córdova asserts (with some exaggeration perhaps) that Palavincini practically repeated the arguments of Justo Sierra and Emilio Rabasa: Córdova, *La Nacion y la constitución*, p. 19 n. See also Lira, "Revolución, derechos sociales, y positivismo jurídico," pp. 83–105.

4. Fernández, José Diego. *La Constitución de 1857 y sus reformas* (1914). Facsimile reissue (2005), introductory study by Manuel González Oropeza. The proposal was endorsed by the Confederación Cívica Independiente, which supplied a "prologue" by Agustín Aragón and Fernando González Roa. The second proposal was *Proyecto de reformas constitucionales* (1916). Antonio Martínez Baez discovered Part 1 of the committee proceedings in the archive of the Cámara de Diputados, through article 58 of the Constitution. Part 2 apparently is lost.

5. Ibid., pp. 515–16.

6. See Tena Ramírez, *Leyes fundamentales*, p. 812; also Medina, "Emilio Rabasa y la Constitución de 1917"; Cosío Villegas, *Constitución de 1857*; Díaz y Díaz, *Emilio Rabasa*; Villegas Moreno, *Emilio Rabasa. Su Pensamiento histórico-político*.

7. DDCC, 1: 388. Lira argues convincingly that Article 1 of the 1917 Constitution, which followed Carranza's view (essentially that of José Natividad Macías, author of the first chief's proposal), was a positivist conception of individual rights, drawn from Ignacio Vallarta: "Derechos del hombre." Rabasa would have certainly agreed with this formulation. Macías had been a founding member of the ELD and a professor there in 1912.

8. DDCC, 1: 396. The reference to Tocqueville is probably from *Démocratie en Amérique*, Vol. 1, pt. 1, p. 169 (Eng. ed. [1954], 1: 173).

9. On the Convocatoria and the Senate, see my *Transformation of Liberalism*, pp. 71–73, 80–83; also Chapter 3.

10. Mention must also be made of the vice-presidency, which Carranza rejected but Rabasa generally supported, though he did not emphasize it in his books. The first chief claimed it was "the means invented by the Científicos (*el cientificismo*)" to hold on to power, in the absence of Porfirio Díaz. See DDCC, 1: 398 (incidentally, his only specific reference to Díaz). However, Rabasa did devote an article to the vice-presidency just before his death. See above, p. 120.

11. Cosío Villegas attributed to Rabasa's influence the presidential regime established in 1917, "which juridically is not far from dictatorship": *Constitución de 1857*, p. 68.

12. The debate took place 19, 20, and 21 January 1917: DDCC, 2: 698–746, 765–70.

13. Ibid., pp. 704–05.

14. Ibid., p. 714.

15. Ibid., p. 727.

16. Medina's oration ran in from pp. 733–41 in ibid.

17. Ibid., p. 770. The committee revised the final version of article 94, increasing the number of justices to 11, and making judges irremovable after 1923. The first ones elected would serve two years (until 1919), the second group 4 years (until 1923). In 1930 Rabasa ridiculed this "unusual and totally original idea," designed to accustom the people to irremovability by degrees: "La Asamblea nacional," p. 299.

18. Some of the following discussion is drawn from my "The Civil Law Tradition and Constitutionalism."

19. Merryman, *The Civil Law Tradition,* p. 2. On the civil law tradition generally, see also essays by Mauro Cappelletti and David S. Clark in Clark, ed., *Comparative and Private International Law*; Lawson, *A Common Lawyer Looks at the Civil Law*; Glendon et al., *Comparative Legal Traditions.*

20. The standard work on the comparative history of the judiciary with emphasis on the revolutionary reaction against the judiciary of the Old Regime in France is Dawson, *The Oracles of the Law.* For the text of the decree of 16 August 1790, see Stewart, *Documentary Survey of the French Revolution,* pp. 143–57.

21. Merryman, *Civil Law Tradition,* pp. 26–27.

22. Passages from Montesquieu (book. 11, chapter 6), quoted by Cappelletti, *Judicial Process,* pp. 192–99.

23. King, "Constitutionalism and the Judiciary in France," pp. 69–70.

24. David, *French Law,* p. 19. It is important to note that Montesquieu's influence on historical constitutionalism entailed his emphasis on the balance of powers between king, nobility, and commons, and not between the executive, legislative, and judiciary, since he saw the judicial power as null. Thus the U.S. notion of separation of powers (or checks and balances), which includes the judiciary, cannot be attributed directly to the influence of Montesquieu. See Palmer, *Age of the Democratic Revolution,* 1: 57–58.

25. In general, see Merryman, "The Public Law-Private Law Distinction."

26. Kelley in *Historians and the Law* demonstrates the ambivalence of the postrevolutionary judicial establishment toward codification, which in part prompted its growing enthusiasm for history and for the German historical school of law.

27. On the evolution of cassation in France, see Cappelletti, *Judicial Review in the Contemporary World,* pp. 12–16. Cappelletti (also in *Judicial Process*) stresses the efforts to strengthen judicial review in post–World War II Europe and notes indications of convergence between the two Western legal systems. However, in France, the traditional Council of State, which was charged with reviewing abuses of administrative action, and the new Constitutional Council (1958) have remained basically political as opposed to judicial entities.

28. Rabasa to Limantour, 1 April 1919. JYL. Rabasa dealt with Raúl Mille, an agent of the publisher Bouret, which also published the Rabasa's *Evolución histórica* in 1920. Bouret published the four novels separately in 1919.

29. Rabasa to Limantour, 25 July 1919; Limantour to Rabasa, 21 August 1919. JYL.

30. Rabasa, *Juicio constitucional,* pp. 133–34. Further evidence of his re-engagement in Mexican legal issues at the moment of his return was his thoroughgoing study: "Juzgar Dos Veces por el mismo delito" (1920). The case dealt with the two different trials and the wrongful accusation (according to Rabasa) of the officer supposedly guilty of not confronting the assassins of Venustiano Carranza on 21 May 1920. Rabasa claimed there had been a violation of Article 23 of the Constitution.

31. Rabasa took exception, however, to the process for ratifying amendments to the U.S. Constitution, in this case the 18th, ratified January 1919. See "La Adición antialcohólica" (1919). He argued that a vote by Congress, confirmed by two-thirds of the state legislatures, "is a fiction of the exercise of sovereignty." The temperance states have imposed prohibition on those opposed to it, and the constitutional masterpiece now contains a precept "that is only appropriate for a municipal ordinance."

32. Rabasa, *Juicio constitucional,* pp. 159–60.

33. Ibid., p. 173.

34. Ibid., pp. 138–39. Rabasa later summarized much of the substance of *El Juicio constitucional* in "Historia sinóptica del derecho constitucional" (1923).

35. Rabasa, *Juicio constitucional,* pp. 173–74.

36. Ibid., pp. 177–87, 202.

37. Ibid., p. 206. In the course of his discussion on the Anglo American judiciary, Rabasa cited and quoted from Cooley, *Treatise on the Constitutional Limitations* (1868, and later eds.). Cooley (1824–98) exerted great influence following the American Civil War, not only for his doctrine of the "implied" limitations on the authority of the states, but also for his interpretation of due process, which strengthened laissez-faire doctrine and opposition by the Supreme Court to regulatory legislation. Rabasa also referred to Haines, *American Doctrine of Judicial Supremacy* (1914) and to Bryce, *American Commonwealth.*

38. Rabasa, *Juicio constitucional,* p. 199.

39. Ibid., pp. 220–22.

40. Ibid., pp. 225–26.

41. Ibid., pp. 229, 210.

42. Rabasa, *Constitución y la dictadura,* p. 193.

43. Rabasa, *Juicio constitucional,* pp. 230–37. There is, of course, an extensive technical literature on the juicio de amparo and a debate on its origins, which is beyond the scope of this study. The standard work is Burgoa, *El Juicio de amparo.* In English is Baker, *Judicial Review in Mexico.* Contrary to the conventional view, Lira has argued persuasively the colonial antecedents in *Amparo colonial y el juicio de amparo mexicano.* Rabasa had dismissed the possibility of colonial precedents: *Juicio constitucional,* p. 232.

44. Ibid., pp. 284–85. He did not, however, favor a specific constitutional provision excluding extraordinary laws from judicial review (pp. 266–67), a measure that had been advocated by José Diego Fernández in 1914 (see above, p. 135).

45. Rabasa, *Juicio constitucional,* pp. 269–83.

46. Ibid., pp. 254–68. Vallarta's treatise was *El Juicio de Amparo y el writ de habeas corpus.* (*Obras completas*), vol. 5.

47. Ibid., pp. 286–87. Rabasa could well have cited at this point a passage from Tocqueville that supported his views: within certain limits, "the power vested in the American courts forms one of the most powerful barriers that have ever been devised against the tyranny of political assemblies." *Democracy in America*, 1: 107. To demonstrate the power of the U.S. Supreme Court, Rabasa also related at some length the unusual case of the Adamson Act of 1916, which established the eight-hour day for railroad workers. In *Wilson v. New*, the Court upheld the law's validity by 5 to 4 even before the act went into effect. Rabasa quoted from the opinion of Chief Justice Edward D. White: Rabasa, *Juicio constitucional*, pp. 290–92. For the context pertaining to the Adamson Act, see McCartin, *Labor's Great War*, p. 34 and passim.

48. Rabasa, *Juicio constitucional*, pp. 278, 322. On the amparo as cassation, see Baker, *Judicial Review*, pp. 175–76; Karst and Rosenn, *Law and Development*, pp. 130 ff. For the numerous late nineteenth-century volumes of court reports devoted to cassation, see Clagett and Valderrama, *Revised Guide*, pp. 406–13.

49. Rabasa, *Juicio constitucional*, pp. 329–33, also 223–224. In these pages, Rabasa cites Haines, *American Doctrine of Judicial Supremacy*. For more recent studies of the U.S. context, see Paul, *Conservative Crisis and the Rule of Law*; Fisher et al., *American Legal Realism*; Horowitz, *The Transformation of American Law*, chapters 1–2; Wolfe, *The Rise of Modern Judicial Review*. Wolfe emphasizes the rise of "judicial activism" after 1900.

50. Rabasa, *Juicio constitucional*, p. 333. In his "Brief Introduction to the Mexican Writ of *Amparo*" (designed to introduce U.S. lawyers to the juicio de amparo), Hector Fix Zamudio states (p. 308): "It is important to note at the outset the lack of a principle in the Mexican legal system comparable to *stare decisis*" (i.e., the power and obligation of courts to base decisions on prior decisions).

51. For Rabasa's early position, see *Constitución y la dictadura*, pp. 188–90. The quote from Hamilton on p. 201 is taken from *The Federalist*, no. 78, pp. 504–05. Hamilton's phrase was: "the judiciary is beyond comparison the weakest of the three *departments* of power." On the issue in France, see David, *French Law*, p. 27. My italics.

52. See Rabasa, *Juicio constitucional*, p. 227; also Tena Ramírez, *Derecho constitucional*, pp. 229, 411–412; Herrera y Lasso, *Estudios constitucionales*, pp. 291–95. Cosío Villegas, presumably following the critics in the Constitutional Congress, dismissed Rabasa's 1912 statement but failed to acknowledge Rabasa's later position. Andrés Lira faults Cosío for his failure to come to grips with Rabasa's juridical ideas or with his two juridical studies: "prologo" to Cosío Villegas, *Constitución de 1857* (1998 ed.). Alonso Lujambio has also defended Rabasa's comparative method against Cosio's criticism: introd. study to Wilson, *Gobierno congresional*.

53. Rabasa in *Memoria del primer congreso jurídico* (1921), p. 21. Rabasa's speech was directed to the conference theme: "Reform of the political Constitution of the Republic, with the objective of organizing the Supreme

Court of Justice as a tribunal that can guarantee the speed of its resolutions and carry out the technical functions entrusted to it by the Constitution."

54. Ibid., p. 24.

55. Rabasa was reacting in part against the Law of Amparo of 1919, which, after a half century of debate (that included Rabasa's *Artículo 14*) on the problem of overlapping cassation functions in federal tribunals and in the Supreme Court via amparo, eliminated cassation in name, though maintained it in effect with the "legality" function of the juicio de amparo. See Fix Zamudio, "Casación," *Diccionario jurídico mexicano*, 1: 428–30; also idem, "Brief Introduction," p. 324, where Fix Zamudio asserts that 80 percent of amparo suits are the cassation type.

56. Rabasa, *Constitución y la dictadura*, p. 195.

57. Ibid., p. 198. Rabasa drew his information on the United States (and the term *Jefferson democrats*) from a Belgian scholar, whom he also quoted: Nerincx, *L'Organisation judiciaire aux États-Unis* (1909), especially pp. 208–10.

58. "Las Invasiones de la Corte Suprema," the title of chapter xv (pp. 209–21) of *Constitución y la dictadura*.

59. Rabasa (*Constitución y la dictadura*, pp. 218–20) quoted from Bryce, *American Commonwealth*, 1:237 and also from Boutmy, *Eléments d'une psychologie politique du people américain* (1902), pp. 189–90, to point out the contrast between the U.S. Supreme Court's respect for the rights of the states as opposed to the "invasions" by the Court in Mexico. Boutmy (1835–1906) was a leading founder of the École Libre de Sciences Politiques and formed part of the conservative-liberal movement that advocated scientific politics and influenced the Mexican *La Libertad* group in the late 1870s. It was natural that Rabasa should quote him and refer to him as "an influential authority." See my *Transformation of Liberalism*, p. 94.

60. Rabasa, *Constitución y la dictadura*, p. 221. The "legally unqualified by origin" doctrine was also important in the dispute over the reelection of President Sebastián Lerdo de Tejada in 1876, when the Court invalidated the election because several state legislatures were deemed under siege at the time. Chief Justice José María Iglesias then claimed the presidency (as de facto vice-president), and Porfirio Díaz launched his rebellion and Plan de Tuxtepec. See my *Transformation of Liberalism*, pp. 85–86. Rabasa does not mention the national issue.

61. Rabasa, "La Barra americana," dated 6 December 1923 (1928), 6–15, in Serra Rojas, 2: 169–76. The book he summarized was Madier, *L'Association du barreau américain* (1922). Madier made only a brief reference (pp. 23–24) to the anti-recall campaign by the Bar Association.

62. Rabasa, "Barra Americana," Serra Rojas, 2: 171.

63. Haines, *American Doctrine of Judicial Supremacy*; Lambert, *La Gouvernement des juges* (1921). Haines, a political scientist whose book was published in 1914, devoted his final chapter (pp. 312–53) to "recent criticisms of the practice of judicial supremacy." He discussed (pp. 343–44) Roosevelt's proposal that became a plank in the Progressive Party Platform of 1912. Both authors ap-

peared to have opposed the inflexibility of the Supreme Court, though Lambert claimed objectivity in what was an exceptionally thorough and detailed study (see p. 236). He directed the Institut de Droit Comparé de Lyon, which sponsored Madier's study; he also supplied a preface to that study.

64. See Betancourt. "Inamovilidad" and Sánchez Pontón, "Algunas Ideas sobre la reforma de las instituciones judiciales" (1922), pp. 1–5, 14–18. Rabasa did not mention specific opposition to irremovability in his 1923 articles, but he did so briefly the following year in an address to the Tercer Congreso Jurídico Nacional marking the centennial of the Constitution of 1824: "Un Discurso" (dated 1924), p. 178. See also note 66 below.

65. Rabasa, "La Inamovilidad de la suprema corte. Primer artículo," 9 May 1923.

66. See *DDCD*, 25th legis, pp. 6, 13–21 (2, 6 October 1911). For the Senate, see *DDCS*, 25th legis., pp. 212–21 (28 October 1911), pp. 278–96 (17 November), pp. 296–355 (November 1911), pp. 379–413 (27 November 1911). It is possible that Rabasa did not take part in the debate because he was completing *Constitución y la dictadura* at this time. See Chapter 3, p. 43.

67. Rabasa, "La Inamovilidad de la suprema corte. Segundo artículo," 12 May 1923.

68. Rabasa, "La Inamovilidad de la suprema corte. Tercer artículo," 16 May 1923. Pimental remained on the Court in 1923 and 1924 and had been on the Court in 1917 and 1918, as had Cruz and Colunga. But the latter two were not listed later. See Camp, *Mexican Political Biographies,* pp. 238–39. Pimentel (1862–1924) and Rabasa had been fellow editors of *El Universal* in 1888. In February 1930, Rabasa claimed that a minority group of senators had improperly refused "to provide a quorum" in 1923, thus preventing the Congress from meeting as a Colegio Nacional to elect permanent judges. By misinterpreting Article 84, the senators left the country without a Supreme Court for three months until the matter was resolved. See Rabasa, "Asamblea nacional."

69. Rabasa, "Sobre La Suprema Corte. Cuarto artículo," 19 May 1923. The constitutional reform of 1928 did not eliminate irremovability but changed the mode of selection of justices from election by Congress to presidential appointment and confirmation by the Senate (a mode Rabasa advocated).

70. Mayagoitia, "Don José Mariano Pontón y Ponce," pp. 375–76. The problems that concerned the Orden Mexicana de Abogados were clearly the same ones raised by Betancourt and Sánchez Pontón in the second Congreso Jurídico (see this chapter, p. 151).

71. Querido Moheno asserted that the 1921 Congreso Juridico "had as its objective to canonize Don Emilio Rabasa," cited in Serra Rojas, 2: 180.

72. See Rabasa, *Gorozave vs. Ruiz* (1924); *SJF* (1924), 15: 1049–65.

73. Rabasa, *Amparo Anastasia Delgadillo* (1924); *SJF,* 16 (1925): 112–28.

74. Rabasa, *Compañía mexicana-holondesa "La Corona"*(1924); *SJF,* 16 (1924): 1746–49. Rabasa's *alegato* is listed by Glass, *Mexico en las obras de Emilio Rabasa,* but I have been unable to locate either the *alegato* or Glass. Luis Cabrera argued the case successfully (apparently against Rabasa): *Sucesión de D. Tomas Valladares* (1924). Rabasa, with Alejandro Quijano and Genaro

Fernández MacGregor, also took on another complex property case, arguing that an amparo in favor of the International Petroleum Company should be overturned because of faulty and even fraudulent documentation. However, I have been unable to find the Court's final decision: *La Compañía mexicana de oleductos* (1924).

75. Rabasa, "Discurso," *Revista jurídica,* 2a época, 3:14. The speech was dated 26 July 1925, commemorating the thirteenth anniversary of the school's founding. The Universidad Nacional Autónoma Mexicana (UNAM) was officially established in 1929.

76. The evidence on Rabasa's teaching of the 1920s comes from student notes on his two courses "Ciencia Política" and "Derecho Constitucional Mexicano" (1928) transcribed by J. J. González Bustamante, Serra Rojas, 2: 339–627; also another typescript version by Alejandro Gamboa, "Derecho constitucional mexicano," which includes a few additional lectures by others. Both González Bustamante and Gamboa were 1929 graduates. The text used in political science was by the Canadian Stephen Leacock, *Elements of Political Science* (1906), which was published in Spanish (1924). Rabasa may have been the translator. For Rabasa's comments on the juicio de amparo and cassation, see Serra Rojas, 2: 590, 619–20; on differences between French and U.S. practices, p. 596; on religion and Articles 3 and 130, pp. 472, 562–66; on property, pp. 605–07. On the 1920s in the ELD, see Arenal, "Los Años del estudiante Felipe Tena Ramírez."

77. Rabasa to Buckley, 22 July, 10 November 1923. WFB. There is no evidence that the financial contributions were ever made public.

78. Díaz y Díaz has made this point in *Emilio Rabasa,* pp. 30–31. Portes Gil graduated from the ELD in 1915 and Padilla in 1914.

79. Oscar Rabasa, "Suprema corte," article dated 20 September 1922.

80. Ibid., pp. 430–31.

81. Oscar Rabasa, *El Derecho angloamericano* (1944), p. 16. Reprinted 1982.

82. The journal *Boletín del Instituto de Derecho Comparado de México* ran from 1948 to 1967 and has continued (to date) as *Boletín mexicano de derecho comparado.* At least two significant comparative studies marked the Institute's twenty-fifth anniversary: Fix Zamudio, *Veinticinco años de evolución* (1968); and Cappelletti, *El Control judicial de la constitucionalidad* (1966) [English version as *Judicial Process,* above n. 11]. See also Cabrera and Headrick, "Notas sobre la justicia constitucional," a clear comparative and bilingual discussion of judicial procedures. On the lack of texts, see Fix Zamudio, "John Henry Merryman and the Modernization of Comparative Legal Studies," in Clark, ed., *Comparative and Private International Law,* pp. 42–43. He was probably referring to the above work by Cappelletti, as well as to David, *Grandes Sistemas jurídicos* (1973) and Merryman, *Tradición jurídica romano-canónica* (1971). All remain out of print, except Merryman, which was reissued in 1989. A straw in the wind indicating change is Serna de la Garza, "Apuntes."

83. "Most distinguished," according to Cosío Villegas, *Constitución de 1857,* p. 174. See also Arenal, "Vasconcelos, Herrera y Lasso y la Escuela Libre de Derecho," 9 (1985): 71–102.

84. Herrera y Lasso, *Estudios constitucionales* (1940); *Estudios constitucionale*, 2d. Ser. (1964); *Estudios políticos y constitucionales* (1986).

85. For Herrera y Lasso's criticism of Rabasa's attack on Article 1 of the Constitution of 1957, see *Estudios* (1940), pp. 252–55; for his views on the juicio de amparo procedure, see *Estudios* (1964), p. 14 and *Estudios* (1986), p. 354; on establishing a court of cassation, see *Estudios* (1986), pp. 379–80; on irremovability of judges and restructuring the Supreme Court, see *Estudios* (1964), pp. 52–54. The respect commanded by Herrera y Lasso is evident in the posthumous testimony by the prominent jurist Antonio Martínez Báez (despite their evident political differences): introd. to Herrera y Lasso, *Estudios* (1986).

86. The three previous statues were to Manuel Crecencio Rejón, the "precursor," Mariano Otero, the "creator," and Ignacio Vallarta, the "realizer" of the juicio de amparo. Rabasa, in Herrera y Lasso's view, should have been recognized as the "consummator." See *Estudios* (1986), pp. 367–76. A statue of Rabasa was finally erected and dedicated in February 2006. See *Foro jurídico*, (2006), pp. 16–24; also Guidiño Pelayo, "Emilio Rabasa en la Suprema Corte," pp. 141–46.

87. Rabasa, *Libertad de trabajo*. He gave the speech 18 September 1922.

88. Leon Duguit, *Law in the Modern State* (1919), pp. xxxvii–xliv and passim. English trans. of *Transformations du droit public* (1913). Spanish ed. [1915].

89. Rabasa, *Libertad de trabajo*, pp. 34–35 (Serra Rojas, 2: 244)

90. Ibid., pp. 44–45 (Serra Rojas, 2: 246-47). The Confederación was established in 1918, was threatened with abolition in 1936, but then revived in the 1940s. Rivero Quijano was also the friend who traveled with Rabasa and his daughter, Concepción, in Spain in 1919. See above, Chapter 6.

91. Also of note is a brief preface by Rabasa to González Salceda, Jr., *Transición pacífica del individualismo al socialismo* (1927), a published ELD thesis. Rabasa praised González Salcedo's discussion of "police power" and other U.S. constitutional doctrines that had permitted, "without changing the texts, the necessary broadening of interpretation (*extensión*) to allow for law to evolve in concert with social evolution." Perhaps the "police power" doctrine, he added, could be applied in Mexico.

92. See Sánchez-Cordero Dávila, "prólogo" to *Libro del cincuecentenario del código civil*, p. 11. Tena Ramírez's long-lost thesis, entitled "La Función del derecho: del individualismo al socialismo" (1929) was recently discovered by Jaime del Arenal. Duguit's work figures prominently in it, and appears to be drawn mainly from French sources, plus a few German works on Roman law.

93. Tena Ramírez, *Derecho constitucional*, pp. 58–65 (cf. 1st ed. [1944], p. 93). CF. statement by Duguit quoted in Eisenmann, "Deux théoricians du droit: Duguit et Hauriou," pp. 44–45.

94. Tena Ramírez, *Derecho constitucional*, pp. 442–43 (cf. 1st ed. [1944], pp. 455–56). He cited Hauriou, *Principios de derecho público* (1927), trans. of *Principes du droit publique* (1910), and inserted a long quotation from the work criticizing procedures of the U.S. Supreme Court. He also cited Lambert, *Gouvernement des juges*, as well as quoting a passage from Abraham Lincoln, warning against the usurpation of public authority by the Supreme Court. The

passage was taken from Corwin, *Constitución norteamericana* (Buenos Aires, 1942), one of the few references to U.S. works by postrevolutionary Mexican jurists.

95. Tena Ramírez, *Derecho constitucional,* pp. 462–63. Although the wording is slightly different, the statement in the 1st ed. (1944, p. 476) is essentially the same, indicating that his views on this subject had not changed between 1944 and 1963.

96. Ibid., pp. 412–13, 416–17. See also "La Crisis de la división de poderes," in *Crisis del pensamiento* (1946), pp. 155–81. For an excellent political analysis, with emphasis on recent decades (including the reforms of 1994, designed to enhance judicial independence, see Domingo, "Judicial Independence"; also Fix Zamudio, "Independencia judicial."

97. Urbina, in O. Rabasa, *Derecho angloamericano,* p. 11.

CHAPTER 8

1. Díaz Dufoo, " El Ultimo Pensamiento de Emilio Rabasa," Serra Rojas, 2: 321–22. Díaz Dufoo included the text of a note from Rabasa, dated 22 March 1930, inviting him to discuss personally the collaboration. On the special position of "Rector" at the ELD, see Arenal, "Un Rector," pp. 358–59.

2. For details on Rabasa's death, including the texts of several eulogies, see Serra Rojas, 2: 311–35. Ironically, one of the student speakers was José Barros Sierra, presumably son of the deputy who accused Limantour in 1912, and against whom Rabasa mounted an able defense. See Chapter 4. It should be noted that just before and just after Rabasa's death Luis Mier y Terán, a recent graduate (1928) of the ELD, argued that the school should bear Emilio Rabasa's name. While expressing great respect for Rabasa, the Junta de Profesores rejected the idea. See correspondence between Mier y Terán and Rafael Martínez Carrillo, 25, 27 February, 2 May 1930. Archivo ELD.

3. Ferrer, "Semblanzas mexicanas. Don Emilio Rabasa"; Díaz Dufoo, "Ultimo Pensamiento," Serra Rojas, 2: 322.

4. Salado Álvarez, *Memorias,* 1: 343–44. Salado Álvarez's daughter, Elena, married Ramón Rabasa, son of Don Emilio's brother Ramón. Personal communication, Manuel Rabasa, the elder Ramón's grandson (March 2005).

5. Silva-Herzog Márquez, "Emilio Rabasa," pp. 291–92. The author, however, goes on to argue that Rabasa secured Huerta's agreement to resign the presidency as a result of the Niagara Falls Conference.

6. *La Libertad* in 1878 was entitled a "conservative-liberal newspaper" (*periódico liberal-conservador*)."

7. See my *Transformation of Liberalism,* p. 136. In a sense Rabasa took up Bulnes's argument of 1903, when he said in 1912 and again in 1920 that the era of dictatorship (or personal government) was over, and that the constitutional stage must follow. However, he did not use the word *conservative.*

8. Tello Díaz, *El Exili.,* pp. 233–34. It should be noted, however, that Casasús had ties to Francisco Madero and to companies supporting the Revolution. Roberto Núñez, a fellow Científico, called Casasús a "traitor." See Chapter 4,

p. 54. Tello Díaz's fascinating account describes, among other things, the elegant lifestyle of the descendants of Casasús and Porfirio Díaz in Paris, in contrast to that of the penniless exiles from the Russian Revolution.

9. See my "Mitos políticos."

10. Don Emilio's son Oscar served as legal advisor to presidents and as director of the Foreign Service in the 1950s; his grandson, Emilio O. Rabasa was secretary of Foreign Relations under President Luis Echeverría (1970–75); his great-grandson, Emilio Rabasa Gamboa, was sub-secretary of the Interior in the early 1990s.

11. See Knight, "El liberalismo mexicano."

12. See my "Liberal Impulse: Daniel Cosío Villegas."

13. Eduardo Pallares (1885–1972), one of the founding professors of the ELD, wrote in 1930 that with Rabasa's death "the era of the liberal constitutionalists has ended." Henceforth, he added, in an antirevolutionary diatribe, the functions of the Supreme Court would in effect be taken over by the National Revolutionary Party, by armed agrarianists, and by militant syndicalists. See "Muerte de Rabasa."

14. See Kelley, *Historians and the Law.* The postrevolutionary context in France was admittedly quite different from that of Mexico.

15. See my "Edmundo O'Gorman."

16. Medina Peña, *Invención del sistema político mexicano.*

17. Monsivais, "Emilio Rabasa: la tradición del desengaño," p. xvii. For Monsivais, Rabasa's juridical writing was "bizantine."

18. González Ramírez, "prológo" to Emilio Rabasa, *Retratos y estudios.* González Ramírez (1904–79), an ELD graduate of 1928, was a prolific publicist on political and international subjects. His praise of Rabasa almost reached apotheosis.

Bibliography

ARCHIVAL SOURCES

Abbreviations in parentheses as used in notes. All Mexican archives located in Mexico, D. F., unless otherwise indicated.

Archivo Bernardo Reyes. Condumex (BR).
Archivo General de la Nación. Fondo Manuel González.
Archivo Venustiano Carranza, Condumex.
Archivo Escuela Libre de Derecho (ELD).
Archivo Histórico "Genaro Estrada." Secretaría de Relaciones Exteriores (SRE). Fondo Revolución.
Archivo José Yves Limantour, Condumex (JYL).
Archivo León de la Barra. Condumex.
Archivo Porfirio Diaz (PD).
Archivo Privado de Arq. Ricardo de Villafranca Rabasa (RVR).
Austin Historical Society, Austin, Texas.
Willam F. Buckley Archive. University of Texas, Austin (WFB).
Buckley-Garrison Collection, Southern Methodist University, Dallas, Texas (SMU).
Edward House Papers. Yale University Library, New Haven, Connecticut.
Rabasa Archive (ER). University of Texas, Austin.
UNAM Archivo Histórico. Expedientes de la Dirección General de Personal.
UNICACH Hemeroteca Fernando Castañon Gamboa. Fondo Victor Manuel Castillo. Tuxtla Gutiérrez, Chiapas.

EMILIO RABASA PUBLICATIONS

Publications are listed chronologically as of first appearance in published form. For a few publications I was unable to locate, see Glass (1975). I have not listed all later editions of Rabasa books, only those used. I have listed all publications reprinted in Serra Rojas, *Antología*.

"A Castelar." *El Espíritu del Siglo* (San Cristóbal, Chiapas), 17 April 1873.

Amparo concedido por la Suprema Corte de Justicia de la Nación contra la ley del Estado de Chiapas, que impone a los abogados postulantes la obligación de asesorar á los jueces legos. Actor Lic, Emilio Rabasa. Oaxaca, Gabino Márquez, 1880.

La Musa oaxaqueña. Colección de poesías escogidas de poetas oaxaqueños, formada y precedida de un prólogo, por Emilio Rabasa. Oaxaca: Gabino Márquez, 1886.

La Bola y la Gran Ciencia; El Cuarto Poder y Moneda falsa. 2 vols. Mexico, Porrua, 1948. First published as four separate volumes (set roman) 1887–88.

Pio Gil, pseud. "La Inundación," *El Universal,* 22 July 1888 (Serra Rojas, 1: 131–35).

Pio Gil, pseud. "Los Tercetos del Señor Sierra," *El Universal,* 9 August 1888 (Serra Rojas, 1: 136–41).

Pio Gil, pseud. "Copias simples de documentos vivos. Juan B. Pérez" (1888?) (Serra Rojas, 1: 152–55).

Pio Gil, pseud. "Otra Vez '*Miau*'," *El Universal,* 6 September 1888 (Serra Rojas, 1: 143–47).

Pio Gil, pseud. "La Cosa juzgada," *El Universal,* 18 Septiembre 1888 (Serra Rojas, 1: 147–52).

"La Enseñanza de la historia en las escuelas pimarias," *La Escuela moderna. Periódico quincenal pedagógico,* 1 (1889): 5–6.

"La Prisión preventiva," *Revista de legislación y jurisprudencia,*1a. época, 1 (1889): 77–88.

"El Arbitrio judicial," *Revista de legislación y jurisprudencia,* 1a. época, 1 (1889): 226–235.

Luis Huller acusado de abuso de confianza a la Compañía Internacional de México. Mexico: Imprenta de Gobierno, 1889.

"El Caso Estrella. La Cosa juzgada en material criminal," *Revista de legislación y jurisprudencia,* 3 (1890): 36–40.

"La Guerra de tres años," *El Universal,* July 1891. 1st ed. in book form: *La Guerra de tres años.* Mexico: Editorial Cultura, 1931. 2d. ed.: *La Guerra de tres años seguido de poemas inéditos y desconocidos,* ed. Emmanuel Carballo. Mexico: Libro Mex, 1955.

Discurso del Lic. Emilio Rabasa, gobernador del estado de Chiapas, ante la legislatura del mismo, al abrir ésta su segundo periodo de sesiones ordinarias. Tuxtla Gutiérrez, 1892 (Serra Rojas, 1: 189–98).

Discurso del Lic. Emilio Rabasa, gobernador del estado de Chiapas, ante la xvi legislatura del mismo, al abrir ésta su primer periodo de sesiones ordinarias. Tuxtla Gutiérrez,1893 (Serra Rojas, *Antología,* 1: 181–89).

"La Difamación y las personas morales. Opinión del Lic Emilio Rabasa," *Revista de legislacion y jurisprudencia* (1895), pp. 27–33.

Fallo pronunciado por . . . en representacion del Sr. Gral. Porfirio Díaz . . . , nombrado árbitro en la cuestion suscitada por el ayuntamiento de "Sayula," cantón de Acayucán, Veracruz, a los propietarios de predio nombrado "Santiago Xomate," del mismo canton. Mexico: Dublán, 1903.

Laudo arbitral pronunciado por . . . designado al efecto por el Señor Presidente de la República en el juicio que sobre reivindicación de los terrenos que forman la hacienda de "La Bolsa" siguieron los Sres. Regino Franco, Vicente de Jesús Guzmán, José Yerena y sucesiones de D. José Santana y D. Ramón Vargas contra su detentador el Sr. Feliciano Rodríguez. Mexico: "La Europa," 1906.

El Artículo 14. Estudio constitucional; El Juicio Constitucional. Orígenes, teoria y extension. 2 vols. in 1. Mexico: Porrua, 1984. 1st ed. (Artículo) 1906, (Juicio) 1919.

"Las Cuestiones de límites entre los estados." 2 February 1911 (Serra Rojas, 1: 226–46).

La Acusación de Don José Barros contra el ex-secretario de hacienda Don José Y. Limantour. Cuatro Documentos interesantes. Mexico: I. Escalante, 1912.

La Constitución y la dictadura. Estudio sobre la organización política de México. Mexico: Porrua, 3rd ed., 1956. 1st ed. Mexico: Revista de revistas, 1912. 2d ed. Madrid: Editorial América [1917]; Mexico, Porrua, 1956.

"Unconditional Surrender" (1915). Unpublished (?) MS.

Martínez, Pablo, pseud. "Un Libro de Francisco Bulnes," Revista mexicana, 22, 29 October; 5, 12 November 1916.

Anon. "Galería constitucionalista. Pastor Rouaix, Secretario de Fomento." Revista mexicana, 21 October 1917.

Anon. "Galería constitucionalista. Jesus Ureta." Revista mexicana, 4, 11 November 1917.

Anon. "Galería constitucionalista. Luis Cabrera". Revista mexicana, 18 November 1917.

Anon. "Galería constitucionalista. Antonio Manero. Autoretrato." Revista mexicana, 25 November 1917.

Anon. "Como se escribe la historia: Fernando Iglesias Calderón."), Revista mexicana, 8, 17, 24 February; 3, 10 March 1918.

Anon. Los Dos Últimos Marquesas de Prado Alegre. Serie de artículos publicados en "Revista mexicana." San Antonio, Texas, 1918.

El Juicio Constitucional. Orígenes, teoria y extension. Vol 2 in 1 of El Artículo 14. Estudio constitucional. Mexico: Porrua, 1984, 1st ed. (Juicio) 1919; (Articulo) 1906.

"La Adición antialcohólica de la constitución Americana." April 1919 (Serra Rojas, 2: 211–14).

La Evolución histórica de México. Paris and Mexico: Vda. de Ch. Bouret, 1920. 2d ed. Mexico: Porrua, 1956. French ed. Paris: Alcan, 1924.

"Juzgar Dos Veces por el mismo delito; proceso del general Federico Montes," El Foro, 3, nos. 46–48, 53–54 (1920) (Serra Rojas, 2: 214–27).

"Una Invención electoral," Revista jurídica de la Escuela Libre de Derecho, 1 (1921) (Serra Rojas, 2: 228–29).

La Libertad de trabajo. Mexico: Victoria, 1922 (Serra Rojas, 2: 230–48).

Memoria del primer congreso jurídico nacional. Mexico: Sanchez, 1922 (Serra Rojas, 2: 188–99).

Cia. Terminal "La Isleta," vs. Gobierno del Estado de Tamulipas. Alegatos de Lic. Emilio Rabasa ante la Suprema Corte de Justicia. Mexico, 1923.

Cia Terminal "La Isleta" . . . anexos a los alegatos. Mexico, 1923.

"Historia sinóptica del derecho constitucional," *Revista jurídica de la Escuela Libre de Derecho.* Vol. 2, nos. 7–12 (1923) (Serra Rojas, 2: 267–83).

"La Inamovilidad de la suprema corte" (4 articles) *Excelsior,* 9, 12 16, 19 May 1923 (4th article entitled: Sobre La Suprema Corte. Cuarto artículo.)

Amparo promovido por la testamentaria Martínez del Río contra resoluciones administrativas en materia agraria. Alegatos del Lic. Emilio Rabasa ante la Suprema Corte de la Nación. Mexico, 1923 (Serra Rojas, 2: 248–67).

"La Barra americana," (dated 1923) *Revista de ciencias sociales,* 4 (1928): 6–15 (Serra Rojas, 2: 169–76).

Compañía mexicana-holondesa "La Corona," S. A. vs. Sucesión Valladares. Mexico: Victoria, 1924.

Amparo Anastasia Delgadillo. Mexico: Victoria, 1924.

Gorozave vs. Ruiz. Mexico: Victoria, 1924.

"Un Discurso de Don Emilio Rabasa" (dated 1924), *El Foro,* 4a ser., 1 (1954).

Alejandro Quijano and Genaro Fernández Mac Gregor, *La Compañía mexicana de Oleoductos Imperio (the Empire Pipe Line Co. of Mexico) vs. la International Petroleum Company.* Mexico: Victoria, 1924.

"Discurso pronunciado por el rector, Señor Lic. Don Emilio Rabasa." *Revista jurídica,* 2a época 3 (1925): 4–16.

Preface to Alberto González Salceda, Jr., *La Transición pacífica del individualismo al socialismo.* Mexico: Cultura, 1927.

"Ciencia política" and "Derecho constitucional mexicano" (1928) transcribed by J. J. González Bustamante (Serra Rojas, 2: 339–627).

"Derecho constitucional mexicano," typescript version by Alejandro Gamboa (1928).

"San Bartolo Solistahuacán," *Excelsior,* 30, 31 December 1929 (Serra Rojas, 2: 287–93).

"Un Vacío peligroso," *Excelsior,* 15, 25 November, 1929 (Serra Rojas, 2: 283–87).

"El Desquicimiento moral," *Excelsior,* 23, 25 January 1930 (Serra Rojas, 2: 293–99).

"La Asamblea nacional," *Excelsior,* 25, 30 February 1930 (Serra Rojas, 2: 299–304).

Rabasa, "El Desprestigio de la vice presidencia," *Excelsior,* 3, 4 April 1930 (Serra Rojas, 2: 304–10).

OTHER SOURCES

Abbott, Lyman. "The Indian Problem." *Harper's Encyclopedia of United States History.* New York, 1905. Vol. 5, pp. 21–27.

Anders, Evan. *Boss Rule in South Texas: The Progressive Era*. Austin: University of Texas Press, 1982.

"Archivo de la reacción" (AR), *El Universal*, September and October 1917.

Arenal Fenochio, Jaime del. "Vasconcelos, Herrera y Lasso y la Escuela Libre de Derecho," *Revista de investigaciones jurídicas* 9 (1985): 71–102.

———. "Pablo Macedo: Orden y abogacía de un científico," *Revista de investigaciones jurídicas* 12 (1988): 19–47.

———. "La Fundación de la Escuela Libre de Derecho," *Revista de investigaciones jurídicas*, Cuaderno, no. 1 (Mexico, 1988).

———. "Luis Cabrera, director de la Escuela Nacional de Jurisprudencia," *Cuadernos del archivo histórico de la UNAM,* 10 (1989).

———. "Los Años del estudiante Felipe Tena Ramírez en la Escuela Libre de Derecho," *Revista de investigaciones jurídicas*, 19 (1995): 343–82.

———. "Un Rector y una escuela liberales: Emilio Rabasa y la Escuela Libre de Derecho," in *Hombres e historia de la Escuela Libre de Derecho*. (Mexico: ELD, 1999).

"Autorizada Opinión del Señor Lic. Rabasa sobre la dotación de ejidos," *Excelsior*, 19 September 1925.

Bagehot, Walter. *La Constitución inglesa*. Eds. Alonso Lujambio and Jaime Martínez Bowness (Mexico: UNAM, 2005).

Baker, Richard D. *Judicial Review in Mexico: A Study of the Amparo Suit*. Austin: University of Texas Press, 1971.

Barthélemy, Joseph. *Le Role du pouvoir exécutif dans les républiques modernes*. Paris: Girard, 1906.

Bassols, Narciso. "La Nueva Ley agraria" (1927). In *Obras*. Mexico: FCE, 1946, pp. 49–52.

Benjamin, Thomas. *Camino a Leviatán. Chiapas y el estado mexicano*. Mexico, CONACULTA, 1990.

———. *A Rich Land, A Poor People. Politics and Society in Modern Chiapas*. Albuquerque: University of New Mexico Press, 1989.

Betancourt, Ignacio Bravo. "La Inamovilidad," *El Foro*, 4, nos. 19–30 (1922), pp. 14–18.

Boletín del Instituto de Derecho Comparado de México (1948–67), continued to date as *Boletín Mexicano de Derecho Comparado*.

Bolívar, Simón. *Carta de Jamaica*. Caracas: Ministerio de Educación, 1965.

———. *Selected Writings*. Ed. Harold A. Bierck, Jr., 2 vols. New York: Colonial Press, 1951.

Boutmy, Émile. *Eléments d'une psychologie politique du people américain. La patrie. L'état. La religion*. Paris: Colin, 1902.

Brown, Jonathan C. *Oil and Revolution in Mexico*. Berkeley: University of California Press, 1993.

Bryce, James. *South America*. New York: Macmillan, 1912.

———. *The American Commonwealth*. 3d ed. 2 vols. New York: Macmillan, 1893.

Buckley, Priscilla L., and William F. Buckley, Jr., eds. *W.F.B. An Appreciation by his Family and Friends*. New York: Privately printed, 1959, 1979.

Bulnes, Francisco. *Los Grandes Problemas de Mexico*. Mexico: El Universal, 1926.

———. *The Whole Truth about Mexico. President Wilson's Responsibility.* New York: M. Bulnes Book Company, 1916.

Burgoa, Ignacio. *El Juicio de amparo,* 32d rev. ed. Mexico: Porrua, 1995. 1st ed., 1943.

Byam, W. W. *A Sketch of the State of Chiapas, México.* Los Angeles: Geo. Rice, 1897.

Cabrera, Lucio, and William Cecil Headrick, "Notas sobre la justicia constitucional en México y los Estados Unidos," *Inter–American Law Review,* 5 (1963): 229–76.

Cabrera, Luis. *Sucesión de D. Tomas Valladares vs. "La Corona."* Mexico, 1924.

———. *Obras políticas del Lic. Blas Urrea.* Mexico: Imprenta Internacional, 1921.

Camp, Roderic Ai. *Mexican Political Biographies, 1884–1935.* Austin: University of Texas Press, 1991.

Cappelletti, Mauro. *El Control judicial de la constitucionalidad de las leyes en el derecho comparado.* Mexico: UNAM, 1966.

———. *The Judicial Process in Comparative Perspective.* Oxford: Clarendon Press, 1989.

———. *Judicial Review in the Contemporary World.* Indianapolis: Bobbs-Merrill, 1971.

Cappelletti, Mauro, and David S. Clark. In Clark, eds. *Comparative and Private International Law. Essays in Honor of John Henry Merryman on his Seventieth Birthday.* Berlin: Dunker and Humboldt, 1990.

Caro, Brigido, pseud. "Don Jose Yves Limantour y no el Dr. Vázquez Gómez, fue el cerebro de la revolución de 1910," *Revista mexicana,* 18 November 1917.

Clagett, Helen L. *A Guide to the Law and Legal Literature of the Mexican States.* Washington: Library of Congress, 1947.

Clagett, Helen L., and David M. Valderrama. *A Revised Guide to the Law and Legal Literature of Mexico.* Washington: Library of Congress, 1973.

Colección que comprende la constitución general de la república . . . y las constituciones especiales de cada de los estados de la federación. 2 vols. Mexico: Imprenta del Gobierno, 1884.

Connolly, Priscilla. *El Contratista de Don Porfirio: Obras públicas, deuda y desarrollo desigual.* Zamora and Mexico: El Colegio de Michoacán and FCE, 1997.

Constant, Benjamin. "Principes de politique applicable á tous les gouvernments représentatifs et particulièrèmente á la constitution actuelle de la France" (1815). In *Cours de politique constitutionnelle ou collection de ouvrages publiés sur le gouvernement représentatif,* ed. Edouard Laboulaye. 2d ed. 2 vols. Paris, 1872.

Cooley, Thomas M. *A Treatise on the Constitutional Limitations Which Rest upon the Legislative Power of the States of the American Union.* Boston: Little, Brown, 1868.

Córdova, Arnaldo. *La Nacion y la constitución; La Lucha por la democracia en México.* Mexico: Claves Latinoamericanos, 1989.

Corwin, Edward S. *La Constitución norteamericana y su actual significado.* Buenos Aires: Kraft, 1942.

Cosío Villegas, Daniel. *La Constitución de 1857 y sus críticos.* Mexico: Hermes, 1957; 4th ed. (Mexico: El Colegio de México. 1998.

Creelman, James. "President Díaz: Hero of the Americas," *Pearson's Magazine* (NewYork), 19 (March 1908): 241–77. Facsimile ed. and Spanish trans. as *Entrevista Díaz-Creelman,* (Mexico, Cuadernos del Instituto de Historia, UNAM, 1963.

David, René. *French Law.* Baton Rouge: Louisana State University Press, 1972.

———. *Los Grandes sistemas jurídicos contemporaneous.* Madrid: Aguilar, 1973.

Dawson, John P. *The Oracles of the Law.* Ann Arbor: University of Michigan Law School, 1968.

El Demócrata, 10 March 1895; 27 March 1921.

(DDCD). *Diario de los debates de la cámara de diputados,* 16th legis. (1892–93).

(DDCD). *Diario de los debates de la cámara de diputados,* 25th–26th legis. (1910–13).

(DDCS). *Diario de los debates de la cámara de senadores,* 17th–26th legis. (1894–1913).

(DDCC). *Diario de los Debates. Congreso constituyente, 1916–1917.* 2 vols. Mexico: INEHRM, 1987 [1st ed. 1960].

Díaz Dufoo, Carlos. "El Ultimo Pensamiento de Emilio Rabasa," *Excelsior,* 2 May 1930. (Serra Rojas, 2: 319–22).

Díaz y Díaz, Martín. *Emilio Rabasa: teórico de la dictadura necesaria.* Mexico: ELD, 1991.

———. "Rabasa y Molina Enríquez: Un Diálogo autoritario en el orígen de la constitución," *Revista de Investigaciones jurídicas,* 13 (1989): 229–87.

Domingo, Pilar. "Judicial Independence: the Politics of the Supreme Court in Mexico," *Journal of Latin American Studies,* 32 (October 2000): 705–35.

Dublán, Manuel, and José María Lozano, *Legislación mexicana.* 34 vols. Mexico, 1876–1904.

Duguit, Leon. *Les Transformations du droit public.* Paris; Armand Colin, 1913. Spanish ed. Trans. Adolfo Posada. Madrid: Beltrán [1915]. English ed. *Law in the Modern State.* New York, Huebsch, 1919.

Escuela Libre de Derecho. Estatuto. Mejico: Escalante, 1912.

Eastman, Charles A. (OHIYESA). *The Indian Today. The Past and Future of the American Indian.* New York: Doubleday, 1915.

Eisenmann, Charles. "Deux theoriciens du droit: Duguit et Hauriou," *Revue philosophique de la France et de l'étranger,* 110 1930), 231–79.

Esquivel Obregón, Toribio. *Desde el Exilio: correspondencia de Toribio Esquivel Obregón, 1914–1924.* Ed. Mónica Blanco. Mexico: INEHRM, 2005.
———. *Influencia de España y los Estados Unidos sobre México.* Madrid: Calleja, 1918.
Excelsior, 1921–1930.
Fabela, Isidro, ed. *Documentos históricos de la Revolución Mexicana. Revolución y régimen maderista.* 5 vols. Mexico: FCE, 1964–65.
The Federalist. New York: Random House, n.d.
Fernández, José Diego, *La Constitución de 1857 y sus reformas . . . Anteproyecto del señor Lic. D. José Diego Fernández* (1914). Introd. study by Manuel González Oropeza. Mexico: Suprema Corte, 2005.
Ferrer, Jorge. "Semblanzas mexicanas. Don Emilio Rabasa," *El Universal,* 15 April 1951 (Serra Rojas, 2: 325–27).
Fisher, William W. III et al., eds. *American Legal Realism.* New York: Oxford University Press, 1993.
Fix Zamudio, Hector. "Brief Introduction to the Mexican Writ of *Amparo.*" *California Western International Law Journal* 9 (1979): 306–48.
———. "Casación," *Diccionario jurídico mexicano.* 2d ed. Mexico: Porrua, 1987, 1: 428–30.
———. "La Independencia judicial en el ordenamiento mexicano," James F. Smith, ed., *Derecho constitucional comparado: Mexico–Estados Unidos.* Mexico, 1990, 1: 379–98.
———. *Veinticinco años de evolución de la justicia constitucional, 1940–1965.* Mexico: UNAM, 1968.
Foro jurídico, 3a época, no. 30 (March 2006), pp. 16–24.
Gamboa, Federico. *Mi Diario,* 1a. Serie, 2. Mexico: Gómez de la Puente, 1910.
———. *Impresiones y recuerdos.* 2d ed. Mexico: E. Gómez de la Puente, 1922. 1st ed. 1893.
———. *Mi Diario. Mucho de mi vida y algo de la de otros.* 7 vols. Mexico, CONACULTA, 1995).
García de León, Antonio. *Resistencia y utopía, Memorial de agravios y crónicas en la provincia de Chiapas durante los últimos quinientos años de su historia.* 2 vols. Mexico: Era, 1985.
García Naranjo, Nemesio. *Memorias.* 9 vols. Monterrey: "El Porvenir," n.d. [1948?], vol. 8.
Garciadiego, Javier. "Movimientos estudiantiles durante the Revolución mexicana," Jaime E. Rodríguez O., ed. *The Revolutionary Process in Mexico. Essays on Political and Social Change, 1880–1940.* Los Angeles: UCLA Latin American Center, 1990, pp. 115–60.
———. "Los Orígenes de la Escuela Libre de Derecho." *Revista de investigaciones jurídicas* 17 (1993): 199–220.
———. *Rudos contra científicos. La Universidad Nacional durante la Revolución mexicana.* Mexico: El Colegio de México, 1996.
Garner, Paul. "The Politics of National Development in Late Porfirian Mexico: the Reconstruction of the Tehuantepec National Railway 1896–1907." *Bulletin of Latin American Research,* 14 (1995): 339–56.

Glass, Elliot S. *Mexico en las obras de Emilio Rabasa*. Mexico: Diana, 1975.

Glendon, Mary Ann et al. *Comparative Legal Traditions*. St. Paul: West Publishing Company, 1982.

González Peña, Carlos. "Rabasa y sus novelas." *El Universal*, 4 May 1930 (Serra Rojas, 1: 128–31).

González Ramírez, Manuel. Prológo to *Emilio Rabasa, Retratos y estudios*. Mexico: UNAM, 1945.

Grieb, Kenneth J. *The United States and Huerta*. Lincoln: University of Nebraska Press, 1969.

Guidiño Pelayo, Jesús. "Emilio Rabasa en la Suprema Corte," *Iustitia* (Monterrey). No. 14, (2006), pp. 141–46.

Haines, Charles G. *The American Doctrine of Judicial Supremacy*. New York: Macmillan, 1914.

Hale, Charles A. "Castelar and Mexico." In Iván Jaksic, ed. *The Political Power of the Word: Press and Oratory in Nineteenth-Century Latin America*. London: ILAS, 2002, pp. 129–41.

———. "The Civil Law Tradition and Constitutionalism in Twentieth-Century Mexico: The Legacy of Emilio Rabasa, *"Law and History Review*, 18 (Summer 2000): 257–79.

———. "Edmundo O'Gorman, Mexican National History and the 'Great American Dichotomy,'" *Journal of Latin American Studies*, 36 (2004):131–45.

———. "The Liberal Impulse: Daniel Cosío Villegas and the *Historia moderna de México*," *HAHR*, 54 (1974): 479–63.

———. *Mexican Liberalism in the Age of Mora, 1821–1853*. New Haven: Yale University Press, 1968.

———. "Los Mitos políticos de la nación mexicana: el liberalismo y la Revolución," *Historia mexicana*, 46 (1996): 821–37.

———. "Political and Social Ideas in Latin America, 1870–1930," *Cambridge History of Latin America*. Cambridge: Cambridge University Press, 1984. Vol. 4, pp. 367–441.

———. The Reconstruction of Nineteenth-Century Politics in Spanish America: A Case for the History of Ideas," *Latin American Research Review*, Vol. 8, no. 2 (1973), pp. 53–73.

———. "The Revival of Political History and the French Revolution in Mexico." Joseph Klaits and Michael H. Haltzel, eds., *The Global Ramifications of the French Revolution*. Cambridge and New York: Cambridge University Press, 1994, pp. 158–78.

———. *The Transformation of Liberalism in Late Nineteenth-Century Mexico*. Princeton: Princeton University Press, 1989.

Hall, Linda B. *Oil, Banks and Politics. The United States and Postrevolutionary Mexico, 1917–1924*. Austin: University of Texas Press, 1995.

Haring, Clarence H. *The Spanish Empire in America*. New York: Oxford University Press, 1947.

Hart, John Mason. *Empire and Revolution. The Americans in Mexico Since the Civil War* Berkeley: University of California Press, 2002.

———. *Revolutionary Mexico. The Coming and Process of the Mexican Revolution.* Berkeley: University of California Press, 1987.

Hauriou, Maurice. *Principios de derecho público y constituciona.* Madrid: Reis, 1927. Trans. of *Principes du droit publique.* Paris: Sirey, 1910.

Henderson, Peter V. N. *In the Absence of Don Porfirio: Francisco León de la Barra and the Mexican Revolutión.* Wilmington: Scholarly Resources, 2000.

———. *Félix Díaz, the Porfirians, and the Mexican Revolution.* Lincoln: University of Nebraska Press, 1981.

Herrera y Lasso, Manuel. *Estudios constitucionales.* Mexico: Polis, 1940.

———. *Estudios constitucionales,* 2d ser. Mexico: Jus, 1964.

———. *Estudios políticos y constitucionales.* Mexico: Porrua, 1986.

Holden, Robert H. *Mexico and the Survey of Public Lands: The Management of Modernization, 1876–1911.* De Kalb: Northern Illinois Press, 1994.

Horowitz, Morton J. *The Transformation of American Law, 1870–1960: The Crisis of Legal Orthodoxy.* New York: Oxford University Press, 1992.

Jackson, Helen Hunt (H. H.). *A Century of Dishonor. A Sketch of the United States Government's Dealings with Some of the Indian Tribes* (1881). Facsimile ed. Norman: University of Oklahoma Press, 1994.

James, T. M. "Law and Revolution in Mexico: A Constitutional History of Mexico's Amparo Court and Revolutionary Social Reform, 1861–1934." Ph.D. diss., University of Chicago, 2006.

Kantorowicz, Hermann. "Savigny and the Historical School of Law." *Law Quarterly Review,* 53 (1937): 326–42.

Karst, Kenneth L., and Keith Rosenn. *Law and Development in Latin America.* Berkeley: University of California Press, 1971.

Katz, Friedrich. *The Life and Times of Pancho Villa.* Stanford: Stanford University Press, 1998.

———. *The Secret War in Mexico. Europe, the United States and the Mexican Revolution.* Chicago: University of Chicago Press, 1981.

Kelley, Donald R. *Historians and the Law in Post-Revolutionary France.* Princeton: Princeton University Press, 1984).

Ker, Anita M. *Mexican Government Publications.* Washington: Library of Congress, 1940.

Keynes, John Maynard. "The Council of Four, Paris 1919," *Essays in Biography.* New York: Harcourt, 1920, pp. 3–30.

King, Jerome B. "Constitutionalism and the Judiciary in France," *Political Science Quarterly* 80 (1965): 62–85.

Knight, Alan. "El liberalismo mexicano desde la reforma hasta la revolución (una interpretación)." *Historia mexicana* 35 (1985): 59–91.

———. *The Mexican Revolution.* 2 vols. Cambridge: Cambridge University Press, 1986.

Laboulaye, Edouard. "Avertissement." Montesquieu, *Oeuvres completes.* 7 vols. Paris, 1875.

———. "Friedrich Carl von Savigny" (1842), *Études contemporaines sur l'Allemagne et les pays slaves,* 3rd ed. (Paris, 1868), pp. 239–310.

———. *L'état et ses límites.* Paris, 1863.

———. *Histoire des États-Unis.* 6th ed., 3 vols. Paris, 1877. 1st ed.: vol. 1 (1855); vols. 2 and 3 (1866).

———. *Historia de los Estados Unidos.* Trans. Manuel Dublán. 2 vols. Mexico, 1870.

Lambert, Edouard. *La Gouvernement des juges et la lutte contre la legislation sociale aux États-Unis.* Paris: Giard, 1921.

Lawson, F. H. *A Common Lawyer Looks at the Civil Law.* Ann Arbor: University of Michigan Law School, 1953.

Le Bon, Gustave. *Les Lois psychologiques de l'évolution des peoples.* Paris: Alcan, 1894.

———. *La Révolution française et la psychologie des révolutions.* Paris: Flammarion, 1912.

Leacock, Stephen. *Elements of Political Science.* London: Constable, 1906. Spanish ed. Mexico: Victoria, 1924.

Lempérière, Annick. "La Formación de las élites liberales en el México del siglo xix: El Instituto de ciencias y artes del estado de Oaxaca." *Secuencia,* no. 30 (1985), pp. 57–94.

Lerminier, Jean Louis Eugéne. *Introduction génerale à l'histoire du droit.* Bruxelles: Hauman, 1829.

Lewis, Stephen E. *The Ambivalent Revolution: Forging State and Nation in Chiapas, 1910–1945.* Albuquerque: University of New Mexico Press, 2005.

La Libertad. periódico liberal-conservador, 1878–79.

Limantour, José Yves. *Apuntes sobre mi vida pública.* Mexico: Porrua, 1965.

Link, Arthur S., ed. *The Papers of Woodrow Wilson.* 69 vols. Princeton: Princeton University Press, 1966–94.

Lira González, Andrés. *El Amparo colonial y el juicio de amparo mexicano.* Mexico: FCE, 1972.

———. "Derechos del hombre y garantías individuales. Vallarta en la Constitución de 1917." *Revista de investigaciones jurídicas* 29 (2005): 575–82.

———. "Revolución, derechos sociales y positivismo jurídico en México, 1870–1920." *Jornadas de historia de occidente.* Jiquilpan, Michoacán, 1987, pp. 83–105.

Lopez Medina, Manuel. Coord. *Memoría del 70 aniversario de La Escuela Libre de Derecho.* Mexico: ELD, 1982.

Lozano, José María. *Tratado de los derechos del hombre. Estudio del derecho constitucional patrio en lo relativo a los derechos del hombre.* Mexico: Dublán, 1876.

Luna Argudín, María. *El Congreso y la política mexicana (1857–1911).* Mexico: El Colegio de Mexico, 2006.

Mac Gregor, Josefina. *Belisario Domínguez. Moral y ética, impronta de vida.* Mexico: Senado de la República, 2004.

———. *La XXVI Legislatura. Un Episodio en la historia legislativa de México.* Mexico: Instituto de Investigaciones Legislativas, 1983.

———. "La XXVI Legislatura frente a Victoriano Huerta ¿Un Caso de parlamentarismo?" *Secuencia* 4 (1986): 10–23.

Macías, José N. *Alegato de buena prueba presentado por ... en representación del Estado de Tlaxcala en el juicio que este estado y el de Puebla siguen ante el Sr. Juez Arbitro, Lic. Don Emilio Rabasa, con motivo de sus límites.* Tlaxcala: Imprenta del Gobierno, 1899.

Madelin, Louis. *La Révolution.* Paris, 1911.

Madier, G. *L'Association du barreau américain.* Paris: Giard, 1922.

María y Campos Castelló, Alfonso. *José Yves Limantour. El Caudillo mexicano de las finanzas (1854–1935).* Mexico: Condumex, 1998.

Mayagoitia, Alejandro. "Don José Mariano Pontón y Ponce: un jurista en una época de crisis. Notas para su biobibliografía," *Anuario mexicano de historia del derecho* 15 (1999).

McCartin, Joseph A. *Labor's Great War.* Chapel Hill: University of North Carolina Press, 1997.

Medina, Hilario. "Emilio Rabasa y la Constitución de 1917." *Historia mexicana,* 10 (1960–61): 177–95.

Medina Peña, Luis. *La Invención del sistema político mexicano.* Mexico: FCE, 2004.

Mendieta y Nuñez, Lucio. *El Problema agrario de México.* 8th ed. Mexico: Porrua, 1964.

Merryman, John Henry. *The Civil Law Tradition. An Introduction to the Legal Systems of Western Europe and Latin America.* 2d ed. Stanford: Stanford University Press, 1984.

———. "The Public Law-Private Law Distinction in European and United States Law," *Journal of Public Law* 17 (1968): 3–19.

———. *La Tradición jurídica romano-canónico.* Mexico: FCE, 1971.

Meyer, Michael C. *Huerta. A Political Portrait.* Lincoln: University of Nebraska Press, 1972.

Moheno, Querido. *¿Hacia Donde Vamos? Bosquejo de un cuadro de instituciones políticas adecuadas al pueblo mexicano.* Mexico: Lara, 1908.

Monsivais, Carlos "Emilio Rabasa: la tradición del desengaño," introd. to Rabasa, *La Bola.* Mexico: Ediciones Oceana, 1986.

Montesquieu, *Oeuvres completes.* Ed. Laboulaye Edouard. 7 vols. Paris, 1875.

Mora, José María Luis. *Mexico y sus revoluciones,* 3 vols. Paris: Rosa, 1837.

———. *Obras sueltas.,* 2a. ed. Mexico: Porrua, 1963.

Nerincx, Alf. *L'Organisation judiciaire aux États-Unis.* Paris: Giard & Briére, 1909.

Neu, Charles E. "In Search of Colonel Edward M. House: The Texas Years, 1858–1912." *Southwestern Historical Quarterly* 93 (1989): 25–44.

"Nuestra encuesta sobre la educación nacional." *El Demócrata,* 27 March 1921.

Palavincini, Felix F. "Un Nuevo Congreso constituyente" (Veracruz, 1915). In *Historia de la Constitución de 1917.* Mexico, INHERM, 1987. Vol. 2, appendix. Facsimile of 1st ed.

Pallares, Eduardo. "La Muerte de Rabasa" *El Universal,* 2 May 1930 (Serra Rojas, 2: 322–25).

Palmer, Robert R. *The Age of the Democratic Revolution.* 2 vols. Princeton: Princeton University Press, 1959–64.

Papers Relating to the Foreign Relations of the United States, 1911. Washington, 1918.

Pasquel, Leonardo. "Biografía." *Boletín de la sociedad de alumnos de la Escuela Libre de Derecho.* Vol. 1, no. 4 (May 1956).

Paul, Arnold M. *Conservative Crisis and the Rule of Law: Attitudes of Bar and Bench, 1887–1895.* Ithaca: Cornell University Press, 1960.

Piccato, Pablo. *Congreso y revolución.* Mexico: INEHRM, 1991.

Pola, Angel. "En Casa de la Celebridades. Emilio Rabasa." *El Diario del hogar,* 20 Septiembre 1888 (Serra Rojas, 1: 101–06).

Proyecto de reformas constitucionales de la Secretaría de Justicia de 1916. Mexico: Cámara de Diputados, 1967.

Puig Casauranc, Manuel. *Organización técnica de los departmentos de "antropología," de "educación rural e incorporación cultural indígena y de investigación físico pedagógica e hygiene.* Mexico: SEP, 1924.

Quirk, Robert E. *An Affair of Honor. Woodrow Wilson and the Occupation of Veracruz.* Lexington: University of Kentucky Press, 1962.

———. *The Mexican Revolution, 1914–15. The Convention of Aguascalientes.* Bloomington: Indiana University Press, 1960.

Rabasa, Oscar. "Breves apuntes sobre la personalidad del señor Lic. Emilio Rabasa." Mexico, n.p, 1956. [I was unable to locate this document or those who quoted from it.]

———. *El Derecho angloamericano. Estudio expositivo y comparado del "common law.* Mexico: FCE, 1944.

———. "La Suprema corte es incompetente para conocer asuntos políticos," *Revista jurídica de la Escuela Libre de Derecho* 1 (1922): 421–48.

Rabasa, Ramón. *El Estado de Chiapas. Geografía y estadística. Recursos del estado, sus elementos, condiciones de riqueza, porvenir agrícola, etc., etc. Datos recogidos por . . . orden del gobierno del estado y publicados por acuerdo del Presidente de la República.* Mexico: Cuerpo Especial de Estado Mayor, 1895.

Ramírez Rancaño, Mario. *La Reacción mexicana y su exilio durante la Revolución de 1910.* Mexico: UNAM, 2002.

Ramos, Carmen. "Emilio Rabasa: Su obra literaria como expresión política," R. Camp, C. Hale, & J. Vázquez, eds. *Los Intelectuales y el poder en México.* Mexico and Los Angeles: El Colegio de México and UCLA, 1991, pp. 665–79.

Richardson, Rupert Norval. *Colonel Edward M. House. The Texas Years.* Abilene, Texas: Hardin-Simmons University, 1964.

Ross, Stanley R. *Francisco I. Madero. Apostle of Mexican Democracy.* New York: Columbia University Press, 1955.

Ruggiero, Guido de. *History of European Liberalism.* Oxford: Oxford University Press, 1927.

Ruiz Abreu, Carlos. *Emilio Rabasa Estebanell: los combates por la vida.* Tuxtla Gutiérrez: Consejo Estatal para la Cultura y las Artes de Chiapas, 2000.

Rus, Jan, "Coffee and the Recolonization of Highland Chiapas, Mexico. Indian Communities and Plantation Labor, 1892–1912," William Gervase Clarence-Smith and Steven Topik, eds., *The Global Coffee Economy in Africa, Asia, and Latin America, 1500–1989*.Cambridge: Cambridge University Press, 2003.

———. "Whose Caste War? Indians, *Ladinos,* and the Chiapas 'Caste War' of 1869." Kevin Gosner and Arij Ouweneel, eds. *Indigenous Revolts in Chiapas and the Andean Highlands.* Amsterdam: CEDLA, 1996, pp. 43–77.

Salado Álvarez, Victoriano. Introd. to Rabasa, *La Guerra de tres años.* Mexico: Editorial Cultura, 1931.

———. *Memorias.* 2 vols. Mexico: EDIAPSA, 1946.

Salmerón Castro, Alicia. "Política y redes sociales a fines del siglo xix: el caso de Rosendo Pineda." TRACE, no. 32 (1997), pp. 48–55.

———. "Porfiristas expatriados: El Exilio de los científicos." Unpub. manuscript.

Sánchez-Cordero Dávila, Jorge A. Prólogo to *Libro del cincuecentenario del códico civil* (Mexico: UNAM, 1978).

Sánchez Pontón, Luis. "Algunas Ideas sobre la reforma de las instituciones judiciales en México." *El Foro,* 4, nums. 19–30 (1922), pp. 14–18.

Saulnier, Frédéric. *Joseph Barthélemy (1874–1945). La Crise du constitutionalisme libéral sous la IIIe République.* Paris: L.G.D.L, 2004.

Savigny, Frederic Charles de. *On the Vocation of Our Age for Legislation and Jurisprudence* (1814). English (1831). Reprint. New York: Arno, 1975.

Sax, Antimaco [José Elguero?]. *Los Mexicanos en el destierro.* San Antonio, 1916.

Schieber, Harry N. "World War I as Entrepreneurial Opportunity. Willard Straight and the American International Corporation." *Political Science quarterly* 84 (1969): 486–511.

Semanario judicial de la federación (SJF) 5th época. Vol. 12 (1923), 2d sem., pp. 884–92; Vol. 16 (1925) 1a sem., pp. 1275–82, 1302–03.

Serna de la Garza, José María. "Apuntes sobre las opciones de cambio en la metodología de la enseñanza del derecho en México." *Boletín mexicano de derecho comparado,* new ser., año 37, núm. 111 (2004), pp. 1047–82.

Serra Rojas, Andrés ed. *Antología de Emilio Rabasa.* 2 vols. Mexico: Ediciones Oasis, 1969.

Sierra, Justo. *Obras completas.* 15 vols. Mexico: UNAM, 1948–93.

Silva-Herzog Márquez, Jesús J. "Emilio Rabasa." *La Constitución mexicana de 1917: Ideólogos, el núcleo fundador y otros constituyentes.* Mexico: UNAM, 1990.

Smith, Robert F. "The Formation and Development of the International Bankers Committee on Mexico." *Journal of Economic History* 23 (1963): 574–86.

Spenser, Daniela, "Soconusco: the Formation of a Coffee Economy in Chiapas," pp. 123–43. Thomas Benjamin and William McNellie, eds., *Other Mexicos. Essays in Regional Mexican History, 1876–1911.* Albuquerque: University of New Mexico Press, 1984.

Stewart, John Hall. *A Documentary Survey of the French Revolution.* New York: Macmillan, 1951.

Stratton, Lorum. *Emilio Rabasa: Life and Works.* Lubbock: Texas Tech University, 1974.

Taine, Hippolyte. "Psychologie du Jacobin," *Revue des deux mondes* (1881), pp. 536–50. Reprinted in *Les Origines de la France contemporaine,* 6 vols. Paris: Hachette, 1876–94.

Tello Díaz, Carlos. *El Exilio. Un Relato de familia.* Mexico: Cal y Arena, 1993.

Tamayo, Jorge L. ed. *Benito Juárez. Documentos, discursos y correspondencia,* 15 vols. Mexico, 1967.

Tena Ramirez, Felipe. "La Crisis de la división de poderes." *Crisis del pensamiento. Ciclo de conferencias de 1946.* México: Colegio de Abogados, 1946, pp. 155–81.

———. *Derecho constitucional,* 2d ed. Mexico, Porrua, 1964. 1st ed. 1944.

———. "La Función del derecho: del individualismo al socialismo." Unpub. thesis. Escuela Libre de Derecho, 1929.

———. *Leyes fundamentales de México, 1808–1964.* 2d ed. Mexico: Porrua, 1964.

Tocqueville, Alexis de. *De la démocratie en Amérique.* J. P. Mayer, ed. *Oeuvres completes.* 18 vols. Paris: Gallimard, 1951. Vol. 1, pts. 1–2 . Rev. ed. 1960. English ed. New York: Knopf, 1954.

Trejo, Rosauro de J. "Causas del odio que el Licenciado Don Emilio Rabasa tuvo a la ciudad de San Cristóbal de las Casas." n.p. (1937).

El Universal, 1888–93, 1917.

U.S. Department of State. *Foreign Relations of the United States. Diplomatic Papers* (1914), pp. 508–10.

U.S. Senate. *Investigation of Mexican Affairs. Hearing Before a Subcommittee on Foreign Relations, 66th Congress,* 1st Session. Washington: Government Printing Office, 1919.

Vallarta, Ignacio. *El Juicio de Amparo y el writ de habeas corpus. Ensayo crítico-comparativo sobre esos recursos constitucionales.* In *Obras completas.* Vol. 5. Mexico: Terrazas, 1896. Reprint 1975.

———. *Obras completas,* 1a. ser. *Cuestiones constitucionales. Votos.* 4 vols. Mexico: Terrazas, 1895–96. Reprint 1975.

Villegas Moreno, Gloria. *Emilio Rabasa. Su Pensamiento histórico-político y el Constituyente de 1916–17.* Mexico: Cámara de Diputados, 1984.

Vos, Jan de. "Los Linderos sudorientales al despuntar el siglo xx; Las fincas huleras en la frontera Chiapas-Tabasco." Mario Humberto Ruz, ed., *Tabasco: Apuntes de frontera.* Mexico: CONACULTA, 1997.

———. *Oro verde. La Conquista de la selva lacandona por los madereros tabasqueños, 1822–1949.* Mexico: FCE, 1988.

———. *Vivir en frontera. La Experiencia de los indios de Chiapas.* Mexico: Instituto Nacional Indigenista, 1994.

Washbrook, Sarah. "Exports, Ethnicity, and Labour Markets: The Political Economy of Chiapas, Mexico, 1876–1911." Ph.D. diss., University of Oxford, 2005.

———. "Indígenas, exportación y enganche en el norte de Chiapas, 1876–1911," *Mesoamérica,* año 25, no. 46 (2004), pp. 1–26.

Wasserstrom, Robert. *Class and Society in Central Chiapas.* Berkeley: University of California Press, 1983.

Wilkins, Mira. *The Maturing of Multinational Enterprise. American Business Abroad from 1914 to 1970.* Cambridge: Harvard University Press, 1974.

Wilson, Woodrow. *Congressional Government. A Study in American Politics.* Boston: Houghton Mifflin, 1885.

———. *El Gobierno congresional. Régimen politico de los Estados Unidos.* Mexico: UNAM, 2002. ed. Alonso Lujambio. Trans. Alfonso Posada, Madrid, 1902.

Wolfe, Christopher. *The Rise of Modern Judicial Review. From Constitutional Interpretation to Judge-Made Law.* New York: Basic Books, 1986.

Index